NO TIMD

Fourth edition
published in 2005 by

WOODFIELD PUBLISHING
Bognor Regis, West Sussex, England
www.woodfieldpublishing.com

© Ken FitzRoy, 2004, 2005

ISBN 1-903953-71-5

No Time on the Ground

....

A former Military, Commercial and Civilian Pilot looks back on Fifty Years of Experiences in the Air

KEN FITZROY

Woodfield

For Sally Anne

and

For the Fighter Collection – pilots, engineers, staff and volunteers who do so much. Not forgetting our boss, Stephen Grey, without whom we would not exist, and a large part of this country's aviation heritage would have been lost forever.

Acknowledgements

My thanks to David Berry, Brian Holt, Chalky White, Peter Hearne and Wally Kahn for their unstinting help and encouragement and to Kit Jenkins for deciphering my scribbles and typing them.

Contents

The Author – a mere lad – Thornhill 1952.

Preface

This is a story of aviation as I experienced it in 50 years of flying; the reader will find little of my somewhat turbulent domestic life. I make no claims to have been a great aviator, far from it, but I have never lost my enthusiasm for flight, and I look forward to half an hour in a Tiger Moth today as much as I did 50 years ago.

A real aviator was once asked how he viewed his aviation career. He replied: "I have squandered my life in the air and loved every minute of it".

I'll drink to that!

Prologue

September 1991. We were flying back to Duxford from Lydd following the Shepway Air Show. The four fighters had just left for their low pass over the airfield, their shadows almost merging with the aircraft themselves as they raced across the ground for their final break. I did my best to follow them in the B25. Taxiing onto the flight line John did a quick mag check, and with the temperatures and pressures in limits, we closed the mixture controls to shut off. Silence reigned. Quickly, I completed the shut down checks and opened the side window. This is always a moment to savour with the soft evening breeze blowing in off the airfield bringing with it a smell of damp grass, hot oil and metal from the engines and listening to the soft ticking noise of cooling metal. My mind wandered back 25 years to my last trip in the RAF in the Britannia. I remember then looking around the empty flight deck and thinking "this is my home, this is where I belong".

How did it all start, so long ago, this all-consuming urge to fly?

Ken FitzRoy

1. Early Days

It all really began in 1934. My parents were taking me up to London from Rickmansworth in their new Riley, a treat after my first term at boarding school; I was 6 years old. Driving up the new Watford by-pass I saw an aeroplane bank low over the road ahead and disappear into a field. No doubt screaming with excitement, I persuaded my father to pull up. There in the field was a bi-plane, engine ticking over and a sign which read '5 shillings for 5 minutes'. I must have been a very persuasive youngster, for the next thing I knew I was following my mother into the rear cockpit and standing on a circular wicker seat, clutching what I now know to have been a Scarff Gun Ring (Avro 504? Brisfit? I don't know). A pair of oversized goggles was thrust on my head and we were off! Bouncing over the rough ground, a sharp turn by the hedge, a lot of noise and wind and we were airborne. That magic moment when the wheels left the ground, the bumps ceasing and the countryside below falling away is still very clear in my mind; it was like entering a new world. When I fly today, that moment of breaking away from the earth still fills me with a great sense of freedom and enjoyment. All too soon we were back on the ground and I was hauled out. I looked up at the pilot (god to me) and there was just a hint of a smile behind his goggles.

I was hooked!

It is strange how some memories are surprisingly clear when others are dulled. Indeed many must be either erased or suppressed forever. That drive in the Riley to London is the only memory I have of seeing my parents together and yet we had lived in the same place, Rickmansworth, since I was born.

One day my Dad took me to see the Hendon Air Pageant; it must have been around about 1936 or earlier. I watched spellbound as a lumbering Heyford dropped "bombs" of chalk on huge skittles from around 1,000ft. The Central Flying School Aerobatics Team performed in Avro Tutors, with their wings tied together – the most wonderful formation aerobatics. And I saw the new Boulton and Paul Overstrand Bomber; the first aircraft with a power-operated gun turret (in the nose position). This all fuelled my already strong desire to fly.

I went to live with my mother, who was Belgian, and we made frequent visits to her family in Europe. Prior to my epic flight our trips were, of course, by train and boat – but the sea was not kind to my young tum, so we now flew. I remember well a trip to Brussels in a Fokker Tri-motor, and more than one in a DH86 Express. On one trip I watched a streak of oil on the starboard inner engine cowling gradually make its way to the rear of the Nacelle and could not understand why it moved so slowly or why it reversed its direction before flying off. Another trip was to Zurich in a shiny metal monster of Swissair, a DC2, but best of all, just before the war, my mother put me in the care of Imperial Airways to fly unaccompanied from Croydon to Paris in a Handley Page 42.

We boarded through canvas tunnels on wheels with all four engines running (I suppose this was to save embarrassment if an engine failed to start). The captain sat me in the first row behind the cockpit (facing rearwards) and left this 9-year-old completely enthralled. Later I was led into the cockpit, very noisy, to see Captain O.P. Jones himself at the controls, sitting behind a wheel that would not have been out of place in a London bus! Some 30 years later, I met OP again at Lasham, at a gliding competition.

"You won't remember me, but I remember you…" started our conversation! We had one other thing in common; we had both flown Stratocruisers (Boeing 377). There are many stories about this legendary pilot, one of which, I believe, concerns the stopping of all 4 engines in a Liberator over the Atlantic. It is said that OP turned round to face the distraught flight engineer and said, "Strangely quiet is it not, Mister?"!

Following my parents' divorce my mother went to live with a Dr MacGregor in Finchley, North West London. She married him a month before the war broke out. He continued to practise as a GP until called up to the RAF and posted to Padgate, a dreadful place near Blackpool. We left London before the worst of the Blitz, but not before a bomb hit the road next to our house and caused much damage to the Tube tunnel below it. It damaged the house which was eventually pulled down. The bomb also opened up the sewers, which flooded into our 'sunken garden'!

But prior to this my mother had flown to Brussels a week before the invasion of the Low Countries to get her mother 'out'. This she achieved on the last civil boat out of Calais. It was just as well that the old lady was rescued; the Hun has a long memory. Our family had been involved in the Great War with Nurse Edith Cavell's prisoner of war escape organisation, and were very lucky not to have joined that lady at the firing squad. The second time around my Uncle Paul, who had been a young medical student in 1917 and also active in helping our POWs, had to flee for his life out of the kitchen window when the Gestapo broke in to round up all likely resistance workers, only two weeks following the occupation of Brussels. Paul walked, hitchhiked and somehow got himself to Nice and to my mother's sister Germaine, who was already involved in getting escapees through the South of France and then, either by fishing boat or hiking over the Pyrenees to Spain and Gibraltar.

Paul eventually made it over the mountains, a journey which would fill a book – the first of many such journeys for hundreds of escapees. One incident remains in my mind, in Spain he used to sleep in cemeteries on his journey to Gib. He awoke one night to the sound of digging. Peering out he saw about 20 men and women digging a large pit. They put down their tools and then, as he watched, horrified, one-by-one the Spanish shot them and pitched them into the pit. Paul always thought Spain posed more of a danger than occupied France and was able to give a valuable insight on escaping to MI9 on his arrival in London.

Germaine was also lucky and survived two arrests and interviews with the Gestapo. Both these interrogations were carried out by a particularly evil man, a White Russian; she never forgot him. After the war she joined her daughter in Darien, Connecticut USA and in 1949 she bumped into the same White Russian in a New York Restaurant. Thinking quickly, she discovered from the Restaurateur, a fellow Frenchman, that this man was a frequent visitor and had refugee status. The FBI was informed, a trap was laid, and Germaine had the pleasure of seeing him arrested. We never knew the outcome of this satisfying incident but we all hoped and prayed that it was painful, prolonged and fatal.

Meanwhile my stepfather had survived Padgate and we moved to RAF Cranwell. I recall watching and listening to the first thousand bomber raids forming up over Lincolnshire in the darkening sky, a mass of aircraft orbiting and gaining height. Two collided and fell some miles away with an appalling noise. The next morning a Halifax flew low overhead with an engine feathered and flaps fully down. I am sure the Hastings had the same hydraulic system; accumulator pressure pumped your flaps up and the system pressure pushed them down – no accumulator pressure equals flaps down. The aircraft had been badly shot up and belly-landed in a field half a mile away, causing great excitement to us youngsters. The crew were OK and we rushed there after school to view the site.

In May 1941 more excitement, a "Queen Mary" transport drove through the village of Leasingham with a strange aeroplane, covered by a tarpaulin, and with an armed guard. It did not seem to have a propeller. I spoke to my stepfather later that day on what I had seen, to be told very firmly 'no more questions and keep quiet about it'. It was of course the E28-39 – Whittle's first jet-powered aircraft. Yet another bit of excitement was caused by a Whitley landing on the West Wing of the College at Cranwell. For many years the temporary roof patch was clearly visible.

Another posting followed to RAF Cosford near Wolverhampton, with yet another new school for me. It was now obvious to my Ma that my educational standards were falling far behind and the decision was made for me to go to a boarding school. So in January 1944, after cramming for my common entrance exam, I entered Shrewsbury School and more importantly to me, was now old enough to join the Air Training Corps.

The ATC was rather looked down upon by those in the OTC (Officer Training Corp) the school having been very much Army orientated (Sir Phillip Sydney and all that). However, we got to fly in aeroplanes, lots of aeroplanes, while our pongo brigade drilled with carbines that had seen service at Ladysmith! I got my backside tanned on several occasions for getting caught sneaking my bicycle into school having been flying at RAF High Ercal, a maintenance unit, when I should have been studying. Flights in Halifax's, Venturers, Martinets, Wellingtons, and Harvard's were my happy lot. My stepfather arranged, in the holidays, for a couple of flights in Horsa troop-carrying gliders on delivery from Cosford to Southern airfields just before D-day. On one the towrope broke and we put down at the small airfield of Whitney. The Whitley tug landed, the towrope shortened and we resumed our journey to Netheravon. Taking off from that somewhat uneven airfield to return to Cosford, the Whitley's props struck the ground and we landed none-the-wiser at Cosford with six inches missing from each blade. On another occasion from RAF Shawbury I struck lucky with a four-hour navigation trip in a Wellington (often called 'the Cloth Bomber', it being fabric-covered). Following a pressing need for the Elsan I walked aft down the catwalk and had just put my foot off the bomb bay step when the cover of the belly dustbin turret (not fitted) flew open, revealing the heaving sea. At the same moment a pair of large hands grabbed me from behind and pulled this wee lad to safety. It was the wireless operator, who had noticed the lid opening and closing in flight and rescued me just in time.

Needless to say, I did not rise to any academic heights at school (I did eventually pass my School Certificate). I guess I must have been easily led by pranksters and troublemakers; I still am. One accomplishment that I recall was stacking up the music master's pride and joy, an Austin Seven, on bricks. I hasten to add that I merely assisted in this operation, for I happened to be passing the music house at the time. Of course, the whole thing went wrong, the owner got in, fired up, let in the clutch and revved for all he was worth. The car fell off the bricks, the back wheels joined the front ones and the whole thing fell apart. It was over a week before I could sit down without extreme discomfort!

In the spring of 1945 I managed by good behaviour to be selected for an ATC gliding course at Hockley Heath – No.4 Elementary Gliding School, near Birmingham. Training in those days was on the Dagling Primary, there were no dual control gliders available, this was real flying by wire stuff, no instruments or fuselage and a lot of loose control wires. The rudder pedals had straps to hold your feet in and you had a joystick; aft movement of which could be restricted by inserting a pin in a bracket thus preventing full up movement of the elevator and a U.T. pilot from becoming airborne in the first goes. Attached to the nose was a cable from a modified balloon barrage winch on the far side of the airfield, the driver of which regulated ones forward speed. At first we were given ground slides just fast enough to practise aileron control, maintaining the wings level then the speed was increased bringing the rudder into play. After half a dozen of these and plenty of advice from the instructor we were given a low hop up to 25 feet where movement of the rudders elevators and ailerons were co-ordinated! A few more low hops and then a high hop to 200 feet. The winch driver had a great deal of responsibility at this stage (we were not allowed to release the cable) it was he who regulated our speed and height. The big day finally arrived and I did my first type rating on the Kirby Kadet, rather like the Colditz Glider but a real machine with fuselage but no instruments. We were now in pioneer country, high hops to 200 feet and then 300, releasing the cable ourselves - eventually to 400 for our A certificate check. The final brief by my sweating instructor, and a wan encouraging smile, "take up the slack" and then "all out" and I was off, my very first real solo and almost my last. Due to a breakdown in communications the winch man thought I was on a circuit and winched me up as far as I could go, about 700 feet. The tow wire automatically back-released when I was over the winch. This was really flying I thought as I sailed on into the sunset, only to suddenly realise I could not land ahead

and turning was to be taught the next day. I managed a skidding 180°
turn and then another nearer the launch point, much, much lower. I
landed still skidding, ripped the skid off without harm to myself. The
instructor, sweating a little more now, ran up, bless him, and popped
me straight into another Kadet to do the same thing again, well,
another high hop again! Later having mastered turns I got my B
Certificate and returned to school one very happy young man, my
head having swollen to twice it's normal size.

During my last term at school I was able to further my gliding at
Castle Bromwich (48 EGS) still on the Kadet.

2. Struggling to Fly

In January '46 the RAF college at Cranwell invited applications for the first postwar course and I applied forthwith. I passed the various interviews and tests until coming a cropper on the medical. My left eye suffered from a slight astigmatism and my sight was not considered good enough. Nowadays it would pass without a problem but in 1946 with some 500 applicants for 40 places, I guess the Service could be choosy. This threw me back into the National Service melting pot and in January 1947 I was called up for the Army at Budbroke Barracks, Warwickshire. I will not dwell too much on the Army for that winter was one of the coldest on record and coal was still scarce. I remember standing in a long queue of recruits in the snow outside the station medical centre, stripped to the waist waiting for a cocktail of jabs. There were not many of us still standing at the end.

After six weeks of square bashing, it came to an end and I applied for the Parachute Regiment and started training at Aldershot. Within two weeks I went down with Scarlet Fever and spent a month in the Cambridge Hospital at Aldershot. I well remember having to lie to attention when the Matron did her rounds! To get fit enough to return to the para training battalion would have taken several weeks and being National Service with limited time it was thought I would be better off in something less physically demanding and so I found myself on Salisbury Plain in the Royal Artillery, training to be a gunner surveyor. For one who had showed very poor mathematical ability at school, it was quite an ordeal, but the 9-month course was very interesting and ever since I have had a fascination for maps.

In January 1948 I was commissioned as a Second Lieutenant into the Royal Army Service Corps and joined an Air Despatch Company, No.54 in Hildsheim, Germany, just in time to get involved in the Berlin airlift. The airlift was great fun, my company being responsible for the loading of Yorks and Dakotas at Wunsdorf and I often had to fly to Berlin on duty. Any time I had to spare I spent at the RAF gliding club at Gutersloh, but I never had time to get enough experience in gliding in anything other than a primary glider. Still, they had a superb German winch that would get you up to nearly 1,200 feet.

Eventually I escaped from the Army in April '49 and in May that year I joined BOAC at Airways Terminal, London in the Traffic Department. By now I had almost resigned myself to being a Penguin, and Traffic offered an opening for overseas service as a Traffic Manager at out stations. However, this was not to be. The corporation decided to employ local staff whenever possible, although this decision was not made until the end of 1950. In the meantime I became thoroughly involved in gliding again with the Surrey Gliding Club at Redhill, where I obtained a Silver C in August 1950. I vividly recall the five-hour endurance test one had to do, flying in a strong southwesterly wind over the Seven Sisters in Sussex, having been launched by winch from the old Friston airstrip at 5 o'clock in the morning. I spent most of that flight over Beachy Head at about 1,500 feet with the occasional beat along the cliffs to Seaford. Sitting up over the lighthouse in the Olympia, I had little forward speed and could maintain my position quite easily, escorted by a host of seagulls who seemed to accept my presence. It was a memorable experience.

Later in the year my whole life was changed by a chance remark I made about my early attempt to get into Cranwell, in the presence of Ann Welch. There have been three great aviation ladies in my life who have helped me to obtain the flying career that I have so much enjoyed. I owe them a debt that I can never repay; Ann was the first. Hearing my story, she suggested I try a different approach. Now that I had a Silver C, I could get 10 hours knocked off the standard PPL course of 40 hours. Why didn't I join the Ultra Light Aircraft Association (the forerunner of the Popular Flying Association) at Redhill, learn to fly at 30 shillings an hour (I earned £10 a week in those days) get my Private Pilot's Licence and apply to join the RAFVR as a cadet pilot? "Who knows," she added, "you might end up in the RAF after all! Go for the medical and see what they say."

I did, and now my sight was quite acceptable for a PPL and the RAF Volunteer Reserve. And so I made the change from motor-less flight to power although I still remained with the Surrey Gliding Club, even after the move to Lasham, in fact, I kept up my gliding activities right through my RAF career through the auspices of the RAFGSA (RAF Gliding and Soaring Association) and eventually achieved a Gold C, number 46 and two diamonds. The third diamond, 500k cross-country, has eluded me, although I have been within 40k of it on the odd occasion.

So I joined the ULAA group at Redhill, under the tutelage of Jean Bird, an ex Air Transport Auxiliary girl and probably one of the best instructors I have ever had. Jean lived in a real gypsy caravan on a dispersal at the west end of the airfield, where we had a small hanger. Our fleet consisted of two Moth Minors, GAFOZ and GAEPR, and the one and only Zaunkonig G-ALUA which I now believe has been returned to its place of birth, Brunswick University. This unique aircraft was the forerunner in design of the Fiesler Storch, the Luftwaffe's Army Co-operation Aeroplane.

My first flight in OZ with Jean was on the 24th March 1951 and thereafter I managed about one a week, all I could afford until going solo on 13th April after 3 hours and 10 minutes duel. The Moth was a delight to fly with its 90 horsepower engine and could out-climb a Chipmunk; its only drawbacks were a narrow track undercarriage and a perforated wooden air-brake underneath the fuselage, which could get snagged in long grass on landing.

One flew the Moth Minor solo from the front seat. This reminds me of one of Jean's endearing tricks; this was to put her Labrador dog in the front seat complete with helmet and special harness and taxi pass some unsuspecting onlookers on the airfield with her head well below the cockpit rim in the rear seat. I am not at all sure that the dog did not even fly with her at times. Jean and Jacky Moggridge, another famous ATA girl, were eventually awarded full RAF wings, not before time, flying Meteors. Jean had some 4,000 hours and umpteen different types in her logbook.

I took my PPL in June and my acceptance test for the VR in August and started flying Tigers with 15 Reserve Flying School at Redhill. During the intervening period, I continued with Jean's outfit, she encouraged us to do cross-countries as often as possible, as far as cash flow would permit of course. I flew AFOZ whenever I had some spare dosh: morning coffee at the Beehive, Gatwick in the morning and tea at Panshanger later was a delightful way to spend a day. I also made it to Croydon before it shut. My last flight with Jean was in April 52, just prior to flying out to Southern Rhodesia for flying training. It was a freebee, a sort of parting present in AFOZ, during which she showed me every conceivable way of killing oneself – for example beating up your girlfriend's house into the wind and then doing it downwind, slow turns to wave to onlookers until we flicked over and started to spin and a lot more! I have never forgotten that flight or the lessons learned and I am sure it has saved my neck on more than one occasion. Twenty years later when I started to instruct on light aircraft at Booker I would pass on to post solo students these little gems. Sadly, Jean was killed flying an Aerovan in 1957.

My first flight in a Tiger with the RAF was with 'Tiny' Marshall, an ex-London bus driver and founder member of the London Transport Flying Club back in the 30s. Tiny stood 6 feet 6 and when sitting in the front seat of a Tiger I am sure he could see over the top wing. Again I was lucky; I could not have had a better teacher. I remember the great emphasis on forced landings without power and Tiny turning around and bellowing, "You've just bloody well killed me again!" when I got it wrong. We were taught always to have a landing area in mind for such an event and I still bear it in mind when out flying single-engine aeroplanes.

The reliability of modern day engines has become so good that a lot of Private Pilots in general aviation give the prospect of an engine failing little thought. I recall when I was instructing on singles and twins, it was often hard to convince students that the day might come when their super reliable 'donk' up-front would cease to rotate. But I did once, just once, have the great satisfaction of being thanked by a new PPL holder for my efforts in hammering home forced landings after his Cherokee suffered complete engine failure on his first solo cross-country as a licensed pilot.

I digress. We even practised re-starts in the air which required the Tiger to be pointed vertically earthward at its max speed of 138 knots plus a few more in order to persuade the prop to turn round. The noise is indescribable; try it sometime! Our boss of 15 RFS was "Scotty" – Wing Commander Scott, a peppery little man and much respected. No.2 was a Squadron Leader Lasch (known as Splash) who was reported to have had over 5,000 hours on Tiger Moths and had the leathery face to prove it. He was quite a character and liked to fly a Tiger below the control Tower windows on occasions.

Perhaps I should mention that Redhill in the early 1950s housed, in addition to the gliding club and the ULAA, Miles Aircraft, Tilman Langley Laboratories, the RAFVR and the Flying Club! It was a very busy little airfield. I remember a garden party hosted by the flying club when dear old Splash gave a superb demonstration of Tiger aerobatics which would have given an air display safety committee a collective heart attack! In his final loop he cut it too fine and just brushed the wheels on the deck. The wheels came off and the rest of it hit the ground, going very fast, and disintegrated into silence… Then, from the middle of the largest pile of wreckage appeared Splash. Taking off his parachute he marched to the clubhouse, glaring at all of us.

There was a similar incident when a student pilot in a Tiger, taking off for his very first solo, unfortunately left his wheels behind on the ground. Not having radio he proceeded to fly his brief first circuit and was obviously very pleased to see the small crowd of onlookers at touchdown, all frantically waving and pointing. Polite to a tee, he waved back. The crunch on landing soon wiped the smile off his face, but apart from a broken nose he was OK.

Sticking to wheelie stories, F.G. Miles had just turned out the new Aries Gemini, with Gypsy Six engines. I don't remember the test pilot's name, but as he came over the clubhouse on the first flight for landing, members on the veranda swear they heard the undercarriage warning horn sound in the aeroplane… Another cruncher!

I was also lucky enough to get several trips in the Oxford. For a new cadet pilot this really was a rare opportunity. I also have to thank Lorne Welch, who took me with him in a Gemini to the Scillies to pick up a load of early spring daffodils. It all seems so long ago, but it was the encouragement of so many people, apart from Jean and Ann, that set me on my flying career.

Night flying was fun, using a single row of gooseneck flares and, of course, no landing lights. Control was by Aldis Lamp from the airfield caravan at touchdown. In the 1950s one was discouraged from using any form of aircraft lighting for landing and takeoff. A lot of airfields still used goosenecks and even those (master diversions) with electric runway lights had no approach lighting, the airfield being in utter blackness apart from the runway flarepath. Some did have the wartime Drem system – a few white lights on poles which, if followed, took you downwind and onto finals – first developed at Drem in Scotland during the war.

By now Korea had flared up and the RAF began to recruit aircrew again. I applied to the RAFVR for a transfer to the RAF and, as far as I remember, was accepted in October 51, having had another medical at CME and passed the aircrew aptitude test at Hornchurch. I left BOAC forthwith and started my two weeks 'camp' (an annual requirement) with the VR at Redhill, cramming in another 40 hours. Since my parents lived at Lingfield I could live at home.

The VR taught me a lot. We had the benefit of some very experienced instructors in a very congenial atmosphere and I was sorry to leave at the end of the year. It had been an interesting time and it really was not until very recently that I realised just what had gone on in those few months. Hugh Kendall had designed and built the first fibreglass sailplane (Crabpot), 'cooking' the wing in a huge oven. Surrey Flying Services still had two DH Flamingos, Miles had produced the Gemini Aries, Ranald Porteus was test-flying the tiny Chilton Monoplane and on the extreme eastern edge of the airfield, near a wartime blister hanger, were parked a couple of Walrus amphibians. Much banging and hammering could be heard from this hanger for some months until one day a third Walrus emerged. Two weeks later it took off, where to I never knew, but I think someone said Australia.

The incident I remember best concerned two quite famous ex-ATA girls who were doing a bit of mutual instruction in a Magister on forced landings. Somehow they managed to stop the engine. The wags drinking on the flying club veranda swore they heard two voices in unison from the now silent Maggie shout, "You have control!" A minute later the aircraft landed just short of the field, with a resounding splosh, in the sewage farm. Neither lady was hurt but understandably no one volunteered to drive their car over to pick them up!

3. Harvards in Africa

Because I had been commissioned in the Army, I was inducted into the RAF as an APO (Acting Pilot Officer), considered as an officer right from the start, so although I did the complete new entry course at No.5 Initial Training School (Cosford) I could at least live in the officers' mess while the other entrants roughed it in barrack blocks. In any case, their lot was a much more comfortable one than mine had been during my first six weeks in the Army in 1947! Another ex-Army officer joined me at Cosford, John Cheesbrough, who became a lifelong friend; we still meet frequently.

One of the more enjoyable episodes of the course was the 24-hour 'escape and evasion' exercise. We were taken in separate groups of four and dumped by 3-tonner to the south of Iron Bridge, on the west bank of the Severn. John and I teamed up with two others. The Police and the local Territorial Army were looking for us and all bridges were being watched. Our task was to reach the old airfield at Atcham and to get there we had to cross the Severn and go over the Wrekin, a 1,000 foot hill near Wellington, at night to reach our destination by dawn. We crossed the river by the old Iron Bridge, which although unsafe and closed to pedestrians, was not being watched. It was dark by the time we reached the vicinity of the Wrekin. The flashing red 'Pundit' warning light on top reflecting in the clouds gave us some help. The Army on the crest were out in force but we managed to creep across within the designated borders and started downhill. Half way down one of our party gave a terrified squawk and screeched that he was sitting on the edge of a precipice. Sure enough, this indeed seemed the case. John eased himself down about 20 feet away and crawled towards him, to find that his feet were just 6 inches off the surface of a path! We made it to airfield and it was a home run.

I got involved as well in the station's gliding club and did quite a lot of flying at weekends. Time passed quickly and was pretty routine, drill – Air Force law, basic aerodynamics, navigation etc – and in May we passed out minus about 20% of our original number. The cadets now became Acting Pilot Officers like John and I and we prepared for our training in Southern Rhodesia. I had also managed a bit more Tiger Moth flying, with Murray Mair, a flight commander. On one trip we spied a lone figure walking around the perimeter track. "Watch this!" he shouted, as he dived on him at high speed, causing him to duck. As we passed over him a second time, even lower, I saw his handlebar moustaches flutter in the wind and realised to my horror that it was Wing Commander Baxter, our commanding officer. Murray never rose above Flight Lieutenant, but then neither did I.

With the end of the course I had two weeks leave to equip myself with tropical kit, pack a trunk, get married, have a honeymoon and turn up at Lyneham to catch a Skyways York for Livingstone.

The 10th June found us at RAF Clyffe Pypard, an ex-Elementary Flying School and grass airfield just south of Lyneham, now used as a transit camp. The next day we embarked in a Skyways York for a three day trip to Livingstone, where we split into two groups, mine going by Central African Airways Viking to RAF Thornhill near Gwelo and the other thirty-odd going to RAF Heany near Bulawayo with John. We landed at 8am on 15th June and to our astonishment were met by the Group Captain, all the Station brass and the Station Warrant Officer, who formed us up in threes for inspection by the Station Master. On being told we were so scruffy as to be a disgrace to the RAF we were marched to our quarters to change into best blue for another inspection in five minutes. Then to the main Lecture Room for a most unwelcoming address by the Station Master, followed by an hour's tirade by the Padre on the evils of sex with the natives and then it was to Sick Quarters for a FFI (free from infection) inspection, all standing starkers with some unfortunates (not me) having 'parts' daubed with gentian violet by the Orderly.

At last we were released to the APO's mess for lunch. Half way through, the chief flying instructor ordered us back to quarters to put on tropical kit for another inspection, then into PT kit to be doubled to the gym and here we spent an hour running around exercising on horses, boxes and parallel bars. I particularly remember having to run round and round with one hand on my head and the other on my hip.

Back to quarters, changed back into best blue (it was winter) and then to the mess for dinner. By now we were dog tired and very despondent and not looking forward to 9 months of this routine. We were just about to sit down to eat when we were ordered into the anteroom, where the Group Captain and the whole Station Brass, Padre, Doctor, etc were assembled, only this time they were in civvies, with broad grins, each one holding two large tankards of beer.

The penny dropped. We had been 'conned' and had just endured the standard traditional welcoming of No. 5 Flying Training School by the senior course, No.8 (we were number 13). The day's events had been a gigantic and extremely well-executed hoax and I am glad to say that all of us took it in good part. It was the relief that I remember best, of knowing that life was not going to be as bad as we had first thought. After a big thrash we had a week's 'acclimatisation' (Thornhill is nearly 4,000ft above sea level). We did very little apart from lectures – bliss! A new course would arrive every six weeks or so and we looked forward to the entertainment of their first day.

Training started in earnest at ground school; I seem to remember we worked tropical hours i.e. work finished about 2pm. First flying detail was quite early, about 6am. Sometimes in the summer months after August, low cloud would form a complete cover at 1,000ft, not very thick, but it took half and hour to burn off and one could get caught out when flying off the circuit at this time of the morning. The locals called it *guti*.

The first flying phase was in the Chipmunk, a delightful aeroplane, and lasted about 10 weeks. I was assigned to Flight Lieutenant Slessor, son of Marshal of the Royal Air Force Sir John Slessor, and I see from my logbook that he took care of me for about 80% of my Chipmunk flying. Our first trip was a survey of the local area from the Shabani River to the South and the round smooth 1000ft granite lump known as Umgulugulu to a dam some 30 miles to the north. In the dry season the Shabani was much reduced in size but contained several large pools where on the first day's detail one could fly down and watch the hippos enjoy an early morning bath. We returned to Thornhill after an hour in an inverted glide, which my instructor apparently always did to test his pupils. Some four hours and forty minutes later I went solo again. I much enjoyed the primary phase. John Slessor, and indeed every other instructor, was an excellent teacher and friend and we still are in touch. Only one incident sticks in my mind; we were half way back on a cross-country from Que-Que, about 80 miles to the north, when I noticed that the port nine gallon fuel tank read one gallon while the starboard showed full. This was not an unusual situation in those days and the full tank usually started to feed at about this imbalance (Mod H207 anti siphon hole in the vent system eventually cured this). It was a very bumpy day, typical for the time of the year and so Sir decided that some aerobatics would induce the non-return valve in the starboard tank to open up and feed the engine. The engine stopped.

My instructor said "Well?" so I set up a forced landing pattern on an area of flat Bundu. John called Thornhill and down we went. I was lucky to have an instructor who was able to turn a potential sticky situation into an unforgettable lesson and example in instructing that I have always remembered. John took over for the landing and touched down on the bone-dry grass and we trundled rapidly towards a large anthill. He jammed the brakes on hard and the aeroplane came to a halt nearly on its nose. Pride was all that was hurt but the ants must have thought that doomsday had arrived. Fourteen years later I was to experience a similar situation, also in a Chipmunk.

Ground school was run mainly by ex-aircrew staff, and jolly good they were too, especially one Master Pilot Taylor, who could make aircraft instruments, a rather dull subject involving gyro's etc, into something really interesting. We of course marched everywhere, except for me, as I was course leader and the oldest at 23, and gave the marching orders. It was at this time that we noticed that one of our number seemed to be unable to swing his arms in the conventional manner. Left foot forward was always followed by the left arm. Rifle drill became hysterical. Anyway, he passed out with the rest of us (more later) and eventually became a Senior Captain and training manager in BEA. Incidentally, my ex-Army colleague John Cheesbrough also became a course leader. It was a very pleasant 10 weeks and the final phase on Harvards proved just as much fun. In fact, looking back, it was one of the best flying experiences that I can remember. Instead of shelling out 30 bob an hour to fly a Moth Minor I was actually getting paid to fly!

We started Harvard flying in early September, just before the onset of the summer and the rains. October is known by the locals as the suicide month because of the high humidity and the heat preceding the rains. Again John Slessor sent me solo before leaving Thornhill and returning to the UK. His dining out prior to departure was the usual rowdy affair and afterwards John drove home very slowly across the airfield to his house. Fumbling for his keys and kicking up a lot of noise he woke his wife Anne up, who thought 'Bandits!' and grabbing John's Webley pistol, opened the bedroom window and fired five shots in the direction of the racket. All missed, thank God, but it had an instantly sobering effect on the intruder!

I liked the Harvard, still do, but it was not until I was re-acquainted with it thanks to John Romain at Duxford in 1993 that I realised just how good this aeroplane is as a trainer and how pleasant it is to fly.

Thornhill had a small gliding club with a SG-38 Primary Glider, T31 two-seater and a Tutor. Whatever spare time I had I used to help out and do a little gliding. I managed to wind up the SG38 to 2000ft in very turbulent dry thermals. Those of you who know the SG38 will appreciate the strength of the thermals in Africa. Half way through training came the mid-course leave. The gliding club had received invitations from the South African National Gliding Association to assist in their National Championships and six of us set out for Bloemspruit airfield near Bloemfontein in the Group 'Pig' (Valetta). It was to be an 'official' visit, Bloemspruit being a military airfield. On arrival we were each allocated to a competitor to help in retrieves etc. I joined up with one Helli Lasch, a Swiss businessman who had lived in Johannesburg for several years. He was the owner of a brand new

Air 100 18-metre sailplane. As luck would have it, the organisers were short of tug pilots so I did quite a lot of towing in Tigers when not retrieving. The Tigers had tailwheels instead of skids and no brakes; one had to plan ahead a lot further than usual when taxiing. The weather was perfect. It was December, fair weather CU everywhere, visibility was unlimited and the temperature was up in the 80s.

In addition to the luxurious interior of Helli's Air 100 he had installed a two-way VHF radio; he must have been among the first to do this. On one flight to a declared goal I was able to drive his American Ford and trailer to his destination and guide him down on the radio to a landing. This must have been an all time first in gliding! Another retrieve took us across the Southern Drakensberg Mountains to, I think, the town of Elliot, some 250 miles from Bloemfontein – a South African record flight. It was dark as we drove through the mountains and reached our destination at about 2am. A short kip and we dismantled the Air 100 and were on our way back by 10. Driving through the mountains, this time in daylight, I gazed in horror at the deep precipices we had so happily negotiated in the dark! Most of this part of the road was not sealed by tarmac; there were no barriers on the road sides, it was a single track and the drop on some stretches was vertically down more than a thousand feet. I have a poor head for heights and I did not enjoy this drive, in spite of the wild beauty of the landscape.

That evening, in complete contrast, we all went to the cinema to see *The Importance of Being Ernest*. Bloemfontein was the capital of the Orange Free State, where most people spoke only Afrikaans. Nevertheless, this very English film played to a full house and received a standing ovation at the end!

After a week of non-stop competition flying the organisers called a rest and day and Helli offered me his Air 100 for a day. It was my idea of heaven – a superb sailplane with a parachute, barograph, full instrument panel and a leopard skin lined cockpit was all mine for the day. I waited until 11 o'clock, having got my barograph officially sealed (luckily), organised a tug and clad only in sandals, shorts and shirt I was off. Releasing at 800ft above the ground (the airfield is about 2,500ft above sea level) I caught a thermal to the newly-formed cloud base at 6,000ft in amongst a bunch of swallows busily catching insects and headed towards a large cloud forming about 10 miles away. I made contact with its thermal about 1000ft above the ground (a bit of nail biting here) circled and started climbing with the variometer jammed full 'up'. Into cloud at 7,000ft, very dark, reducing the bank to about 30° we climbed rapidly in very smooth air with the altimeter winding up at an unbelievable rate later measured at 5,000ft a minute. Past 10,000ft and still strong, smooth lift, tapping the altimeter in sheer disbelief, 15,000ft, oxygen on – oh Lord it is only quarter full! – very dark and cold now, ice inside and outside the canopy and on the wings, snow coming in through the air vents. 20,000ft and starting to get very turbulent, my lily-white legs now covered with snow. The turbulence increased and I barked my shins more than once on the bottom of the instrument panel. I increased bank to stay in the narrowing circle of lift and it gradually got lighter, we were suddenly tipped out of the side of the cloud in brilliant sunshine at 24,000ft. Lots of ice on the wings, chilled to the marrow and with the oxygen reading zero I headed downhill. The speed brakes had frozen shut, I should have remembered to exercise them, so our rate of descent was not all that high, despite the weight of ice. I saw a dam I recognised through a gap in the cloud; it put me some 40 miles south of the airfield and I headed for home in and out of cloud. At 8,000ft I saw Bloemfontein. The ice left the ship, I began to thaw out and I soared away in great happiness for another two hours before landing at about 3pm. Following the examination of the barograph I found that I climbed well in excess of the minimum height of my 'diamond' height. A memorable day, 7th December 1952; I shall always be grateful to Helli for his generosity.

Another week of competition of flying followed until on the penultimate day the weather began to change. The temperature and humidity increased and several large CU clouds were developing upwind of the airfield. The task for the day was scrubbed, but Helli, never to be deterred, thought a squall line would develop and he wanted to soar along in front of it, a feat that he had once accomplished, flying flat out straight and level for some 60 miles. Would I tow with him? Certainly.

An hour later and it was time to go, a well developed squall line was lying a few miles upwind and moving rapidly in our direction. If I took off now I would be able to release the glider in the right place, fly around the storm to the south and land at Tempe airfield at the other side of town. Alas there was a fumble with the glider, Helli was not even in the cockpit and the rising dust was a mile away. This was no place for a Tiger. I released the rope yelled to the airman on my wing tip to get as many people on to the glider as possible to hold it down, opened the throttle and took off well ahead of the rising dust but alas not of the wind! The left wing dropped, hit the ground with a crunch that I can still hear followed by the nose, wheels, right wing and I ended up back at the take-off point upside down. I soon discovered, as others have done, that it is impossible when hanging in your straps to undo your harness turn-buckle and at the same time get your hand on the ground in time to break your earthbound fall on your neck.

Helli faired much better and the Air 100 survived unscathed. I never discovered what caused him to fumble so badly; the met office measured the wind at 67 knots, the onlookers thought my gyrations were quite entertaining but the local Civil Aviation man was not a happy bunny. Paperwork kept him busy for two days. Helli and I took well-deserved flak for thinking that we could get away with such a caper. We returned to Thornhill a few days later to finish off the last week of our half term leave. My wife, Pam, then still working for BOAC, had managed to get a seat out to Bulawayo (and back) in a Comet doing crew training and we had a few great days in Victoria Falls before she returned to London on Comet YP.

Before she left I jokingly said "if the window blows out don't hang on to your next door neighbour because you will all go out like a string of sausages." Prophetic words indeed; YP crashed near Elba after the pressure hull had ruptured two years later.

We got stuck in to the last months of the Harvard phase of the course which was quite concentrated because the rains had started which effected the flying programme but I did manage another visit to Bulawayo for a long week-end to visit friends, this time by night-train, a so called express. Railways in Rhodesia were narrow gauge, the rolling stock late Victorian. Steam was the motive power with huge Garret engines much in evidence. The night sleeper was something of a time capsule; the compartments were all fitted out in beautiful mahogany and brass work. Bulawayo was only a 100 odd miles away but the journey took all night at the standard 25 miles per hour and there were many stops, it was a great experience.

In January the Station Master hosted a wedding reception in the mess for one of the students of the Senior Course and his bride, a daughter of one of the staff. There was a great party and our gallant lad had somehow obtained some red roses at great expense for the occasion. Because the Senior Course was a bit behind, he had to fly the following night on a duel cross-country, the aircraft did not return. At 4.00 a.m. I was woken up to get our course to the briefing room pronto for a dawn search. We were to be observers in the back seat with a staff pilot flying. At dawn 10 Harvards lined up abreast on the edge of the airfield and as one, took off in line abreast. I don't suppose I shall ever experience a more exhilarating take off. As we climbed to 1000ft, we peeled off in turn to search the track of the lost aircraft one-mile apart. The sun came up over the horizon casting long shadows over the Bundu turning the Kopjes red; a breathtaking sight. The wreckage was found 40 miles away on track at the foot of a pile of rocks, the loss being attributed to thunderstorms. The funeral took place the next day of our fellow student; on the coffin were the red roses, a more poignant gesture I cannot imagine and one that I remember vividly today. The instructor, one of our most popular, was buried the next day.

Night flying began shortly afterwards. One of our number, Phil Pickford, got airborne with his instructor for his first night flight in the Harvard. Just after take-off his instructor told him to land immediately instead of climbing away from the circuit. On landing, Phil kept the engine running while his mentor went back to the crew room to retrieve the detachable control-column for the rear cockpit!

Our flying usually began at dusk with a little upper air work and then into the circuit before it was too dark! I had a Flight Lieutenant Graham-Bowman after John Slessor as my instructor and it was he who introduced me into the joys of aerobatics on a full moonlit night; great fun. I got on well with G-B. It was with him that earlier, when doing a detail on spinning, that each thought the other had control, a classic error which I am sure has been repeated many times. The first two turns of a spin on a Harvard are accompanied by a lot of shuddering after that the spin becomes smoother and the rate of rotation increases rapidly. We were well into the fifth or sixth turn (I lost count) when a strained voice said, "I think you had better recover" to which I replied "I thought this was a demo, sir!" The Harvard normally takes nearly two turns to recover from a spin; this one took at least twice that number!

I well remember my first night cross country in the Harvard to Heany for a touch and go landing and return to Thornhill; dual then solo. It was a lovely clear night with stars so bright one could see the wings in their light. Early in the flight I became aware of a deep red glow under the cowling, my instructor said nothing so I pressed on, so I presumed it was OK It was only on throttling back that I twigged it, exhaust pipes glow red at night! The next night one of my colleagues on another course did the same exercise only on the solo trip he flew all the way down to Heany with his landing gear down, did his touch and go, returned to Thornhill with his gear up and landed wheels still up, slithering across the grass to the Station Master's garden. I think he became a navigator which reminds me that our course started with 32 and ended with 16 (no fatalities). Sadly we were later denied the welcoming ritual for the new course because they were delayed in the U.K. (I was going to be Group Captain!)

On one side of the airfield lived Ma Bogie, 80-year-old widow of Colonel Bogie, one of Rhodes' Pioneers. The colonel's statue stood in the main square of Gwelo and was frequently attired in strange garments by Thornhill students. We were forbidden to fly over her house, under the pain of death, at any time but there was one excuse, a fouled up practise forced landing with a burst of power at the last minute but even this eventually was not accepted after more complaints from the irate widow. She was a remarkable old lady.

In early January the weather people got very excited by a cold front sweeping across Southern Africa from the West Coast. Apparently this only occurred once in a blue moon. Sure enough the temperature dropped overnight from the mid 80s to 48° Fahrenheit and it took two days before it started climbing up again during which we shivered in our Summer Khaki drill uniforms. The weather after this seemed to change, we had some Northerly winds from the Uganda swamps, concern over mosquitoes and malaria were voiced. Indeed, nearly all my course found itself in sick quarters with the shivers and shakes for about a week and we only just crawled out in time for our own passing out parade. It wasn't malaria apparently but I often wondered because for the next 20 years or so I occasionally succumbed to 12 hours of shivers.

The day of our final checks came on 11th February '53 we all got through although one had to be re-examined; this lad, the one who had difficulty swinging his arms, managed the take-off OK but turned the wrong way for downwind into the Chipmunk half of the airfield and landed with the Chipmunks scattering in all directions. I see from my logbook that we finished the course with an aerobatics competition; I managed a 2nd having unfortunately flicked out at the top of a loop. The Wings Parade was on the 20th, Group Captain Cassels a famous pre-war pilot presiding; I think it was the proudest moment of my life. I managed to collar, with a lot of luck, the Best Flying Results trophy, the Cup of Honour and a distinguished pass which led to a Permanent Commission. Believe me, luck played a big part.

And so we were dined-out, packed our gear, said our farewells and flew to Livingston by Viking, where we joined up again with the other 'half' of our Cosford entry. It was good to see John Cheesbrough again. We were thirty-six boisterous and happy chaps as we boarded the Skyways York for Entebbe and home.

But it did not quite work out like that… We took off from Entebbe at night, as it was a little cooler, but 30 minutes later shut down the starboard inner engine and returned to Entebbe. We spent the rest of the night and the next day on the ground while the Flight Engineer, assisted by the BOAC Station Engineer, worked on the engine. Towards evening the BOAC man was overhead saying to the Captain, "If I ever see another of your aircraft in this state I'll ground it!" With these encouraging words we got airborne again. At 10,000 feet the same engine was shut down, but instead of returning to Entebbe we pressed on to Wadi Halfa, occasionally sinking to 8,000 feet and then, with full power applied, we clawed up again. After an hour of this seesawing the Flight Engineer came aft and asked for help in moving baggage from the rear hold to the front of the cabin.

"We seem to be a bit tail-heavy at this speed," he explained.

In later years I found out that the safety height on this route is between 12,000 and 14,000 feet!

We had on board a Flight Lieutenant Chris Waugh, one of our instructors, who was going home and, in fact, about to join East African Airways. An old York and Lancaster pilot, he was appalled at the performance of the flight crew, because he knew the route well and thus our proximity to the peaks. Landing at Wadi Halfa we expected the beast to be fixed. Not so. On we went to Fayid, shutting down number three engine after take-off and flying on in the heat at 3,000 feet. I don't know what Chris said at Fayid but the York Captain was replaced, the engine fixed in half an hour by the RAF (the supercharger had kept slipping out of gear) and we were off to Malta for a night stop, then Lyneham, home and leave ... and the next part of our course.

4. Vampires, Goblins *et alia*

March saw us in Norfolk at No.3 F.T.S. Feltwell, not far from Kings Lynn, for a months acclimatisation flying (Harvards) to be re-acquainted with the vile English weather and improve our flying on instruments and the Lorenz landing system (S.B.A.), and do some ground controlled radar approaches and other pilot-interpreted radio aids to landing in bad weather. After the Rhodesian summer the fenland landscape came as quite a shock. The cold wind howled across the airfield from the northeast, the skies were overcast for much of the time. But at least we were not cadets any more but highly trained and competent Royal Air Force Pilots – or so we thought.

We practised the pattern 'B' instrument procedure. This was quite a challenge; one had to fly four "sides" of a square, adjusting height on each leg, and included 270º / 450º turns at the end of each 2-minute leg as well as changing height. The theory was to return to your point of departure after precisely 16 minutes! It formed part of the RAF instrument rating for nearly all aircraft for most of the 1950s, and was a very good co-ordination exercise.

I remember walking out on the apron for my first sortie, a local familiarisation with an instructor, which we considered a bit *infra-dig* for after all, were we not now fully qualified pilots who had wings on our flying suits to prove it? I started out on the wrong foot by forgetting that I was at sea level and not at 4,000ft in Rhodesia and rammed on full throttle way past the +3 pound maximum boost pressure.

"I thought you might do that," said the voice from the rear seat.

Sweating a little, I took off and headed for Kings Lynn. It was a lovely morning for early March: 6/8 strato-cu at about 2,000ft with a little sea fog around the coast, which encroached a couple of miles inland near the Wash and was moving southwards. We did the required local area familiarisation and then the voice said, "How are your aeros?"

I had done rather well at Thornhill in aeros, so I thought I would make amends for my clanger on take off by doing my usual sequence.

"OK," said the voice, "all yours, and we will then return to base."

A quick glance at the altimeter showed 5,000ft and a good look round and then up with the nose, a boot full of rudder and into the spin, recover, up to a stall turn and a Cuban Eight – my repertoire knew no bounds! It was a lovely morning. Eventually I levelled off just above the strato-cu and headed south to Feltwell.

After a couple of minutes the voice said, "I have control. Very nice – I particularly liked the entry with the spin. Yes, very enjoyable from here."

We flew on, just skimming the cloud tops, always a fun pastime.

"By the way..." said the voice, "what's that over there on the starboard wing?"

I looked, gasped, choked and started to sweat again as we passed a church steeple poking through the "cloud" at our level.

Silence. I thought 'My God, I have blown it this time!'

At last the voice spoke.

"I am quite sure you will never do anything so stupid ever again. READ YOUR ALTIMETER!"

In late February we all got leave and said our farewells, for now we would be split among the many Advanced Flying Units. I was rather chuffed, for I left with another 'above average' assessment, but much chastened after my performance on that first day. Fifty two years later I related my tale of that first trip to another survivor of No.13 Course, Phil Pickford.

"You were not the only one making blunders", he replied. "I got lost on my first solo at Feltwell – too many roads and railways, unlike Rhodesia, which seemed to have just one of each! I was looking for a field (too proud to use the radio) on which to land and ask the way, when I spotted this large one right underneath me – it was Feltwell!"

The next move was to 242 Advanced Flying School (A.F.S) at Tarrant Rushton in Dorset on Meteors and Vampires, the home of Flight

Re-fuelling Limited. The A.F.S. was a "lodger" unit here and our first line servicing was all civilian, courtesy of Flight Re-fuelling. Our quarters were at RAF Grimsdyke, a small Nissan-hutted establishment near Salisbury, requiring a daily bus ride to T-R of some 20 miles. I had an instructor who was from Central Flying School (CFS) and had gone there straight from Cranwell College (known to us lesser mortals as 'Sleaford Tech') – a new departure for the air force, for one usually got a little squadron flying before being considered for CFS. But the RAF was expanding rapidly and there was a shortage of Instructors. We did not hit it off right from the start, his opening words being, "You're quite a bit older than the others, aren't you?" He taught by sarcasm and there was much sighing when I got things wrong.

The system at the time was to do about 5 hours dual in the Meteor VII, a 20-minute solo flight and then fly the Vampire V for all ongoing solo work with further dual in the Meteor. And so it was through to the end of August. We did a lot of formation flying, in pairs and fours and, of course, solo flying. We were introduced to clay pigeon shooting (advocated by that famous wartime fighter pilot Johnny Johnson, now a Group Captain) to learn about deflection.

We also visited Southern Radar at Sopley near Christchurch, once part of the defence radar network in 1940. This was now an underground bunker with a vast rotating radar antenna on top. We worked with Sopley doing upper air practice interceptions during our flying. Low-level cross country flights were also on the syllabus, usually leaving Tarrant to the South and passing close to the Isle of Wight before entering the low-level route. Sometimes (solo) one could deviate a little and pay a noisy visit to the keepers on the Needles Lighthouse just on the southwest tip of the Isle of Wight. Those who were more daring (?) flew through the gap between the largest of the five islets leading to the light, always West to East, until one pilot passed a civil Auster (rather close) going the opposite way!

It was on one of these flights that I was told, just after take-off, to contact Sopley Radar, given a vector to steer maintaining 1000ft and report on an unknown aircraft (bogie). I picked up the 'bogie' near

Sandown; it was a USAF B-47 six jet bomber, essentially a high-level flyer. To cut my story short, I followed him over Southampton (he was considerably lower than me) then to Salisbury. I had to leave him to proceed on his unauthorised low level escapade just south of Coventry because I was getting low on fuel and returned to Tarrant. I heard later that the B-47 pilot had quite an eventful day beating up places, but I never heard any more about it!

I managed an 'average' assessment, which was fair enough and elicited a snide farewell comment from my erstwhile teacher. There had been one or two incidents on the way, two bent Vampires, which made me a little unpopular. The first came when my Goblin engine swallowed a stone off the runway during a pair take off; I was number two. I heard a loud bang behind my head just as the two of us got our wheels up; a violent vibration shook the Vampire so badly that the instruments became a blur. I pulled up behind my leader, turned down wind, throttling back from 10,200rpm to about 4,000 – just above idle, to ease the vibration, called "downwind engine failure", put the wheels down and turned into land. The vibration had eased a little so I could read the airspeed. With a bit of flap we landed half way down the runway and went straight into the cornfield at the end, stopping the engine on its HP cock – no fire.

Later we found that a segment of 80 degrees of the cast alloy impeller had failed, gone through the engine, melted and coated the turbine and jet pipe a bright silver.

"Too far behind your leader," said my instructor. "Bound to get stones".

Two days later I had done a solo cross-country to Valley in Anglesey and had to stay the night because fog shrouded T-R in the afternoon. I left the next morning and got half way home when the fog rolled back and I had to return to Valley. By now the aircraft was pretty cold, especially the front windscreen, which only had a very crude hot air supply around the canopy to warm it and which ceased to operate at all once you throttled back the engine on landing (the Meteor had an electrically-heated panel). It was a known fact that when returning from upper air work one might have to fly fast at low level to warm the windscreen, to guard against external fogging that sometimes formed in damp conditions on a cold aircraft. I must confess that I should have realised that the close proximity of the sea to Valley might well cause this. It did, and it caught me out just over the railway embankment which ran across the landing path on this particular runway, some 20ft off the ground. The turbulence over this at the time did not help, but I thought I could make it looking round the windscreen. No way. We hit the ground with a hell of a thump short of the threshold and I put one undercarriage leg through the wing and smashed the other as we ground to a halt.

I stop-cocked the engine; there was a lot of smoke. I pressed the fire extinguisher; more smoke. I left the aircraft somewhat rapidly, discovering that you cannot run very fast with a seat-type parachute and dinghy strapped to your rear end. Of course I should have gone round again and I have kicked myself ever since. The A.F.S. sent a Meteor 7 to pick me up, flown, of course, by my instructor, who enjoyed explaining my errors all the way to T-R.

So I left Dorset for South Wales and RAF Pembrey, home of 233 Operational Conversion Unit (Vampires). After a dismal drive through the Industrial Area of South Wales I reached Llanelli (known to us as "Slash"), about 6 miles from the airfield and the nearest town. The thing I remember most about it was that every time one went into a shop everyone started to speak Welsh. The RAF was not exactly welcome. Before very long, of course, Pembrey closed down and there was much wailing and ranting at the loss of income and employment that the service brought to the area.

A similar situation occurred later at Newquay, Cornwall and I dare say elsewhere. There the Station Master was asked by the Mayor to keep his airmen out of Newquay during the holiday season.

"Certainly," said the Station Master. "I will go even further and keep them out of the town in the winter." There were no more complaints!

We were attached to the tactical squadron and started formation flying, low-level cross-countries etc. Two weeks later an instrument rating in a two-seat Vampire TII (new to the station at that time) and then more formation flying. One detail saw four of us climbing through 20,000 feet in cloud in close formation with the leader when he suffered a Barostat failure. This device was a bit of a Woolworth job to regulate the fuel flow at height. It usually failed closed, which left you with very little power, or just seized at whatever power setting you had on. On this occasion it failed shut. The leader called "Break!" and we all broke in various directions. After having your eyes glued to your leader for 15 minutes in cloud the sudden transfer to instruments in close proximity of three other Vampires is somewhat alarming.

In late September I got lost on a low-level cross-country in a Vampire V and only just made it back with much less fuel than the minimum recommended (which was, I think, 50 gallons – one used 35 gallons in a circuit) and found myself in deep water. My fault entirely. With one bent Vampire and a wrecked Goblin already to my credit the authorities decided that perhaps I should try something else, so I left Pembrey somewhat despondent and wondered what my future would be in the RAF. After several interviews with Group Captains and above I went on leave to await my fate.

It was during this time that my stepfather, who had established himself as a GP again, at Lingfield in 1946, decided that the new NHS was not for him. Indeed, as he explained to me, he was drowning in paperwork. He made many dire predictions on the NHS, all of which, regrettably, have come true. The crunch came one day when a gentleman in a bowler hat, striped trousers, etc, visited him to explain how he should run his practice, how much time he should devote to each patient and so forth.

"Right," said my step-pa. "Please come with me," and politely showed him the front door. A few weeks later he was in the USA, taking his final Medical exams all over again. A month later he departed the UK with Ma, Grand-ma and four children, to Connecticut USA and enjoyed a highly successful career for the rest of his life.

In early November I got a posting to No 201 A.F.S. Swinderby for a multi-engine conversion onto the Varsity. Someone must have looked kindly at my file in the Air House! Swinderby is about 15 miles south east of Lincoln on the Foss Way. A three-runway wartime airfield with hutted accommodation it was one of dozens of such airfields in the area, of which only Scampton and Waddington survived the peacetime cuts. I remember the food in the mess was excellent and the whole establishment had a happy atmosphere and I am glad to recall that the CFI gave me an 'above average' assessment, which boosted my morale no end.

In the early 50s the Varsity replaced the Wellington T10 as the aircraft for twin conversions and multi-crew training. This aircraft was a great improvement on the much-loved Wimpey; it had a nose wheel and hydraulic disc brakes with anti-skid. The engines were 1950 horsepower Hercules 264s and very reliable. The Varsity had no vices and in the fully-stalled position with the stick hard back one still had aileron control. The inside looked more like an airliner than a military aircraft; not a patch of bare metal skin to be seen anywhere. There were five, I think, fully-equipped stations for trainee navigators and signallers and a bomb-aimer's window in the belly.

If a fault could be found it was in the heating department; day flying in winter was not too bad but at night with a blackout curtain drawn between the flight deck and the cabin, the front end froze. I can remember dressing for a long night flight in pyjamas, woolly underwear, uniform, two pairs of socks, flying boots and suit, gloves and sweater and watching the icicles form around the outlet valve of my oxygen mask. We usually flew on these trips above 15,000ft. Three feet behind my seat and curtain the navigators were in shirt sleeves and complaining about the heat.

But the Varsity was a delight to fly, had a good single engine performance (almost performance 'A' standard) and the serviceability of the Hercules engines was excellent. However the old problem of "coring" in the oil coolers of this type of engine was still there and the oil temperature and pressures had to be closely monitored in cold weather. Coring could occur in very cold conditions when the oil in the cooler started to congeal and led to high oil temperatures.

I had arrived at Swinderby in the winter of '53, a particularly cold one again. Ten days of ground school and then into the air with a crew consisting of another pilot, two UT navigators and two signallers. These poor souls had to endure their pilot's attempt in going solo before they could start their navigational exercises. My first sortie was upper air work, followed by an introduction to circuits and landings. My introduction to circuits came to an abrupt end. The Varsity had toe brakes – a new innovation – but if one took one's big feet off the floor and put them on the rudder pedals, the chances were they would also cover the brake pedals – as I suddenly discovered. My first landing run was about the length of a football field, amid much smoke and noise of expiring tyres, to say nothing of a suddenly overcrowded flight deck full of assorted navigators and their impedimenta. My Instructor, a chap called Hicks, kept very calm but I could sense that he was not pleased. Anyway the very next day there appeared in the landing checklist a new line: "Heels on the Floor".

A Varsity at Swinderby.

The course progressed and the weather got worse and I managed to solo in 8 hours. Next came an instrument rating prior to night flying and cross-country navigational exercises. In those far off days it was customary to do single engine flying with one engine actually shut down rather than throttling one back to simulate a duff engine and so on instrument ratings one could expect the examiner to shut the fuel cut-off on an engine after take-off and then watch you fly, feather the correct motor (hopefully) set up a single engine climb to the Swinderby NDB. A lot to be said for the old saying: "dead foot; dead engine".

My instrument rating took place on a cold January afternoon with a Northerly wind, low cloud and impending snow. After take off under the I.F. screens the examiner switched off the fuel on the starboard engine, the critical one. I went ahead and shut it down and continued to climb to 3,000ft as briefed. As I levelled off the instructor said, "OK that's fine, I will re-start it for you," and promptly switched the port engine off! After 46 years two things remain in my memory of this event: the first is the deafening silence and the second is the seemingly instant reading on the A.S.I of 60 knots instead of 120. A voice invoked the son of our maker and shouted "dive and unfeather starboard!" I stuffed the nose down (it seemed an age before I saw 100 knots come up) and started the unfeathering drill. My instructor closed the port throttle but left the pitch in fine, then switched the I.C.O. on again. There was an appalling propeller surge accompanied by protesting backfires, but by then I had the starboard engine running and was gingerly increasing power. Normality, if one can call it that, returned and at about 1,800ft I started to climb again. The detail was terminated. That evening we got another aeroplane and completed the instrument rating, this time sans crew in the back.

The next event was to be the night solo. Flight Sergeant Tony Hinds took me for this. He had been an instructor on Harvards in Southern Rhodesia for a while and the evening promised to be a relaxing one on a fine, cold but clear winter's night. We did the requisite duel circuits at Wigsley, our satellite airfield, but on landing the aircraft went u/s with a hydraulic leak. Tony Hinds detailed me to fire up the spare Varsity, fly over to Swinderby, only 5 minutes away, and do my three landings. I had a new co-pilot this time, who had only just started the course, and three signallers in the back for air experience. All went well until on very short finals for landing, at about 20ft, on throttling back the engines, I lost all feel on the elevators; the back pressure that I had been holding just vanished. The aircraft hit the ground with quite a thump, which induced the crew to make known their displeasure. I taxied round for another go, muttering that I must have been a bit slow. On the next landing the same thing happened, but this time the landing was really heavy, so I abandoned the details and put the aircraft u/s. Today, after a few more hours under my belt, I might have realised the cause of this phenomenon; somehow the airflow over the tail was being destroyed at low air speed, a rigging problem or something. Being a mere lad at the time I put down on the form 700 exactly what had occurred.

At seven o'clock the next morning, after three hours in bed, I was on the carpet in front of an irate Wing Commander who accused me of abandoning a detail without permission (a sin in Training Command usually punishable by death), hazarding my aeroplane, wasting his and the Royal Air Force's valuable time and causing him to get up early to do an air test. And no, I could not go to breakfast until he had returned from the test. When he did return I was again summoned. He looked at me across the desk, a look that only senior officers seem to manage, and then said, "sit down lad." I nearly fell over. "Your technical description may have been a little vague, but I have just experienced exactly the same symptoms and more. You did the right thing." When I finished the course I stayed on a few weeks doing staff pilot duties while awaiting a posting to Dishforth on Hastings.

I have pleasant memories of flying the Varsity. I learned quite a bit about navigation, which stood me in good stead on the Coastal Command Course at St Mawgan a couple of years later. In fact, we had some crews who were going direct to Coastal from Swinderby. For their benefit we had a four-hour Navex over the North Sea, the pilots keeping a plot solely from estimated drift, time, airspeed and heading as viewed from the cockpit, with a Mercator chart on their knees. In the back the Navs worked away in a more conventional manner. It was surprising how accurate the pilots 'plot' could be. It was to prove useful when I eventually joined the Kipper Fleet. On more conventional nav exercises the pilots would obtain true bearings from various airfield on VHF for the benefit of the Navs.

One station we always worked when up North was Silloth, where there was a WAAF operator in the control tower with the sexiest voice I have ever heard. Some unkind soul said he had seen her during a diversion to Silloth and said she weighed 18 stone. I don't believe it!

Before I left for Dishforth I heard the full story of the Varsity that caused me so much trouble on my first night solo. The pilot who flew it prior to my flight that morning had picked it up brand new from the Maintenance Unit at Shawbury. On the way home he had performed some not very good barrel rolls. He is, I believe, still in hiding!

My days at Swinderby came to an end and I left for RAF Dishforth for a Hastings second pilot's course. Dishforth is on the Great North Road, 8 miles east of Ripon in the Vale of York. In fact, the main runway 16/34 ran parallel and in close proximity to this road. Another runway 09/27 was very close to the edge of the A1. We did two weeks of ground school on the Hastings as second pilots in those days we were not to be qualified (or trusted) to land the beast and we sat in the right hand seat for flying on our captain's solo details. I suppose we filled the letter of the law that the aircraft had two pilots and in reality many of the QFIs gave us landings on the QT. The same occurred on the squadrons. It had been an interesting experience as many of our captains were ex-wartime pilots with tales to tell. Dishforth was a very busy airfield with Hastings and Valetta flying going on 24 hours a day, much to the entertainment of the users of the Great North Road. We were encouraged as second pilots to fly the station's Chipmunks and Tiger Moths and the one and only Oxford to keep our hands in.

5. Hastings Squadron

After six weeks I was posted to Lyneham on No.511 squadron. Lyneham is some ten miles west of Swindon. Work on the airfield started in 1939 and the airfield opened in May 1940. Although part of the last expansion programme for the RAF for more permanent airfields, the war intervened confining the permanent work to the building of the runways and hangars. The domestic side was almost entirely hutted. It still was in 1953. On the western edge in 1940 there stood the largely derelict Bradenstoke Abby; after the war an American saw it, bought it, and transported the whole edifice stone by stone to America for his home! Lyneham was now the main base of Transport Command with TC headquarters at Upavon. It was a very happy station (and Squadron) and I did my first tour there and my last on the same Squadron. I arrived there on the 15th April, started the arrival procedure and eventually checked into the old wartime wooden Mess for lunch. There I met Perce, another new second Dicky. Perce was a Liverpudlian given to strong Trade Union views and an admirer of Nye Bevan. We sat opposite each other to eat, both feeling a little strange and out of place. Perce grabbed the tomato ketchup bottle and proceeded to shake it vigorously. To my horror the top flew off and the contents covered the Squadron Leader sitting next to him. Perce was blissfully unaware of this and continued shaking. In the afternoon we turned up at 511 Headquarters for the CO's welcoming interview. Perce was in first to find his new boss still trying to remove the ketchup.

Talking of meals, we had one "Batchy" Brown on the station, once a pilot, now a navigator having lost an eye playing squash (an injury not as uncommon as one might think). He was a bit of a leg-puller and is remembered for letting his glass eye drop into the soup and then calling over the latest new WAAF waiter to complain. One always knew when this had happened by the inevitable loud shriek from the poor girl.

I was now able to move my wife and small son to a house near Lyneham at Wootton Bassett. It was a rather cold and cheerless place but cheap (!) with open fires and a hot water system that defied comprehension. But it was home. Years later we would build our own house in the same village.

We had four Chipmunks at Lyneham for our use and were again encouraged to fly them as much as possible. One day a friend of mine (who later became my fleet manager on Vanguards at BEA) took off for some formation flying with another "chippie". Boys will be boys and soon they were dog fighting over the Wiltshire countryside with all the zeal of a Von Richthofen and Ball. Indeed the radio language between the two as they fought tooth and nail was realistic with machine gun sounds made with the mouth and reflected the hate each felt for the other! I know this to be true because one of them inadvertently kept his thumb on the r/t transmit button during the encounter. The WAAFs in the tower had to be evacuated to spare their blushes.

The station had a gliding club – one of the first in the RAF Gliding and Soaring Association – called the Moonrakers. It was run by one of our captains, Ted Morris, still a good friend, and we operated in the grass area that was to the east of runway 18/36, which gave us enough room for a 1,000ft winch launch. We had a small space in a hangar for our two tutors – a T31 and a Gull 4. Our workshop was the fuselage of a Hamilcar tank-carrying glider, several of which were parked around the airfield. The construction of the Hamilcar was superb and despite some 10 years in the open, the huge nose door opened like a well-oiled safe with no sign of warping. We lowered the fuselage by draining the hydraulic oil from the main u/c oleos and jacked the tail up. We removed the 20-ft long hardwood tank-bearing floor ramps and turned them into workbenches. Glider wings could be stacked in the tail and the fuselages worked on in the freight area. The Lyneham maintenance unit had quite a store of aircraft in the various grass covered 1936 hangars around the airfield. In some were Tiger Moths on their noses, dozens of them; Spitfires abounded in others. I wish I had had £50 to spare for a Tiger or about £500 for a Spit at the time.

After a year the gliding club moved to RAF Netheravon, a grass airfield on Salisbury Plain. It was an historic site. The original World War One wooden hangars were still in use and the Mess was pretty well in its original state. In the ante-room the footprints of Wing Commander "Wings" Day [of Colditz fame] had been safely preserved crossing the ceiling! A small room off the bar served by a hatch contained a large table and some chairs – this was the 'Glide Inn' where Generals Eisenhower, Montgomery and others often met to discuss the plans for the airborne D-Day landings. No lady had ever set foot in there and when Her Majesty the Queen visited the station in the early 1950s it was said she observed the tradition by only putting her face round the door.

Sometime after I joined 511 I went to RAF Detling near Maidstone for an ATC (Air Training Corps) Glider Instructors' course and on return got stuck in to instructing on the T31. Our Gull needed recovering so we worked on this during our spare evenings. I see from my logbook that I did the first cross-country in the Gull 4 in April 55, to Oundle school. I remember this well, as I nearly left my landing too late and had to use the first eleven cricket pitch with a match in progress. In July the RAFGSA entered the National Gliding Championships representing the RAF for the first time, under the management of Air Commodore Paul, who was really responsible for getting the GSA into being. Despite the fact that gliding was the only way for ordinary airmen to actually fly, the RAF did not seem too interested. Money was hard to get hold of from the Sports Board, and yet here was a way to get the ordinary airman really interested in flying, improve his self esteem and thus probably do his routine job a lot better. For many years it was an uphill struggle to get the Air House to recognise this fact. The Army on the other hand had an extremely active gliding club at Lasham and the Navy an equally enthusiastic one at Lee on Solent. Both took part in the Championships for the first time as did a team from RAF Bicester, the Headquarters on the RAF GSA under the famous and very popular

Warrant Officer Andy Gough. Anyway, the Moonrakers were entered with the Gull 4, now newly refurbished, resplendent in cream painted hull, varnished wings and clear doped fabric – flown by myself and Corporal Stan Wells. Between us and the retrieving team we won the Kemsley Cup Team Class and the Minavia inter-service team trophy. To achieve this we all had had to take our annual leave – no official time off for gliding clubs. Things did improve later after this and not before time.

I suppose I remember this competition better than I do the others I took part in, it being the first. Air Commodore Paul established a tented camp for all RAF participants at Lasham for a week's practice followed by ten days of competitions, and turned out to be a surprisingly good camp cook! The weather was glorious. Sailplanes in 1955 had about the quarter of the performance of those today. In still air the Gull IV could perhaps be persuaded to fly four miles in a straight glide from 1,000ft – today an all-fibre glass 18 meter span sailplane will make about ten to twelve miles! So cross country flights were mainly in the order of seventy to eighty miles, as my log book shows, for the competition week. Out and return flights and triangular tasks were hard work into wind, involving much circling in thermals in between quick straight dashes to the next one.

To retrieve the Gull we had an ancient Ford Shooting brake with a V8 engine and wooden body, very prone to overheating and with very poor brakes. On one retrieve from Bridport, going round a bend in Romsey too quickly, full emergency braking was needed. In front was a line of Rolls-Royces slowly going across our path into the drive of an imposing mansion. With the handbrake on (operated by the co driver) and the driver furiously pumping the foot-brakes, we managed to avoid the cavalcade, which is just as well because the first one sported the Royal Standard. HM The Queen looked at us rather disapprovingly but the Duke had a broad grin on his face!

I like to think our success in this first championship did a lot to getting gliding recognised, at least as an approved sport!

The primary role of Transport Command was providing support for our overseas bases. Our secondary role was to support the Army in the training of paratroops. We also dropped supplies by air, including such items as jeeps and guns. Two of these vehicles were carried under the belly of the Hastings on a special beam, which caused a considerable amount of drag. The release mechanisms were not all that reliable and on more than one occasion the premature departure of one or both jeeps caused embarrassment. If you were unlucky enough to have the rear jeep go and the front hang up then your aircraft was way past the nose limit of the centre of gravity and a high speed landing on some long runway, usually Boscombe Down, was needed.

In order to appreciate what the paras went through, we were encouraged to do the short parachute course for aircrew. I volunteered and went to Abingdon for two weeks ground training (the Army did four but we were not required to carry the same equipment, thank goodness) do two jumps from a balloon and two from an aircraft. The parachute jumping instructors were really quite kind to us, but after two weeks of hard physical exercises, exit trainers, leaping from the top of the hanger attached to a rope which drove a fan which simulated the rate of descent and the thump you would receive on landing for real, I was exhausted – in fact in the morning my shoulders and neck ached so much from practise landings and rolling that the only way to get my head off the pillow was by pulling it up by my hair!

They say that after your first parachute descent you are never again quite the same person. That first jump from a balloon at 1,000ft at Weston on the Green lives on in my memory forever. I was the last of six of us to go. As each jumped we all moved towards the door and consequently the floor began to tilt in that direction. There could be no turning back. With a yell of "go" from the PJI, I fell out of the door. I remember the crack of the static line being pulled out of my pack; 180ft further down the last tie broke and the canopy opened (bless that WAAF packer). I looked up at it, mesmerised. Then a shout from the ground. "Get out of your seat! Check for twists, hold your lift webs, check drift, legs together, bend knees, roll…" crunch, it was over. I felt a feeling of relief, joy and surprise that has never been matched.

The 'X' type parachute was designed to minimise the usual jerk one received when the canopy of a parachute opens, by allowing the rigging lines to be fully deployed first before the canopy. It made for a very gentle retardation instead of the awful jerk in tender parts associated with the conventional emergency chute.

The aircraft jumps were less intimidating than the balloon, the slipstream accelerated the rigging line extraction and before you could catch your breath you were floating gently downwards. I remember the Hastings giving us an easy exit with the inboard engines throttled right back. The Valetta, being a twin, was different. In fact one hit the slipstream just below the door and shot under the tail plane horizontally and rather adjacent to it. Our third jump was our last, as the aircraft went u/s, but being 'in the business' the Wing Co let me back the following weekend to complete the fourth. I got another one as a bonus. Incidentally, reserve chutes were not an option in those days, though I believe the US Forces equipped their troops with them.

I liked the Hastings, and if it had any faults they lay in the pneumatic braking systems, typical of aircraft of that time. The Hastings brakes were operated by a lever on the control column. Heat was a major problem and constant short operations of the brake lever were often needed just to cool the air in the sacks behind the brake shoes. Many are the tales of brakes failing. Ted Morris once landed at Kai Tak, Hong Kong (the old Kai Tak – no long runway 13 in those days) and lost all his air pressure. I never went into Hong Kong at that time but I remember Ted telling me that on finals over Kowloon on runway 07 one had the touchdown point hidden from view by buildings until you were committed to land. Overshooting on runway 07 was not an option because of the high ground to the east and this I can understand from later visits in the 60s. Anyway, Ted landed on a hot gusty day and started braking, the runway was 5,000ft long but the landing distance was considerably less and at the end was one of those wide monsoon ditches with gently sloping sides. The brakes failed when they had almost stopped, very near the end, and the aircraft slowly but inexorably continued towards the ditch, so they shut down the engines. Over the lip Ted was aware of a strange figure in shorts leaping up and down and urging him to stop.

"Sorry," said Ted, "we can't," and at that stage the aircraft tottered over the lip and gently down into the ditch, crunching numerous dinghies that had been parked there. It then reached the other side of the slope and rolled backwards on a slightly different track and crunched some more. By now the strange figure in shorts was purple with rage, as he had just seen his own boat flattened. Senior Officers can get very irate at times!

Our own Station Commander was Group Captain Charlie Slea, much loved and respected by all from the lowest airman upwards. He was a real gentleman and made Lyneham one of the happiest stations I have ever been on. The old wooden Mess was eventually pulled down to make room for a runway extension – not before time because the cockroaches, who had been there since the war, had grown to terrifying proportions. If one came in late from night flying the cook invariably left you a meal in the kitchen under metal covers. The cockroaches were quite capable of surmounting this obstacle. Charlie Slea drove the first bulldozer right through the entrance when the demolition began years later.

But it was a happy Mess, run by Mr Quick, an ex-Chief Petty Officer who had been Lord Louis Mountbatten's "minder" during the war and who gave the place a nautical air. For instance, bedrooms were called cabins. Mr Quick weighed about 18 stone, mostly muscle, and was not to be trifled with. However between the three squadrons we had several very large chaps too – Tiny Topham, Andy Wilson, McClaren, to name but a few. One night Mr Quick got rather obstreperous during a dining-in. Tiny lifted him up by his lapels off the floor and gently sat him on the bar; you could have heard a pin drop.

Several members had vintage cars too, Bentley's, Lagondas and me with my 1929 Roesch-Talbot 75. I was the second owner of this car and it had its original tyres and only 15,000 miles on the clock. I bought it for £150 and sold it (much regretted) for £200 when I moved to the Kipper Fleet! One of our members, Mike Sproul, had a beautiful 1934 Bentley, his pride and joy. When he was away en-route the battery shorted out and the car caught fire and was destroyed. No one knew how to break this to Mike when he returned some days later.

I re-iterate our main purpose was the maintenance of our overseas bases; in those days we still had an Empire of sorts. The transfer of personnel including families on posting was mostly done by the Hastings and Valetta aircraft, with the help of a few Comet Mk IIs, although these were used more for the up market echelon of the Services. After the civil Comet disasters of the early 50s these few aircraft had a limited life of about 3,500 hours, I believe, before they had to be scrapped. Priority freight, especially aircraft engines formed a big part of our loads, the aircraft often flying in the PCF role – freight in front, passengers behind. This was in the days before roller conveyors were fitted as a permanent fixture to aeroplane floors and our aircraft floor had a thick plywood cover over the metal decking. Heavy freight was loaded by means of a winch (the Hastings had a tail wheel) situated behind the flight deck door and we were able to drag the items up the steep slope of the floor. Then everything was lashed down with chains, tensioners and 'S' hooks.

The turbulence encountered flying at 8,000–10,000ft in some parts of the world would today make your average airline crews hair stand on end. We had no radar, weather forecasts were not that accurate and the unexpected encounter with the inter-tropical front a frequent occurrence. In the flight deck my briefcase and other items were often airborne; and we sat strapped tight in our seats, gritted our teeth and put our faith in old Sir Fred Handley-Page. The Air Quarter Master had his work cut out, not only looking after the passengers but he had to keep tightening the tensioners on the chains that secured our freight. One of us, usually the second dickey, often gave him a hand; it was good training for us young chaps.

The passenger seats faced aft and were extremely strong (stressed to 9g I believe) and rather uncomfortable but they saved many a passenger's life in numerous crunches. In July '53 a group of Transport Command Senior Engineering officers were going from Fayid to Benina and on to the UK – V.I.P style – and some had insisted on more comfortable seating. York seats were provided (these faced forward) and off they went. Near Benina they started to get oil sludging in the oil coolers – this was on old problem on the Hercules engine and was mainly due to the RAF having to use re-claimed oil, no doubt as an economy measure brought on by a parsimonious Treasury. On this occasion things were so bad that they were soon down to one serviceable engine and ditching was inevitable. Flight Lieutenant Wright pulled off a highly successful ditching. The standard rearward-facing seats for the lesser mortals remained secure and they were safe but the VIP York seats all came adrift and both seats and VIPs ended up in a heap behind the freight. On impact the wings parted company with the fuselage and floated away with the dinghy; the tail plane also separated. The second dickey, Mike Geldheart [an old friend], being the most junior, had to swim quite a way to retrieve the dinghy while the rest remained relatively dry in the fuselage. All survived.

Route flying was usually very gentlemanly; one kept the same aircraft and night stopped one's way eastwards in fine style. But the word 'slip' was creeping in and we started flying as such to Fayid in the Canal Zone, slipping at Malta and sometimes Fayid. Our arrival at Fayid was usually at dawn and we departed some four hours later. My old boss in the Army (Colonel Lindon, of 54 Company RASC in Germany) was quite close to Fayid and I often popped in to see him. Early one morning I was crossing a stretch of sand to Operations. On my left was 2,000 miles of the stuff and on my right the Station Master's quarters. Suddenly a head shot out of an open window and roared "get off my garden!" Despite the fact that the British had had a presence in the Canal Zone since the days of Lawrence, the accommodation was still mostly tented. I remember the latrines were a long line of buckets with seats, I think about 12, separated by Hessian partitions. A ditch in the sand ran just behind these buckets for obvious reasons. One day some wag who had obviously had too much sun poured petrol down one end, lit it, and retired; the resulting exodus from 'el bogs' was rapid and confused, but no parts suffered any serious damage. Later we had a choice of the Kipper Fleet or Valettas at Aden or Fayid ... not a difficult choice to make.

We had several Poles and Czechs on the Squadron and one, called Jan, was an ATC Controller. He had escaped from Czechoslovakia in 1949 by stealing a Russian ANT II biplane, filling it up with friends and family (34 I think) and flying at low level to Manston in Kent, where he ran out of fuel. I asked him why he did not land in France. "You joke, my friend!" was his reply.

We also had one or two signallers as well as navigators, all of whom had served in the RAF during the war. One trip with a Polish signaller I remember well. This lad used to keep in touch on HF with friends and relations still in Russian hands using the aircraft radios. On this particular trip he was skimming through obscure frequency bands when he picked up an HF voice broadcast, in fact it sounded like a telephone conversation. He switched it to intercom so we could all hear an extraordinary conversation between Army HQ Middle East and the War Office, giving details of future troop movements, situation reports and a lot more, all in plain language. We reported this when we reached Malta and on landing at Lyneham the next day we were met by a bevy of Special Branch and Intelligence people. Our report had caused quite a rumpus. We all got chastised (especially the signaller) for "listening to frequencies that were not germane to our flight"! No one seemed the least concerned that less friendly chaps might be doing the same! We were sworn to silence – kept until now.

We had many other destinations. I went to Shaibah several times, which hadn't changed much since the First World War; you could go down to Basra if you were so inclined and watch public executions and other unpleasantness. It was hot – about 125° F – and the stone huts with Nissan tin roofs were like ovens. The sanitation (!) featured the inevitable latrine buckets. There was a met man on the station on his second tour; he loved it! He persuaded me to play squash one night in the open court; I think I lasted 5 minutes. At Aquaba, famous for Lawrence's raid, the two airport "buildings" consisted of the fuselage of a Valetta and that of a Dakota. Mafraq and Amman come to mind, flying low over the Hedjaz railway and seeing the havoc caused in the First World War by Laurence, wrecked trains everywhere, bridges still blown, in fact it was like a time warp. About 25 years later I visited the old station in Damascus; it was still in use.

I have delved into my log book and extracted a fairly typical month's work down the route, all times are flying times for those interested [NB the RAF required only take off to landing times in one's log book]. I hope it is of interest...

HASTINGS 330

20.08.54: Take off from RAF Lyneham at 0700 for Castel Benito and (eventually) Hong Kong. Returned with an engine out to base. Time 2 hrs.00

HASTINGS 338

22.08.54: Another try for Castel B. Down the radio ranges to Marseilles and then direct to Libya. Time 6hrs.30

23.08.54: To Khartoum after a restful night (picking up much gin at 3/- a bottle) in the old Italian Air Force Officers quarters which had also served as a brothel! Took-off at 0800 to the south over the Roman ruins and across the desert to Kufrah, Jebel Uneiwat (Nasser's corner) and Khartoum. Much evidence of earlier activities of the 8th Army still around. Hot in Khartoum and spent part of the night getting rid of a large camel-spider. Time 7hrs35

24.08.54: To RAF Eastleigh, Nairobi, taking off at 0400. For once a fairly cloud-free day, the scenery magnificent and we chuntered down at 9,000 feet via Malkal, Lake Turkana, Nakuru. 8/8 strata-cu over Nairobi so we did the usual "let-down" into the Rift Valley and then whipped across to Nairobi under cloud base. Time 5hrs30

25.08.54: Dawn take-off for a day return to Lusaka. The Hercules engines were prone to damage from oil sludging. An extra TEC Filter had been fitted to all engines with a pressure gauge at each end. A differential pressure of 15 PSI indicated a severe sludge problem and required the engine to be shut down. Three hours out and No.3 engine was shut down for this reason. Much draining of oil and filter replacements at Lusaka but we now had a doubtful engine. Refuelled with 2 gallon Petrol Tins, up to 1700 gallons! Time 5hrs15

26.08.54: Back to Eastleigh via M'Beya and its duty CB which some said was due to the NDB! Dodoma, setting sun showing Mt Killy in all its glory. Mt Lengai (which I was to see erupt from a Britannia many years later), then damn good nosh at Laverini's. Time 5hrs 50

27.08.54: To Aden, keeping Mt. Kenya on our right, Addis then down the escarpment to the Perin Islands and Khormaksar. "Dinty", my Captain decides to demonstrate for my benefit a constant power approach to Runway 09. Forty miles out, minus 4 Boost and down the slope we went from 9000 feet, taking flaps, U/C as appropriate. It all looked very good indeed but a lit late with "slow cut, ENG", a bounce that would have cleared Buck House and round again! Free beers for the crew that night. Time 5hrs 20

28.08.54: Went to the camp cinema last night. First time in Aden and I asked the doorman if the cinema was air-conditioned? "Oh yes, Sah"; and as I took my seat I noticed the roof was missing! So we departed for Mauripur, Pakistan, where many deals would be struck with gin for carpets. Past Salalah, Masirah Island, (I wonder if the door marked "TV" in the lounge in later years still leads the unwary out into the desert?). A few battered Halifax's at Mauripur. There would be one less on our return. Time 7hrs 55

29.08.54: To Negombo, Ceylon, down the left side of India and the Western Ghats with their monstrous Cunimbs. How come Sutcliffe's Met book said Cunimbs could not go higher than 33,000 feet? No 3 engine sludged up again, feathered. Dinty landed in torrential rain on that tree surrounded runway. Bit of an ace, was our Dinty. Time 6hrs 35

30.08.54: Air Test. Same problem on No. 3. Much work on the ground again, all helping Ginger our flight Engineer. Time 1hr05

31.08.54: Set off for Changi at Dawn. This used to be a night leg but without weather radar it proved to be too hairy. Routed via Car Nicobar, Phuket; a very rough ride. Five hours into the flight No 3 engine clogged up again accompanied by a reduction in main oil pressure: Feathered. "Pan" call put out and the Duty SAR Pig (Valetta) got up from Changi and met us near Phuket. We had two spare Merlin's on board plus some 20 passengers so we were rather heavy. Above Malacca No 1 engine expired with some internal failure (sleeve I believe) and was feathered. Now we were down to two and down to 1200 feet. "Usual" preparations for ditching. The Pig took us onto left base for Changi Runway 02. Dinty took the wheels at 300 feet, the flaps a little lower and slipped old 338 onto the end of the runway with a satisfying squeak – then cut the engines! I learnt a lot that day. Time 7hrs 20

01.09.54: Rest Day

02.09.54: Air test, following a new No 1 engine. New plugs, harness, oil filters etc. on No 3. Aircraft still required a lot of work. Time 4hrs20

03.09.54: Rest Day

04.09.54: Rest Day

05.09.54: Change of plan. Not going to Hong Kong (groans) but to Fiji (cheers) with returning Fijian troops including one "striker frame" containing a paralysed soldier plus a full medical team. Left before dawn for Kemoyoram, Jakarta. Watched another Hastings do a perfect three-pointer on that billiard tabletop runway – 20 feet off the ground! The aircraft stopped flying and sustained severe damage (CAT IV). Captain retired not long afterwards and joined the CAA! Time 2hrs30. On to Darwin via Bali, Southern Timor. Passed through the ITF with severe turbulence. Stretcher plus occupant broke loose and a spare Merlin engine began to stretch its chains and 'S' hooks. Tried the old trick of selecting 400kcs on the Radio Compass and steering away from the needle to avoid the storm cells – not much use! Time 8hrs40

06.09.54: Short night stop, remembered by a snake in the ground-level loo. Onto RAAF Amberly near Brisbane; a route remembered years later with Royal Brunei. New filters for No 3. Time 7hrs05

07.09.54: To Nandi, Fiji passing New Caledonia and through (or along!) the ITF again. A very rough ride, in which my briefcase, grey, canvas, Navigators for the use of, containing a liberal supply of medicinal gin hit the cockpit roof with dire results. Time 7hrs05

08.09.54: Cleaned oil filters on No 3 and changed the oil. A very convivial evening in the Mocambo Airport Hotel, then made of wood. One crewmember came within an ace of burning it down by setting fire to his bed. Moral: do not smoke while asleep.

09.09.54: We launched ourselves westwards for Amberly shutting down No.3 engine yet again. Time 8hrs10

10.09.54: And so to Darwin on all four. Another convivial night in downtown Darwin, then consisting of corrugated iron huts. At a dance we could not get any of the girls to cavort with us until they discovered that we were visitors and not "new Australians"!! I remember seeing the train that ran south to Birdup about a third of the way to Alice Springs. Never did find out why it was not extended to Alice. Time 7hrs25

11.09.54: To Changi direct – we were empty. Time 9hrs00

12.09.54: Rest day – aircraft u/s with hydraulic problems

13.09.54: To Negombo. Two u/s Hercules engines on board and UK bound families as passengers. Rough ride over the Bay. No 3 engine began to get sludged again, but a new engine awaited us in Negombo. Time 8hrs10

14.09.54: Air test Time .30mins

15.09.54: Air Test, more TLC needed on our new engine. Time .30mins

16.09.03: To Mauripur on all 4 Time 7hrs15

17.09.54: To Habbaniya, that oasis in the desert not far from Baghdad. Landed on the new "Plateau" runway. Time 7hrs50

18.09.54: 0800 start for Castel Benito, down the oil pipeline, which replaced the ploughed furrow of the 1930s. To Palmyra, Homms, that fantastic Castle of the Kraks, to be visited years later when with Syrian Arab Airways. The crew and passengers all had the infamous "Hab meat pie" and hard-boiled eggs in the lunch boxes. The crew's pies were always binned; the eggs departed in the usual way through the Verey Pistol housing. Sometimes one could suspend an egg in the airflow rushing up the tube! A long gentle approach over the Bay of Sirte to Runway 18. A lot of passengers suffered from acute food poisoning and spent the night in the sick-quarters. Time 8hrs15

19.09.54: 0400 Takeoff for Lyneham. Up the Rhone Valley on the Radio Range, to Dunsfold and into the welcoming arms of Lyneham GCA. A very tired crew with all heads nodding in unison. We checked to ascertain if Swindon Town Football Club had done well as this affected the temperament of one of our resident Customs officers. Nice to be home again. Three days off, two days of station duties and then off again on the 26th! Time 8hrs20.

It was now a time of change. My posting notice came through with a choice, a tour on Valettas in Aden (unaccompanied by family) or coastal command on Shackletons. I chose the 'Kipper Fleet'.

6. The Kipper Fleet

In September '55 I left for Coastal Command and St Mawgan, the School of Maritime Reconnaissance. I was sorry to leave Lyneham and Transport Command; the tour on Valettas would have been as Captain. Coastal Command – usually known as 'the Kipper Fleet' – was something new to me and sounded interesting; it also had the added attraction of a spell on the RAF's last Lancasters at St Mawgan. These aircraft had had their dorsal gun turrets removed but retained the tail and nose ones, minus guns. This gave more room inside the fuselage for anti-submarine detection equipment and a lengthened navigation table to accommodate two navigators side-by-side. I arrived there in September 1955 in the middle of a glorious summer that lasted well into November. The school was equipped with the last 16 Lancasters (ASR Mk3s) in the RAF. It was a 12-week course giving all new aircrew a sound indoctrination into the activities of Coastal Command, and for pilots in particular a concentrated course in Navigation up to a standard which enabled them to complete six flights as Navigators, with the staff Nav as a silent observer; you just could not trust pilots with a pair of dividers and a sextant too much! Ground school consisted of basic navigation, astronavigation (Astro), use of Consul and Loran and, of course, dead reckoning navigation, and we certainly sweated a lot in the Nav trainer doing simulated four hour flights. We had to 'shoot' 60 star shots on terra firma with a sextant and plot them in our spare time. In theory of course the position lines obtained should have all gone through St Mawgan, however I have to tell you that this was not always the case!

There was also much time spent on anti-submarine tactics, sonar buoy exercises, Anti Surface Vessel Radar (ASV) attacks, search and rescue and co-operation with the Royal Navy (why do the Navy always refer to the RAF as 'crab fats'?)

I do not think I have ever worked so hard as under the excellent supervision of the staff navs. Navigators of old often said that they did all the work while the pilots sat up the front with their minds in neutral and their thumbs well hidden! I think they had a point. The hardest part for me was Astro (I was very bad at maths at school, still am) but it is an absorbing subject and up to leaving the RAF in 1967 I still managed the odd 'three star fix' when the opportunity arose.

These were the days before inertial navigation systems, satellites and other goodies. We had limited help from Consul, Loran and Gee – wartime aids requiring special charts for each aid. These were overprinted with a lattice from which the aircraft's position could be established when interpreting the various signals emanating from the ground stations. But we did have a radio compass, a radar altimeter and, of course, the ASV radar. A word of caution came with the Radar Altimeter (essentially a low-level flight detection aid); in very calm seas the radar pulses transmitted to the sea surface could penetrate it instead of being reflected back, giving a totally false reading. It had to be used with caution, but it was extremely accurate. However, in the science of sub-hunting at the time, any radio transmissions of any kind would be picked up by our quarry, with the inevitable result, so when engaged in these activities it was back to basic dead reckoning navigation, astro and for searching, sonar buoys (passive) and the 'mark one eyeball'. I hope detection has improved in the last 45 years.

We started flying after the fourth week and alternated flying with ground school as and when the weather permitted. I see from my logbook that I completed 12 flights, each of them about 5 hours duration. I am afraid that I have lost all my old logs and charts but I do recall my first three star fix on a rather rough night flying at around 1,000ft. My "cocked hat" or triangle of position lines encompassed the whole of Northern Ireland, which would not have been too bad had we not been well south or Cork at the time. However, I did improve and I found the whole business of navigation quite fascinating. The Lanc was not the best of flying platforms, wallowing at around 1,000ft or lower for work with maps, charts, sun guns (sextants) and I must admit I did on occasion review my last meal.

But up front, practising depth charge attacks etc, it was pure joy to fly, and the snap, crackle and pop of the Merlin exhausts when throttling back on landing is a noise I treasure. The silence after shutting down the engines, opening the window, sniffing the air and listening to the tinkling of hot metal cooling down was pure magic, and still is. I also met up with Tug Wilson, a staff pilot with whom I had shared a room at Aldershot prior to commissioning in the Army in 1947. We both felt that we had now purged ourselves of our Pongo past. Sadly some Air Ministry penguin ordered the scrapping of every single Lancaster, for the sum of £700 a piece, an act of sheer vandalism.

We exercised a lot with the submarine training flotilla at Portland, which operated some of the famous wartime 'U'-class boats. We would be allocated an exercise area off Portland containing a lurking submarine, drop our sonar buoys in a domino five pattern and assess the noise level of the submarine's propellers received at each buoy via VHF. From this we could track the sub and mount an attack, using 7½ lb practice bombs. If successful the sub would surface or release a flare. We were permitted to drop 7½-pounders on subs at periscope or snorkelling depth, the bombs being fitted with a pre-impact device which broke to ensure that the small explosive charge would not damage the pressure hull. On one particular cold, misty dawn I was tactical nav, trying to make sense of the sonar buoy plot, when the front gunner sighted a periscope about half a mile to port, too close to turn and attack, so we did a timed run and turn and my fellow trainee up front started the final run in.

"Bomb doors open, cameras armed!" he cried in great delight.

We saw the periscope dead ahead, just as the rest of the boat broke the surface. Quite carried away by the excitement he dropped the stores and pulled up and round. One bomb hit the casing and to our horror the conning tower lid flew open, emitting a great cloud of smoke, followed by a large number of white jersey'd matelots pouring onto the casing and shaking their fists. It transpired that at *le moment critique* a flash electrical fire had started in the control room, hence the hurried rise to the surface, where the commander, on pulling open the hatch, was confronted by a Lanc roaring over at 50ft, four bellowing unsynchronised Merlin engines and the crack of a bomb hitting his boat. Having survived two exciting years at war unscathed he was not a happy chap, as I later discovered on a school visit to Portland. But we did have a good working relationship with the submarine school at Portland, with aircrews getting a little sea-time under the water and submariners flying with us.

At the end of the course we sorted ourselves into crews (the Shackleton carried 10 or 11 crew) and left the tranquillity of Cornwall for the unknown beyond Hadrian 's Wall, namely Kinloss. No.236 OCU trained crews on the Mark I Shackleton and the Lockheed Neptune; a twin engined American anti-submarine aircraft of which I believe we had one Squadron. The Mark I Shack was the last of the line of the Manchester, Lancaster, Lincoln breeds. It had four Rolls Royce Griffon engines (derived from the Merlin) giving up to 2500hp, each driving two three bladed contra-rotating propellers. This allowed smaller diameter ones to be fitted than would have been the case had normal single propellers been used. This enabled the engines to be fitted closer together and nearer the fuselage which in turn lessened the effect of the loss of an outboard engine on take-off. On take off (in still air) there was no tendency for the aircraft to swing (like the Lancaster) because the causes of swinging, slipstream effect, torque effect, gyroscopic effect and asymmetric blade effect, were cancelled out. Smaller propellers also permitted shorter main undercarriage legs thus bringing the fuselage quite close to the ground facilitating easier maintenance and arming of the bomb bay. The interior of the aircraft was spacious (one could stand upright) and had a large Perspex nose with the radar scanner underneath it: this would be my favourite place for a nap! Unfortunately, the designers had discarded the excellent Lancaster type cockpit for a more conventional one. A few Squadrons had the MKII with a more pointed nose and positions for twin cannon to be fitted each side of it. On both these marks there was no internal sound proofing, just bare metal skin – it was noisy!

I arrived at Aviemore on the Inverness Express on the 15th November, it was a delightful sleepy little village in those days where the Station Masters wife cooked a magnificent breakfast for all passengers on the branch line train to Elgin for the sum of two shillings and sixpence. None of us had had much sleep having enjoyed the company of James Robertson Justice, the actor, in the buffet bar most of the night. What a character; as large as life off the stage as on it and a born raconteur.

Kinloss in the early 50s was still a hutted camp close to the airfield. It was bitterly cold, the ground covered with snow and frozen solid. We slept in huts 'heated' by coal stoves and coal was in short supply. Never mind, ground school was soon over and we started flying the mighty Shackleton Mk I, sharing the airspace with Royal Naval Air Station Lossiemouth close by where they flew Sea Hawks and often exercised with us. Much friendly rivalry existed between the stations. On one occasion a commando type raid by the Lossie pilots 'stole' all of the mess silver, this was in retaliation for the erection of a flagpole on their airfield hoisting ladies undergarments.

I see from my logbook that we started flying on 29th November after two weeks of ground school. We all graduated as First Pilots; i.e. we flew the aircraft from the left-hand seat and acted as Co. Pilots in the right hand one. The first three weeks were essentially flying the aircraft in the circuit, Instrument let-downs and emergency drills: the operational side of our Coastal Command role was covered in the New Year.

Christmas was fast approaching and I believe we got five days leave to go home – for me in Surrey with Pam and her parents. Returning to Kinloss (still frozen) and the cold cheerless huts and abominable coal stoves, we started flying again in earnest. However, there was one more event that we all looked forward to – New Year in Scotland.

The party started early in the Mess on the 31st and by the time the clock struck midnight it was in top gear. After the usual singsong and a few words from the Station Commander, dancing with gay abandon was resumed, the Whisky flowed, and there was a lot of hooting and roaring! At ten past midnight the Station Master, accompanied by the Padre banged on the top table for silence. "It is the Sabbath" he said, "the bar will shut in five minutes"! I seem to remember the Staff members (mostly Scots) did not seem surprised; the course members were dumbfounded! One cue at 0015 the bar shutters came down and the Mess quietly emptied. Not to be dismayed we thought we might try a bit of "first footing" in the Married Patch (Quarters) armed with lumps of coal and whisky. We were not welcome, anywhere! So ended my one and only New Year in Scotland; I still remember it in shock to this day.

Flying Shacks in the circuit was a cold business as the Dragonfly combustion heater did not operate below 104 knots. Student pilots were cleared in both seats so we all graduated as first pilots. We did some Arctic fish patrols at a time when the Icelanders were upset about fishing rights. I have seen trawlers in gale force winds with a crew breaking off ice from the rigging with axes while I sat at 500ft in shirtsleeves. The weather in the winter in the North Atlantic was a revelation to me. Even after reading about the war time convoys and seeing newsreel footage during the war, a full gale in these waters has to be seen to be believed. One could fly down vast troughs, and a Shack had a wingspan of 120ft, in the waves and be unable to see over the crests. A signaller of my crew took a photo with a K20 camera of a trawler perched on a crest above our wingtip. We submitted it to Coastal Command in the annual photo competition but it somehow got 'lost in the post' and I got a rocket.

The Mark I had a mid upper turret with two 20 mm cannon and we all enjoyed blasting away and on rare occasions hitting a target. We did a few depth charge drops; these were wartime stores and rather unstable. They were dropped from 100ft which was quite exciting. Some gung-ho boffin in Coastal Command decided that we could do the same at night but sanity prevailed. The time was fast approaching when all sorts of other gadgets were being developed and we already had a homing torpedo in the inventory. Later on one occasion I had a DC hang up on the bomb carrier. After a very gentle landing we stopped, put external power onto the aeroplane and shut down the engines. Handing over to the station Armament officer I bravely led my crew away at a speed that must have equalled the four-minute mile. On another occasion a colleague was doing radar attacks on the Kinloss radar buoy in the Firth one night and on his final run in dropped two practice bombs. When his target pictures were developed they showed the bridge of a very large tanker with a very angry gent gesticulating in an unseemly manner.

I have cause to remember my final long-range patrol out into the North Atlantic. For the Navs it was a dead reckoning exercise; just three drift winds, no radar, Loran or radio bearings. It went quite well, we found our target, a Cunarder off to the USA and after an exchange of pleasantries using the Aldis signalling lamp, we turned for home via Flannan Island and Lewes. As pilots we were expected to keep a rough DR plot on our chart largely based on headings and airspeeds, as already mentioned. It was interesting to see that these could be surprisingly accurate at times. Some hours later and about 50 miles from Flannen Island we entered cloud at 1000ft and I dropped 200ft in the clear. A few minutes later we were in cloud again so I returned to 1000ft. Staff Nav came up for a breather and I said, "I thought we should be near Flannen" he looked a bit puzzled and returned to the Nav table and switched the radar on. After a moment the screen came to life and showed a coastline running north and south about 5 miles ahead. By the time he shouted, "climb" we had already had plus 18 boost and 2750 rpm on the Griffons and had become upwardly mobile. At the wash up the Nav had admitted that he had "lost" one degree of longitude somewhere and was invited to see the Nav leader. I am glad to say that he learnt quite a lot that day, we all did and our Nav eventually became a Specialist Nav and rose to high rank.

The course came to an end and we got our postings, the most un-popular pilot went to Bally Kelly (justice here). Interesting place BK, the local branch line ran across the airfield and aircraft gave way to trains. Most of us, myself included, returned to Cornwall to St. Eval and St. Mawgan. I left Kinloss in the middle of February 1956; it was bitterly cold the ground was still snow covered and frozen and the wind still howled in from the Firth, I never returned. I joined 206 Squadron at St. Eval and acquired a small bungalow at Rock on the Camel Estuary opposite Padstow. To get to work by road meant a detour of 14 miles via Wadebridge. Sometimes I left my car at

Padstow and took the Ferry to Rock (5 mins) saving a long drive. It seemed appropriate that I should brave the sea in all its moods before flying over it. Rock was a lovely spot and our bungalow was right on the water's edge, next to a café run by Jim and Alice and umpteen children. Jim had been an opera singer of some repute and occasionally he would burst into song for all to hear. One day he failed to hit a high note. There followed a minute of silence then "That's it Alice, I am finished"! He never sang again. Most visitors came by the open boat ferry from Padstow and were few in number; it was before the days of mass tourism which has now devastated parts of Cornwall. We were very happy there.

I was crewed up with a Flight Lieutenant Robinson, a Canadian on exchange duties from the RCAF, replacing the co-pilot who was Tourex. Much of 1956 was spent on Maritime exercises and towards the end of the year we started to track Russian submarines transiting the Western approaches en-route to the South Atlantic, detecting and tracking them with sonar buoys. On one occasion the quarry surfaced, hauled up our buoy, gave a friendly wave and headed again for the deep! In 2001 a Foxtrot submarine of a similar type that we had tracked lay moored in Folkestone Harbour and is now open to visitors. It is a fascinating insight to submarines of that era. I got checked out in the Station Flight Anson which was great fun: this being a time of little restriction of flying and I took full advantage of this freedom to visit other airfields (and friends) on the slightest official pretext.

Twenty four-hour search and rescue cover was provided by St. Eval and St. Mawgan with the Shackletons loaded with full fuel and Lindholm survival gear, and with crews on one-hour standby. This mark of Shackleton did not have a fuel jettison system consequently once airborne with a full fuel load; one could not get down to landing weight for about 7 hours. One moonless night we were launched to illuminate every buoy off the South Coast in the vicinity of the Solent to search for a Lascar stoker who had fallen off the stern of a tanker! One of the problems with low level searches especially in rough sea conditions was salt spray drying on the windscreen; what it did to the rest of the aluminium structure I dared not contemplate! To get rid of this one could use the wipers and some of the de-icing fluid, but this was not a good idea as it tended to smear, and in any case we only had a limited supply of the fluid, which was best used for its correct purpose. One crew fitted an old one-gallon oil can on the left side of the nose, just by the first pilot's knee, filled it with water and fed it to two small nozzles (taken from a car's screen washer system, I believe) via lengths of rubber tubing with a "bulb" within reach of the pilot, which he could squeeze when he felt the need, thus squirting water onto the windscreen (this part of the system came from a doctor's blood pressure machine!) But it worked, and was incorporated in most of our aircraft; search not for a Modification Classification number because you will not find one! When the Mark III aeroplane came on line it had a more high-tech system.

Most of our serious searches were for missing aircraft way out in the Atlantic and involved flights of 15 hours or more to enable us to cope with these long flights the Shackleton was fitted with a galley and a couple of rest bunks and before flight we drew rations and utensils in order for a hot fry up to be produced by the duty cook (we all took it in turns). My memory goes back to those long patrols! Dawn in the middle of the grey Atlantic. We have been lurching over the sea at a 1000-ft for 8 hours; the din of four Griffins hammering against the bare metal fuselage is beginning to get to me. We have just dropped a smoke float to check our drift; it had been leaking a little, not unusual, and a stench of carbide combines with the smell from combustion fuselage heaters. This coupled with the usual 'Shack' aroma of hydraulics, glycol and petrol makes a potent atmosphere and through it all comes the reek of burnt sausages and bacon, fried egg and tinned tomatoes all in the same large pan; baked beans were banned. Happy days!

In July a formation of nine Shackletons performed a fly pass, my logbook fails to indicate where. I do remember it was a pretty tight formation (we were in the box) and we had practiced diligently for some days, that's a lot of rivets flying close together. I recall that as we closed up and thundered in over our destination, someone in the lead ship ahead of us ditched his rubbish from lunch through the flare chute and covered our windscreen with a resounding smack. Luckily there were no tins in it.

In October we took a Marine Commando out to Cyprus – Suez was in the offing. I think we reduced our crew to five and squeezed on 32 marines plus kit. We put 6 in the nose and 2 in the aisles between the pilot's seats. On take off as the tail came up and the nose descended these 8 leaned further and further back until the two in the aisle were almost horizontal! It was a cold eight hours to Gibraltar, our first stop, as the fuselage heaters could not be used for fear of singeing bodies. We took no further part in Suez as other things had been planned; a Christmas Island atomic test – Operation Grapple in the South Pacific. This was going to involve the squadron for the whole of 1957 during which I did three tours, the first two with Robbie and the last on my tod with the same crew. In June Robbie returned to Canada and was missed by all.

Christmas Island was discovered by Captain Cook on Christmas Eve 1777; he remained there for a week to observe an eclipse of the sun. The island is 5ft above sea level and is the largest coral atoll in the Pacific, shaped like a crab's claw. Being only 2° north of the equator (1100 nautical miles south of Honolulu) the climate is humid and hot but a strong Easterly trade wind blows most of the time and keeps the temperature down to about 80° Fahrenheit.

The airstrip had been built by the Americans during the war on the North Coast and the runway had been resurfaced. The population had gone from one District Commissioner and a dozen Gilbert and Ellis Islanders to some 3,000 servicemen, army, navy, RAF and scientists and technicians from Harwell, the Atomic Warfare Research Establishment (AWRE), all under canvas. Other inhabitants were thousands of large land crabs and a thriving colony of black rats, survivors of many shipwrecks. The shore of the eastern side of the Island was covered with old timbers and spars from numerous shipwrecks probably dating back two or three hundred years. The rats and the crabs would often be joined in battle and much was the carnage. Needless to say that living in tents in close proximity to this wild life posed a problem. There were two schools of thought; the first advocated the surrounding of ones tent with anti-crab boards. The second, and one which most of us adopted, was to keep the tent sides raised four inches off the sand and thus allow the invader to pass through! Living under canvas was not my idea of heaven but in the pleasant climate with a cooling wind it was not too bad at all. Strangely, we enjoyed plenty of water for showers and laundry, this came from boreholes and although slightly saline it was a great bonus. For the cookhouses an ancient wartime distillation plant left behind by the Americans was persuaded to work again and provided nearly pure fresh water.

The squadron task was mainly gathering weather information and we carried a competent met observer on these flights plus all the required instrumentation. We would fly to a far distant area and do a stepped climb from the 1000 millibar level (almost sea level) to our maximum height in "S" gear of 16,000ft, stopping at 100 millibar intervals for 10 minutes to take readings. At 16,000ft the temperature was well below zero a fact that seemed to discourage the fuselage heaters from working and the sweat that had accumulated on our shirts and 'shreddies' at sea level now froze. The squadron also provided search and rescue cover and more importantly, constant patrols of the designated prohibited zone looking for shipping and any other unwelcome visitors. Two aircraft were fitted with special camera mounts for medium level photography of the bomb bursts.

Robbie and I left St. Eval on the 19th January 1957 in our trusted Shack WG529 (now reduced to saucepans). Fitted with a Decca Navigator system for use near the islands where a temporary Decca chain had been installed. However, all we had on board to negotiate the USA and Canadian Airways was one radio compass, HF/MF and VHF radio, and radar. Oh yes, and two navigators! It was radio range flying all the way. Our route was the winter one, Azores (Lages), Bermuda, Charleston South Caroline, Biggs Airforce Base El Paso, Travis Airforce Base San Francisco, Hickam Airforce Base Honolulu – known locally as Hikalulu and night stopping at each place. The Portuguese Airforce were our hosts at Lages and we were well looked after. However, the Portuguese idea of an English Breakfast caused much trouble half way to Bermuda; we were served steak, fried egg and bread and a half inch layer of cloves of garlic (chopped) over everything!

We reached Christmas Island on the 7th February having suffered a 10-day stopover at Travis with a broken tail wheel leg – not my landing! We were well entertained by the United States Airforce and when new parts failed to arrive, our hosts manufactured them in their workshops. I was also lucky to get a two hour conducted tour of a strategic air command bomber – the mighty Convair B-36.

During this unscheduled stopover we ran short of dollars. Since I was the crew imprest account holder I set off with Reg our Nav to the British Embassy to negotiate more funds. It was a Sunday (my mistake). After much banging on the door an irate retainer appeared in carpet slippers whom I took to be the Janitor and addressed him as such in a reasonably friendly manner. "We need some more funds you see", I explained. "Do you know who I am" it roared, "I am Sir Edward Haddow, the Ambassador – go away". I turned up on Monday to find a very helpful staff who not only apologised for his Excellency's attitude but more importantly gave us our funds.

We spent the whole tour doing met climbs and visiting outlying islands such as Penryn and Malden and others including the odd night at Hickham! We did mail drops at Palmyra on the Northern most edge of the Line Islands of which Christmas Island is the centre. Palmyra Airfield was no longer usable and was littered with wrecked aircraft and buildings including the tail of a Liberator sticking out of the lagoon. In fact it looked like an MGM film set of the Pacific War. Anyway, the AWRE boffins who were based there certainly appreciated the mail.

We flew WG529 back to St. Eval in early April having suffered 'another enforced delay' at Bermuda with an engine change. USAF at Kindley field were unable to accommodate us (shame) so we ended up at the Elbow Beach Surf Club (hurrah). Such a good time was had by all that when the aircraft was ready for an air test five days later, it took Robbie and I a whole day to extract the crew from their various 'quarters'. Some of this "good time" can be attributed to the arrival of an ancient two funnel, straight stemmed troop-ship, circa 1920, named the Captain Hobson which docked on the penultimate day of our enforced sojourn, in Hamilton Harbour. This venerable vessel had called in at Christmas Island on its way from Singapore to the U.K with tour ex service personnel including a bevy of Army Nurses, to embark some Royal Engineers. The ships' crew and passengers had been very hospitable during their short stay, and they had sailed for the Panama Canal about ten days before we left in WG 529. The reader can imagine our delight when we saw her steam into port; our trip home now began to resemble the classic race between the Tortoise and the Hare! There was a great party that night at the Elbow Beach, which continued aboard ship: marred only by a request in the morning for an air-test!

Our return to the Island in early May was via the northern route Keflavic, Goose Bay, Edmonton and Travis. I think we were selected for this routing to deter us from succumbing to further unserviceabilities in exotic places. This stint on the Island included a photographic sortie for the test over Malden Island on June 19th. This involved some accurate navigation and co-ordination with the Valiant dropping the bomb. We had to be at the right place in the allocated Decca racetrack pattern at the right time in order for our fixed cameras to photograph the moment of detonation. We flew on autopilot with our eyes covered by eye patches and tight shut even then the flash penetrated our patches and the burst was forty miles away!

Just prior to this we had flown to Bora Bora near Tahiti taking boffins and recording equipment returning six days later. Bora Bora is the most beautiful volcanic Island in the whole of the South Pacific with a 2000ft peak in the centre and surrounded by a circle of Atolls enclosing the world famous lagoon and it's coral forest. On one of these Atolls, the Americans had built a long coral airstrip in 1942. After landing it looked as if it had not been touched since the war. Clearance to land was obtained on the radio from the local Gendarme a Monsieur Persard, a Frenchman who was also Mayor, Fire Chief, Judge and Jury, Jailer, Immigration Officer, Policeman and official welcomer. He was also the only white man on the Island. He met us and took the crew to the main island in his boat and escorted us to the hotel, a large rambling tin roofed edifice run by fearsome Madame Bouchine who could have doubled as 'Bloody Mary' in the musical *South Pacific*. Plumbing was a large tank of rainwater and a shower and the loo an earth privy or two. The natives were very friendly, and delighted to see us just as soon as they realised that we were not American. Bora Bora had been a supply point during the Pacific War and at times there had been some 6,000 troops here. Half way up the mountain there are still a pair of 8" guns – no one knows how they got up there and no one is prepared to get them down again. Eleven years later, all traces of the occupation had been erased and the Island returned to its pre-war paradise by the French. Regrettably today, in the year 2002, I fear it has become a very exclusive holiday retreat for the so-called rich and famous. On reflection I now knew how the Bounty's mutineers must have felt when they first sampled Tahiti. Our time was our own for five idyllic days, swimming in the lagoon by day, fishing over the reef and much feasting and dancing under a full moon. I could still speak fluent French, which was an asset; I charged the other crewmembers a beer for every time I had to act as an interpreter. I still have my grass skirt somewhere.

The sad day came for departure and we found most of the population at the airstrip to say farewell. Old WG529 was garlanded with flowers over the engines, propellers, tail and rudders and inside as well. Our ground engineer tried to escape like a Bounty Mutineer but he was caught and was secured on a crew rest bunk. Mournfully, we said farewell, fired up the engines, the flowers going in all directions. Robbie did the lowest fly past I have ever seen from inside an aeroplane (or outside for that matter) and we headed north, six hours of flying and not a word spoken.

Returning to St. Eval at the end of June, we said farewell to Robbie in fine style and for the next three months pursued routine Kipper Fleet activities. Robbie Robinson is worth more than just a passing mention. Not only was he a great Captain but a good friend as well. Not long after he had returned to Canada he was promoted and went on to command a Squadron of RCAF Argos anti-submarine aircraft, a derivation of the Canadair CL44 with Pratt and Witney piston engines. I was lucky to inherit Robbie's crew with an addition of another co pilot, Gordon Acklam. One of the nice things about this Squadron, and possibly the others too, was that we kept the same crews as far as possible, and just as importantly the same aircraft, in this case WG529. Doing long fifteen to sixteen hour flights it was essential to know every crew members capabilities for to relieve the strain on all concerned we changed positions and duties (within reason!). The five signallers' would rotate through the two side observers positions, the radio compartment, the sonic / anti submarine seat and the H2S (Radar). You cannot expect a radar operator to be really efficient at his job on a search for more than forty-five minutes of watching a trace on a radar tube go round and round twenty times a minute! The pilots rotated with the two navigators and flight engineers – I always ensured there was one pilot in his seat and the navigator would never allow two pilots into their empire! I recall a flight or two with a temporary co-pilot whom I shall call Peter. At the end of three days I told my flight commander "Dad" Church that Peter was an idiot and should be chained to the ground, he agreed. Twenty odd years later I flew with Peter as his First Officer in British European Airways. He had not improved.

Search and rescue flights continued to be high on our activity list and I remember an SAR search for a DC4 at about 500 miles west of Lands End. After six hours of scouring our allocated area, Flint, our Flight Engineer, who happened to be in the nose at the time, saw some yellow objects and a lot of large pieces of what looked like wreckage. Sending off a situation report to Plymouth having marked the area with smoke floats, I saw a ship some 20 miles away. It was a single funnel Cunarder heading for the USA. The sun was going down by the time I made voice contact with the bridge watch and convinced them that an investigation might save lives. During this discussion I discovered that Cunard Captains do not like to be told what to do but in this case I had no choice. The liner hove to about a mile from the wreckage and lowered a motor boat, while we waited and circled overhead. Ten minutes later an irate Captain called up to say that the wreckage was a dead whale which had been dead for some considerable time and furthermore the CINC Coastal Command was going to get an earful from the Managing Director of Cunard which he hoped would snowball onto me. Worse was to come; as the liner got underway it passed through the trail of noxious gasses from the whale just as dinner was being served! It took a long time to live that one down.

I got a few stripes back. Sometime, I cannot remember exactly when, we were on exercise to try and locate the Nautilus, America's first nuclear submarine that was visiting the United Kingdom. It was a visual and sonar buoy search in rather misty conditions at dawn, and we had only just arrived in the search sector, when about a mile away the waters parted and up shot Nautilus! Why I still do not know. Anyway tally ho and a quick simulated attack with pictures of the swirl – she never did surface completely and had gone within a minute. I did not attend the wash up on this exercise but I have it on good authority that the United States Navy thought we had some secret gear for deep-sea detection and were very worried indeed. I believe the truth was withheld from them until right at the end of the day.

Just before leaving for Christmas Island again I had to fly a Shackleton up to Bovingdon for some replacement parts for the Decca. Throttling back on landing at Bovingdon the starboard inner Griffon decided to 'gulp' its oil – not an uncommon occurrence in Griffons. We lost the lot; all 26 gallons spurted out through the breather in a matter of seconds and onto the runway. The result, an angry Station Master who was about to fly off in his Anson and now could not move until the runway had been decontaminated, and the cure for gulping? Fill up with oil, pressurise the system and head for home. It was good to escape again to the South Pacific.

I set out for Christmas in the company of three other Shackletons on the 19th October via the Southern route, Bermuda etc. We were all delayed for a couple of days at Biggs Airforce Base, El Paso, by weather. In fact I had been first delayed at Charleston with a complete spark plug change. It was fortuitous because my mother came down from Connecticut by train to see me. The boss, who had gone ahead with the other two aircraft got a message back to us to say that the wind was picking up at El Paso and we should not delay. I think he thought I was up to my old tricks again of going unserviceable in exotic places. Anyway, we made haste all the way and nine hours later were homing in on the El Paso radio range, 242 kilo cycles, I seem to remember, to discover that Biggs had a 45 – 50 knot crosswind, rising dust and blowing sand. To cap it all there were balls of mesquite rolling across the runway in the hot southerly wind. I agreed with Gordon my co-pilot that when I said 'cut' he would close two and three and four engine throttles and help on the rudders, I would keep number one running. I crabbed in with the runway appearing through the centre and right-hand windscreen. I called "cut" and with a boot full of right rudder from both of us she sat on the runway and stayed! With bursts of number one throttle and a great deal of hard work on the rudders we managed to keep straight down the full 10,000-ft of runway. Taxiing was another problem altogether with the rudders thrashing around in the gusts and we collected some good bruises on our ankles. Flint, our Flight Engineer, who had survived the war on Lancaster's came up and quietly said "well done Captain". I was lost for words.

Next day we made a pilgrimage to Juarez in Mexico only a few miles from the base, across the Rio Grande Bridge which is the border, to be introduced to the delights of Tequila. I am afraid my memory of this sortie is a little hazy which is just as well. I do remember that we lost one of our pilots who I believe succumbed to the charms of a lady called Delores. He was next seen the following day crossing the bridge towards United States Immigration wearing only his 'Y' fronts and a poncho and sitting astride a donkey from which he refused to be parted. I believe he is still known as 'Poncho' to this day.

We arrived at last on the Island and spent most of our time flying clearing patrols in the prohibited zone in readiness for the first test on Christmas Island itself, over a target 2 miles off the South East point and some 25 miles from the airfield and main camp. D-day was the 8th November. On the evening before I took off for the last rounds of the zone. We were to land by 0700 on the 8th, refuel and take up a safe position behind an old Quonset hut on the edge of the apron and await the test. A brilliant full moon turned night into day and we had just finished our fry up (10lb Red Snapper caught by me) when Smithy on radar called up "ship ahead 20 miles". What! Diving down with the landing lights on, sure enough there was a ship, an old wartime rusty Victory ship called the Effie heading straight for ground zero! The Navy dispatched HMS Cossack to intercept her and I spent the remaining two hours to dawn trying to wake someone up in the rust-bucket, dropping our official warning leaflets and firing off all our flares and photo flashes to no avail. Eventually someone woke up at dawn, and got the message and the ship turned south. Cossack caught up with her and sent a boarding party over just as she cleared the danger zone. We returned to the Island completed our refuelling and stores replenishment, ran to our funk hole with 15 minutes to spare and listened to the tannoy from Mission Control. It was an eerie feeling sitting under the palm trees listening to the countdown and hoping that the mad Scientists had got it right. At last the thing was on its way down for a high burst. I think the initial flash is the thing I remember most despite facing away from the explosion with hands over my tightly closed eyes, I still saw my finger bones quite clearly – just like an x-ray. Then came the heat, like an electric fire just behind my head. At bang plus 15 seconds we could get up and look. The upper shock wave was moving rapidly outwards in an expanding circle, clearing the sky of all cloud. Then the ground shock waves arrived with a thunderous bang and wind. It rained coconuts and sent us scampering across the apron to the aircraft. The Air Traffic Control Officer who was driving his jeep towards the tower swore that he saw an airman running in excess of 30 miles an hour and overtook his jeep. There then followed a sobering few minutes watching the evil purple and red fireball climb high above us into the stratosphere, lowering its mushroom like stalk as it rose.

A week later we were at Hickham again helping in the search for a Pan American Stratocruiser that had gone down near the weather ship between San Francisco and Honolulu. Despite several 16-hour searches, nothing was ever found. That evening we had a few drinks in the bar at Hickham Officers Club with some American pilots who had also been on the search. The Hickham club is situated next to the Pearl Harbour channel and of an evening one could watch the ships go by and the sun go down, it was very pleasant. On this occasion Gordon turned up a little late at the bar and demanded a Shakespeare. This foxed the barman and after a lot of argument he eventually produced a multi-coloured drink which I since discovered was based on a "Volcano", consisting of Raspberry Liqueur, Blue Curacao, and Champagne to which he had added some Bacardi rum. The Curacao on top was well alight. Gordon looked upon this with horror "all I wanted" he said "was a beer" to which the barman replied "oh you mean a Falstaff". Gordon had to drink this concoction and we put him to bed about half an hour later.

Returning to the Island we prepared for our departure and the end of 206's involvement with Grapple. One morning we were woken up by the Tannoy blasting out a tidal wave warning! Sitting 15ft above sea level we felt a little apprehensive. However, there was no need to panic. The boffins explained; an under sea quake near the Aleutians had started a pressure wave expanding in all directions. In the open sea nothing would be visible but the sloping shore of the North Coast of some of the Hawaiian Islands would allow the wave to build up and come ashore and cause considerable damage (it did). Christmas Island being an Atoll with a vertical undersea wall of coral was safe (!) despite the fact that the surge would be travelling at over 200 knots when it passed. Sure enough at the predicted time of 1300, all the water between the shore and the reef about 100 yards away drained off, it went very quiet then a large swell appeared and spilled over the reef with a muffled roar and everything returned to normal.

A farewell party was held to speed our impending departure and a great time was had by all – except one. He had returned to his tent quite early, somewhat the worse for wear, and had fallen asleep with his hand over his face. On waking in the early hours, his arm having been deprived of blood was therefore immovable. He opened his eyes and mistook his hand for a land crab; the scream of terror I can still hear to this day.

We attempted to leave for Hickham on 17th November but low oil pressure on No.2 engine required a return to the Island. The engineers got stuck into the engine and we took off for an air test. Same symptoms, after 20 minutes the oil pressure dropped to zero, the oil temperature increased. Landing again the Wing-co (Engineering) had a look and after more engine runs said that it was the gauge and there were no spares! I asked for another air test which annoyed him rather, and he decided to come too. Sure enough 20 minutes into the flight the oil pressure read zero "keep it going" he said, "my responsibility"! Forty minutes later the engine blew with oil, steam and bits escaping from the cowling. After landing the cowlings were removed and most of the engine fell on the tarmac; I still have a mangled big-end as a paperweight. We left a couple of days later with a new engine, reaching home on 3rd December. On 5th I flew 529 to Bally Kelly where she was later scrapped. R.I.P. The crew dispersed, I am sad to say, but they left me with a beer mug suitably inscribed. As I look at it now forty five years later I am trying to remember where they went, and if they should read these scribbles I would like them to know again how much I appreciated their help, after all, they were my first crew and I was a very new sprog Captain! Gordon Acklam stayed in the RAF and retired as a Wing Commander, Reg Castle (navigator) eventually went to British Aerospace at Woodford and brought his expertise to the Nimrod and embryo Nimrod early-warning aircraft. Flight Poutney (engineer) joined British Airways as an engineering instructor, Maurice Smythe (Nav) returned to his home in New Zealand. I regret I have lost contact with the signallers, Ginger Baker, Jock Cormie, Peter Lazerus, Mick Carter and Eric Smith (Best crew cook); but I remember seeing Eric on a newsreel in the sixties rescuing a trawler crew off the Cornish coast as a helicopter crewman, for which he was awarded a well deserved George Cross.

206 squadron was now destined to convert onto the Mark 3 Shackleton and moved to St. Mawgan – St. Eval was to be closed down. So flying the old Mk 1's virtually ceased. It was during this period that the Cornish Gliding Club started up operations at Perranporth. This was a wartime three-runway airfield built near the northwest cliff edge some 20 miles south of Newquay. The site had once been an old tin mine and there were many ancient uncovered mine shafts dotted about to trap the unwary. In some places circular dents in the runways and taxiways could be seen where the foundations had collapsed. Some of these were as much as three feet deep. In early January I started to instruct in the new club and generally tried to be helpful. Soaring over the 400ft cliffs in a strong wind in a T21 watching the waves crashing against the rocks and listening to the screech of seagulls was a real joy. One had to take care on landing because the 'curl over' effect of the wind off the sea, caused severe down drafts half a mile inland. In fact I had kept up my gliding activities with the Moonrakers at Upavon and often flew up there at weekends in the station Chipmunk. Those were wonderful days. Throughout my air force career I was heavily involved with RAFGSA and took part in some half a dozen championships.

We started our ground school for the Mark 3 under the direction of 'Doc Foster' our Chief Training Captain. Not having anything to fly I availed myself of the station Anson on several occasions one of which was nearly my undoing. I found a report in my files not long ago; Sir, it started, I have the honour to submit the following report on a forced landing. I was authorised to fly Anson Mk 19 VM334 from St. Eval to Bovingdon and return on the 7th December 1957. The report went something like this: -

I took off from St. Eval in VM334 that afternoon with the Station Commander, Wing Commander (Admin) and other lesser mortals, to deliver same to Bovingdon for a dining-in night at Coastal Command. I was to return empty to St. Eval that evening. It was a lovely cold winter's afternoon with clear skies and crystal clear visibility. Since I would be returning at night I took a Navigator with me, one Flt Lt Dozey. Our Anson's radio fit and navigation equipment was pretty basic; one P-12 Compass, one ten-channel VHF set, a TR1154-1155 HF + MF set and GEE MK II.

The trip to Bovingdon was uneventful and we landed at 1630, I organised some fuel and had a word with MET; no problems here, St. Mawgan, St Eval and St Merryn would remain CAV OK (Open) though a build-up of isolated cumulus could be expected from Exeter westwards, probably reaching 8000ft.

The forecast wind remained Northerly at 2000ft at about 15 to 20 knots. I returned to the aircraft to find that no fuel was available – the Bowser driver had gone to tea. No problem, we still had 90 gallons remaining, more than enough for the flight plus reserves, the Cheetahs using about 32 gallons an hour at weak cruise settings.

We took off at 1700, passing Benson and getting a VHF true bearing for good measure. After that the VHF went dead. We passed north of Swindon to avoid Lyneham and tried in vain to raise them on VHF. At about 1750, having climbed to avoid Exmoor, we entered cloud which became very turbulent. The windscreen flashed over completely with ice; so it was into Hot-Air on the air intakes, full power and prop de-ice and climb as rapidly as possible. One of the quirks of the Anson is that if the aircraft suffers a yaw due to outside forces the rudder swings in sympathy; disconcerting for the unwary.

I saw the reflection of several lightning flashes ahead and eased over on to a more North Westerly heading to avoid them. Passing 6000ft I realised that the ASI was stuck on 100 knots and that the aircraft was becoming very sluggish to control – had to be ice. I kept full power on past the normal five minute limitation as Daz came up front clutching his map (navigators cannot move in aeroplanes unless holding a map!) "What about a GEE fix"? I asked. "No GEE" he replied. "OK", I said "Keep trying to raise someone on VHF". We suddenly came out of the side of a towering Cu at 7000ft and I was able to reduce power a little. We had collected a lot of ice. I turned west again and Daz called "I can see a coastline to the north, looks like South Wales and those lights to the right could be Swansea". I had a brief glimpse of a ragged collection of lights and water and then more cloud. I decided to head south for home on our wildly swinging

P-12 and eased our heavy Annie up to 8000ft. About 20 minutes later we came out in the clear, with a brilliant star-lit night with a sea of cloud about 4000 below. I throttled back the Cheetahs to Max Endurance settings and descended.

We had now been flying for nearly one and a half hours so I did a fuel check. Switching the fuel gauge selection to the four tanks in turn showed readings of near zero in all tanks and no gauge needle movement, a phenomenon peculiar to Ansons in very low temperatures and it was very cold! Still we had to have (?) at least 35 to 40 minutes fuel left! Time to review the situation; here we were over a sea of cloud, no sign of any ground; not even Dartmoor showing up. No radios, no ASI, no GEE and one unhappy looking Navigator mirroring my thoughts! I decided to fly the standard emergency triangular pattern for those "lost in space with no means of support" and hope that some wide-awake radar operator would see us before heading north again. Daz agreed.

As I started the first turn I became aware of a faint glow to the South East, a solitary sign that there was life on earth. I said, "I think this is for us" and Daz nodded as he checked the fuel gauges yet again! Fifteen minutes later we were overhead the glow and I could just discern a rotating Pundit light showing White and Green and then runway lights! I descended towards this heaven sent haven, carried out the no-radio joining procedure and landed at 1855. As we taxied round to the apron I said to Daz "When we shut down grab the first bod you see and ask him quietly where the hell we are". As I put the parking brake on I looked up at the Tower and to my horror I saw the words: "JERSEY AIRPORT"!

We stayed the night. Next morning I flew back to St. Eval to lots of explaining and lots of flak, to be the subject of many jokes from the rest of the Squadron for a very long time! In conclusion, after my foray to Jersey the Engineers found that the P-12 compass was overdue a swing and was much in error – I should have checked the date on the deviation card! The VHF aerial connection had broken. The Pitot head turned out to be a 12 volt one instead of 24 volt and had burnt out. The wind at 8000ft over the Western UK that night was

010°/45 knots – I should have anticipated this increase. As for the "fix" near Swansea – must have been Torbay! I am glad to say that Daz survived the flak (it was really my fault) and went on with a successful career.

A month later I converted to the Mark 3. I was flown up to Woodford in the Anson, plus some of my crew, with Doc Foster to collect our brand new aeroplane and do a little bit of conversion flying on the way home. Nearer St. Eval we tried a stall! Throttling back and raising the nose we waited for the usual stall warning shudder but this time before the nose had a chance to drop, the left wing went down to near the vertical in the blink of an eye and without any aileron buffet whatsoever. We recovered after quite a loss of height. Doc said "I don't think we will do that again, when I did my conversion with Avro's we only took it to the initial buffet"! Later, stalling spoilers were added to the leading edge of the main plane inboard of number 2 and 3 engines in a similar manner to those fitted on a Shackleton Mk 1 and 2. This made the wing drop less marked. The only other problem that we had was the nose wheel failing to lock down, old Doc had to put one down on its nose. This was soon fixed by strengthening the floor around the nose wheel jack. The Mark 3 had good soundproofing, an excellent galley and rest area and all sorts of new anti-submarine gadgets, but I only got to fly it five or six times. For reasons, totally unconnected with flying, or the Stations Masters daughter, my tour came to an abrupt end with the words of the Station Master ringing in my ears "please be off my Station by tomorrow"! The following day I was on a Beverley course at Dishforth.

7. 'Be Off My Station by Tomorrow!'

Driving away from St Mawgan the next day I pondered on the effects of my sudden dismissal. On the plus side I had escaped from Coastal; usually, once in the Command one remained for at least two tours. Now that Christmas Island was over with there was little hope of any further adventures overseas, other than a posting to Bally Kelly (oh no!) or Gibraltar. Talking of Gib, I suppose I had better come clean about my ignominious departure from St Mawgan. The previous week my boss, Wing Cdr John Preston and I had been summoned by the Station Commander to hear that I had been selected for a job as Personal Assistant to the Commander-in-Chief Gibraltar. I knew that these sorts of posts were always voluntary assignments so I asked for the weekend to think about it. The SM made it very clear that it would be a big mistake to turn it down. From a career point of view he was right.

"Talk to him, John," said the SM as we left his office.

Back in the Squadron the Boss looked at me with an amused grin on his face. "He's right, you know; if you do well as a PA you're made!"

I said I could not see myself as a lackey and I was probably far too tactless to put up with the trivia of C-in-C's cocktail parties and endless similar functions, apart from which I wanted to fly!

"I don't blame you Ken," he admitted. "I don't think I would like it either. We'll go and see the old man on Monday."

So I duly declared my non-acceptance … to be told by an irate Group Captain, "You had better think again, because I have already accepted on your behalf and I am NOT changing that!"

My Boss took my side (and a lot of flak) and we left.

Sad to relate, John was killed a couple of years later, while flying as a passenger in an Anson from St Mawgan to Valley, when his pilot hit the top of Snowdon in bad weather.

In retrospect my sudden exit opened the door to a much more interesting career that I could only have dreamed about … but that was all in the future.

In 1995 I attended a lunch at the RAF Club and bumped into a long-lost ex-Coastal friend. I told him my tale and he laughed. He said, "I live quite close to old B-J, I'll give him your regards."

"Yes," I said, "and my thanks for giving me the heave-ho!"

I learned later that my comments were not well received!

Back to Dishforth on 3rd March '58, the day after I had left St Mawgan, it was good to be back; the Vale of York abounded with friendly people and pubs, and in York itself there lurked a thriving nightlife within the city walls.

The Beverley, what can I say? Forty-seven were built, several were written off and now only one remains, thanks to the stalwart efforts of the Royal Corps of Transport at Beverley in Yorkshire. It is sad to remember that the Royal Air Force Museum at Hendon allowed theirs to rot until it almost disintegrated and then got rid of it. With fixed gear, four Centaurus engines, which gave a maximum cruising speed of 130 knots, and a wingspan of 162ft, it earned its name as the original petrol-cooled, oil-burning, drag-master.

I recall once flying into the Mistral near Orange in the Rhone Valley, registering a ground speed of 62 knots. [A train once overtook a Bev on this route.] However, despite its ungainly and ugly appearance it was surprisingly agile and endowed with excellent STOL qualities. It could land from 50ft in 350yds – the technique being to do a slow approach with full flap and hit reverse on all four complaining engines when the main wheels were just off the ground. Take off to 50ft could be accomplished in about 450 yards from a standing start. An even shorter distance was achieved (I only tried it once) by using 25° of flap and full power, as Blackburn Test Pilot Timber Woods once demonstrated to me; it was quite impressive. The Beverley in this configuration was reluctant to stall, so at the start of the take off roll the co-pilot held the control column fully aft with instructions to keep it there "or else". Full power applied, the nose lifted at 60 knots and she climbed out at an impossible angle at about 67 knots, well below safety speed (!). At 1000ft the procedure was to slowly lower the nose, achieve a 120 knots, reduce power and mop the sweat from ones brow.

I suppose the Bev's Achilles heel(s) were the engines – 4 x 2,850 brake horse power simply was not enough and resulted in some strange payloads [viz: 1,000 lbs for 3,000 nautical miles or 40,000 lbs for 200 nautical miles]. When one remembers that this monster was in the design stages at the same time as the Lockheed Hercules, one should question the thinking of those who wrote out the specifications in the Air House. Admittedly they wanted a short-range heavy lift and para-dropping aircraft, but it still had to transit to the theatre of operations and it did this at only a few knots above the para drop speeds. The continued use of high power and RPM on the sleeve-valve engines (never less than 2400 RPM) resulted in high oil consumption and a time between overhauls of 600 hours (later reduced to 400). [The Airspeed Ambassador, with the same engines, achieved a time between overhauls of 2,000 hours!] An oil consumption of 3 gallons per hour per engine was considered OK, and to top up the engine oil, two 52-gallon overload tanks were fitted in a fair-sized compartment between the wing spars in the centre section, accessed through a hole in the front one from the flight deck. Oil was hand pumped at a rate of 8 strokes per gallon, using [I was told] a Sunderland bilge pump. The reasons for this extraordinary method were unbelievably: 1) it was cheap to install; 2) there was always someone who wanted to visit the flight deck and could be diverted into the 'dog kennel' to pump; 3) electrical pumps often failed; 4) There was a surplus of bilge pumps. There was also an uncomfortable crawl required, along the front spar to the rear of the engines (accessory bays) – a journey not to be taken in flight by anyone suffering from claustrophobia!

In practice we found that the real drawback in operating the Beverley was the role change. The Hercules came on the market with built in roller conveyors, folding seats and a rear freight door that could be opened in flight. The Beverley required the huge rear doors to be removed (and parked) for heavy drops and replaced for para operations. The Beverley was also blessed with power-operated controls with no manual reversion [unlike the prototype].

But the old lady handled well, was nice to fly, if noisy, and was incredibly tough. It was unfortunate that she was handicapped by a lack of power and reliability – or should I say, an excess of drag.

Ground school lasted some 6 weeks, with 2 weeks spent on the engine alone. The Met man was one Mike Hunt; later to gain fame as one of the first TV met men. Mike produced notes for each of his lectures, which became known as 'The Dishforth Met Notes for Aircrew', and are to this day considered one of the best met books ever produced. He went on to write a special set for the Far East Air Force and when I joined Royal Brunei Airlines in 1983 I was handed a copy of Mike's FEAF notes. I still have both sets, now bound.

Flying started on the 29th April. Dishforth was even busier than before, with twin-Pioneers, single-Pioneers and Beverleys all mixing it with the older residents – the Hastings and the Valetta. The Beverley always attracted the attention of motorists on the A1, and it is said that someone in a hot-rod once overtook a Beverley on its take-off run. On another occasion a Hastings landed in a field just short of Runway 9, bounced over the A1 and landed safely on the runway.

I had just completed my first solo cross-country (to Stornaway) when Dad Owen, our flight commander (training) asked me if I would like a free lunch and a tour of the Blackburn works at Brough. Having said 'yes' I discovered I would miss the Mess 'hooley' (ladies night) that weekend and I would also have to pick up the last Beverley and take it to Shawbury on the Sunday. 'Never volunteer', I thought to myself. Anyway, on 28th May we set off for Brough in the Station Anson with a brand new crew, only half way through the course. After a quick tour of the works, during which we saw the new NA39 [later to become the Buccaneer] and the Beverley production line. It was interesting to see that the Beverley was built from the bottom upwards, the keel having first being laid, like a ship. Then to the Executives Club for a splendid lunch, a few words and toasts and at about 4pm I asked where we would be staying.

"Staying?" said the Managing Director. "Oh no. You have to take the aircraft now!"

After more curses on Dad Owens' head and several black coffees we climbed into XM112 and fired up, with a request for a low flypast. I did my best, bearing in mind that I had only 15 hours on type. The Air Quartermaster, who was sitting in the glass nose (foolish fellow), thought I had forgotten that there was some 30 odd feet of metal under my seat.

For recreation York provided a host of good pubs and good company and I teamed up with one Brian, a Navigator, in various forays. Wednesday afternoons were still designated sports afternoons, but not the sort of sports that Brian and I had in mind. One of our more infamous capers was to visit the City Variety Theatre in Leeds in the afternoons, where Phyllis Dixie was giving her last shows before leaving the stage and revealing all (well, nearly). In those days such artistes had to remain stationary when in 'the full Monty' – although on close inspection from the front row this was not always achieved. Anyway, we sat through the whole tedious performance and noted the punchlines of the comedians. Then we made a phone call to the mess and as many of the course that could come met us in a local bar. There the punchlines were committed to memory and we occupied the front rows of the theatre. Every time a comic came to the punchline of his joke, some twenty stalwarts shouted it out at the top of their voices. Eventually the Theatre Manager wrote to the Station Commander, demanding that an officer be sent to each performance to keep his airmen in order!

The course completed, I joined 53 squadron (Wing Commander Bas Taylor) at Abingdon in June. The squadron offices and dispersals were on the north side of the airfield, in an area known as 'Sleepy Hollow'. This was next to the bomb dump, which was also the home of the squadron mascot, an evil-smelling and ill-tempered goat with an appetite for bicycle tyres. 53 was anything but sleepy and I was plunged into a packed training programme to qualify in para-dropping, heavy dropping and other similar activities, including low-level cross-countries. The first one I did was with an NCO co-pilot called Albert [he was Polish; no one could write or pronounce his name, so we simply called him Albert]. Albert had the DFM and bar and looked at me with a somewhat jaundiced eye. He was due out of the service in a few weeks and was just filling in time on the Beverley. I should add at this point that the Bev was flown "solo", the second pilot being trained in the aircraft systems but not in handling, similar to the Valetta and Hastings crews; a more daft philosophy I cannot imagine. Our low-level route took us north-eastwards to Cromer, returning via Thetford, where we would do a simulated para drop over the Army training ground. At the briefing our Nav leader stated that the maximum height was to be 500ft – and forgot to mention the lowest one! We were the second aircraft in this exercise and the planned route took us over Woburn Abbey. It was not long (5 minutes) after the first aircraft had passed over the stately pile before the Duke was on to Air House complaining about the noise. I took off an hour later in a heavy drop aircraft, i.e. no rear doors, with a band of parachute instructors along for the ride. I must explain that people who make a habit of jumping out of aircraft like to stand near open doors and this flight was no exception. The gaping hole at the rear of the freight bay was full of PJIs, some standing, some sitting near the edge (with safety harnesses), all peering over the sill at the ground slowly passing by. Albert enjoyed this and did most of the flying; I think it reminded him a little of flying Typhoons in the Falaise Pocket in '44. He was all smiles. With Woburn in sight we veered to starboard and started to overfly the village of the same name. The Beverley, with all four Centaurus bellowing at well below 500ft, cast a giant shadow over the ground; it must have been an awesome sight. I could see cars stopping and people staring up at us. We followed a policeman proceeding on his bicycle, who looked up, made a valiant attempt to get his notebook from his pocket and collided with a lamppost. He must have seen the gestures from my onlookers in the tail and possibly heard their laughter. I give him his due; he had my number and it was soon (5 minutes) passed on to the Air House.

On returning to Abingdon I found an irate Station Master (again) waiting for me, but thanks to my boss, managed to avoid the firing squad this time. My CO, Bas Taylor, was, I think, the best boss I ever served under and I am sorry to say that he is no longer with us. When the weather was duff and it was market day, Bas would lead a sortie into Abingdon and much fun was had by all, I think we behaved ourselves … well, most of us did. By the end of July I had rented an 18th Century cottage in Standlake, some eight miles west of Abingdon, and moved the family in. This was a delightful house full of beams, low ceilings and vast fireplaces. By sheer coincidence the village was the home of one of the pilots on my course in Rhodesia, Phil Pickford, now with British Overseas Airways, and an ex-flight commander from our Initial Training School at Cosford, Tim Hodges, now retired.

One day we were visited by two French Air Force C-119s, complete with paratroops. Since I still spoke fluent French the Boss asked me to fly with the lead ship and guide them to Weston-on-the-Green airfield for a demonstration drop. Once airborne, out came the Gauloises! As we started our run-in to the DZ they all stood up, hooked up their static lines and continued to smoke. The red light came on and they shuffled towards the doors. Having been trained in the highly disciplined exit drill of our own Airborne Forces I was horrified at this apparent casualness. Worse was to come; the Green light flashed and there was a mad rush for the doors – no semblance of an orderly line – but somehow they all got out on a "first come, first served" basis and pretty quickly too. After landing I asked the crew if this was the normal procedure.

"Mais oui, mon vieux," was the reply, with a Gallic shrug!

In June word reached us that one of our number from the course at Dishforth had crunched a Beverley in Arabia. Apparently he had just taken off from Beihan, a strip in Southern Arabia some 100 miles North of Aden, when the loss of an engine necessitated a return to the "airfield". On landing the nose wheel dug into a patch of soft sand and the whole of the aircraft turned over on its back. The only casualty was unfortunately the signaller, who was killed. It said much for the aircraft that it remained pretty well intact upside down.

Abingdon is one of the oldest stations (circa 1920?) and the Officers Mess was a very pleasant building, reflecting the architecture of the day. In the anteroom hung a painting by David Shepherd of a Beverley landing at Beihan with full reverse thrust on, blowing clouds of sand everywhere. In the right hand corner he had painted an Arab and a couple of camels, standing quite still. When it was pointed out to him that the camels and the Arab would have been in full flight seeing and hearing the Beverley, he agreed to paint them out. I am lucky to have one of his prints of this event at home.

All our servicing was done in the open while waiting for three huge hangars to be built to accommodate the airplanes (the tops of the fins were 40ft high). The contractors built the roof first, with all the electrics, heating and plumbing installed at ground level and then the whole roof was jacked up as they built the walls, thus avoiding the problems of installing equipment in the ceiling at such a height. Unfortunately they got it wrong and for months the hangar was filled with enough scaffolding to build a high-rise block of flats whilst they rectified the faults. I never did see them in use.

A social event now occurred that I think deserves a mention. One of our co-pilots (just retired from Britannia Airways) got engaged to the daughter of an Air Marshal. Bob and I flew a lot together; he was soon to move on to Hunters. The wedding was set in the highest traditions of the service, complete with a Guard of Honour and swords; the reception was to be at the RAF Club. I and five others formed the Guard of Honour. One of the five was Brian! Brian still had a gift for always getting into trouble through his numerous escapades, which would fill a book. Unfortunately I got caught up in some of them and I therefore blame him for my not reaching air rank. Anyway, we drew weapons, white gloves, etc, and in our 'best blues' headed for London, early on the day, in order, as Brian said, 'to lubricate ourselves for our duties'. Despite Brian we managed to turn up at the appointed time and in due course formed up outside the main door of St Clement's Danes Church. To the tune of "Here comes the Bride" we drew our swords and formed an arch. Brian, damn him, was opposite me, trying not to laugh, for he had left the end of his scabbard dangling from the tip of his sword, I think quite deliberately. With the end of mine, I managed to flick it off behind me just as the Bride and Groom appeared. Brian was purple in the face with suppressed hysterics, I was not much better and the Air Marshal was of a similar hue with displeasure. I knew if I looked at Brian and our eyes met, the solemnity of the occasion would be lost. Brian, of course, compounded the situation by asking the Air Marshal where the RAF Club was!

Later that month I got involved in the development of new ways of dropping stores from aircraft, most of which are now commonplace, such as flying a few feet off the ground and using an extraction parachute to drop the palleted stores straight onto the dropping zone. This leads me to the tale of the 'Italian Job' – no, not the Michael Caine film, but close…

I had positioned our Beverley in heavy drop roll at Netheravon for a demonstration in front of some top NATO brass. As we got out of the aircraft we were confronted by a number of excited Italian Mountain troops, resplendent in best uniforms and complete with their famous feathered hats. The cause of this commotion was sitting on the tarmac, lashed to a pallet with parachutes, and took the shape of a rather splendid new shiny Howitzer. As an ex-gunner I could see that this was a well-designed little weapon and apparently the only example of a new line in artillery. They wanted me to drop it in front of the Brass from 1,200 feet. There was just one snag; their plan was not to use an extractor parachute but to invoke gravity, manpower and a very high nose up attitude in flight to drop the gun. I said I did not think it would work but one of the C-in-C's henchman said that I had better *make* it work.

We took off with the gun near the rear exit of the freight bay. Trundling slowly across the airfield without flap and the nose as high as I dared, the Nav switched the green light on, the pallet retaining clamp was withdrawn and … nothing moved. My dispatchers heaved and strained, aided by some still-excited Italians, and slowly, ever-so-slowly, got the platform moving. It fell off, just within the viewing area, but not one of the Italian parachutes opened fully and the gun hit the soft chalk barrel first and almost disappeared.

The Italians ceased to be excited. I never found out what went wrong, because the squadron was soon on its way to Cyprus, but I suspect that 2,000 feet would have been a better dropping height.

The Middle East beckoned us in June and about half of the Squadron was dispatched to Nicosia in the company of Hunters, Hastings, and Vallettas. We were to train for a possible airlift to Amman; trouble had been simmering for some time between Syria and Jordan (*plus ça change*). We were fortunate to be billeted at the Dome Hotel in Kyrenia, a town on the North Coast that was considered safe from EOKA terrorist activities. Years later I discovered why; Grivas, the EOKA head, had one of his headquarters there, in the old Castle, under the very noses of the security forces.

All crews were issued with service revolvers and five rounds; the chamber "under the hammer" being left empty. This was to prevent the death of your mate if you mistook him for a gunman and pulled the trigger. In effect it ensured your own death if you really needed the weapon in a hurry. Royal Air Force crews are not really *au fait* with handguns; none of us had had any training and several incidents inevitably followed. On one occasion a somewhat exuberant signaller, returning to his room full of good Cyprus plonk, put all five rounds into his wall mirror as he opened the door. On another occasion someone slipped on the outside steps of the Dome and let off a few more rounds. I remember getting into a crew bus to return to Nicosia one evening when some wally shouted, "there is a Cyp in the road with a sten gun!" Those inside the bus wanted to get out, drawing their guns at the same time; those outside wanted to get in and go. The result was a heaving mass of bodies. Someone laughed and the whole thing dissolved into a Buster Keaton style farce.

Our favourite watering hole was the Octopus, run by the glamorous Lotty and her ex-guardsman boyfriend. Lotty was a law unto herself and God help you if she fancied you, for she would undress you in a flash – in full view of the entire bar. I came in one night with a 206-squadron tie on (an Octopus on a dark blue background). Two seconds later Lotty had cut it in half and nailed it to her trophy board.

Happy times!

We did a lot of practice flying, para drops etc, and also low-level cross-countries. Our redoubtable boss once led six of us (I was the last one) round the Northwest coast of Cyprus, then flying eastwards towards Kyrenia (very low – no coppers here) and then through the Kyrenia pass to Nicosia avoiding St Hilarion Castle, well below the ramparts. If anyone knows that narrow gorge they will realise that flying through it in a 162ft wingspan airplane is not a job for the faint-hearted … but it was great fun.

We started a lift to Amman, carrying mainly ammunition. I see from my logbook that I did eight sorties in seven days. It was during this period that I made the acquaintance of a lad called Stew, who had joined my crew as second pilot. On one trip we had the first Bev to be fitted with a Mark 10 auto-pilot, a welcome modification to ease our 16-hour duty days (these went back to 19 hours again with the auto-pilot installed).

I took this beast to Amman one night, with orders not to use the auto-pilot; the instruction manuals had not yet arrived. Being a democratic leader of men, I took myself to the dog kennel to pump oil from the overload tank into one of our engines. This was a mistake; no sooner had I started to pump when the Bev stood on one wingtip in an uncoordinated turn, sending me into the scuppers. Much shouting was coming from the flight deck. Stew had decided to experiment with the auto-pilot. Calm returned. Half an hour later the air Quarter Master came up and said he could smell fuel downstairs. Glaring at Stew I left my seat (foolish chap) to investigate the supposed leak in the freight bay. The aircraft lurched again to a steep bank and sent me scampering up the ladder to the flight deck in time to see Chas, my Nav, about to attack Stew with a straight edge. Stew had done it again.

We discharged our cargo and set off for Nicosia. Beverleys at this time were fitted with propeller interruption switches to stop any spurious electrical current from changing the propeller pitch in flight [i.e. like going into reverse]. These were later replaced by under-carriage weight micro-switches. The switches were in front of the co-pilot and were put 'up' after take off and 'down' just before landing, effectively locking the props in positive pitch while in flight.

With switches down on finals into Nicosia I landed, selected reverse and braked to a halt. Cancelling reverse I increased power to taxi (one needed quite a bit of poke to get the thing moving). Without further ado the aircraft rocketed backwards [one thing one must do in this situation is to use the foot brakes]. I ran the throttle to idle in time to hear Stew say, "Oh sorry, I moved the switches…"

The last I saw of Stew was him running across the apron, followed by a very angry Navigator, still clutching his straight edge.

On returning to Abingdon life got back to normal for a few weeks. I did some flying at old Sarum for the Para's, including short field landings (as previously described) and managed to put 18 inch grooves into that soggy airfield. For recreation I often flew a Tiger Moth belonging to No.47 Squadron Flying Club – a civil one. I think the charge was £10 per hour plus petrol. It must have been the last Tiger flying that I did until meeting up with another Tiger in 1997.

But there really was little time for recreation. In October we were off again to Nicosia and Jordan; more trouble with Syria. I recall we flew into Amman in the early dawn, not knowing if we were going to be able to land our troops, or drop them by parachute. We over flew Northern Israel ignoring protestations from Lydda and Tel Aviv – apparently they were not privy to our activities. We were able to land at Amman and spent a week there while the politicians tried to sort out the problems. Eventually after the United Nation's "intervention" we pulled out our troops and equipment, flying a United Nations observed route over Syria and then to the Coast. I was one of the last Bevs, if not the last, out of Amman and I had on board two Arab horses plus grooms, a gift from King Hussein to Her Majesty the Queen. With an hour to go to the United Nations deadline for our withdrawal, the starting motor on number three engine packed up. The Bev was not cleared for three engine ferry flights but I thought we just might be able to air start before we actually got airborne on the take off run. The boss, bless him said "you can either stay or try a start on the runway – either way I will back you". So we feathered number three, wound up the remaining three engines and let go of the brakes: with 3,000 yards of runway it should work providing we jigged a bit once airborne to avoid the hills! At 70 knots Bob unfeathered number three and after a few protesting bangs it joined its companions just as we lifted off. We all breathed a sigh of relief. No sooner into the cruise when smells of hot food wafted through the aeroplane: the grooms had started their little paraffin stoves amongst the straw and horses and were busy cooking! To convince an Arab, who does not speak English, above the din of four Centaurus engines that this was not a good idea only meets with blank stares, so I positioned several fire extinguishers and airmen around the campfire. I must say, whatever they were cooking smelt jolly good. Just before the Syrian border we were buzzed by a couple of fighters which then got very close. Bob shouted, "they're Migs" to which I replied "they're Hunters". Needless to say a Mig-Hunter formation flying at 130 knots is a bit tricky: reducing to a 100 knots soon got rid of them! Unfortunately the press got hold of my merry quip about the Hunters which rather displeased the C in C Transport Command: why I cannot think. Believe it or not, the last 40 minutes of the flight were uneventful. We landed and handed the aircraft over to one Ron Wing, complete with grooms, cooking utensils, straw and horses who then flew the aircraft on to Abingdon and to a Royal reception of TV cameras, press and top brass and Jordanian officials. It was ever thus!

It was about this time that Flight Lieutenant Peter Lewis who had been on my Wings course in Southern Rhodesia started secret negotiations with the Guinness Breweries at Park Royal. Just how this came about is a mystery but the outcome was that "Guinness" adopted 53 Squadron. The Squadron made many happy brew-tasting visits to Guinness over the years. Guinness were marvellous and designed and produced the famous Guinness tie (a Toucan with a Beverley tail and undercarriage), and presented the Squadron with a gallon silver beer mug and one of their ties that could be wrapped around three people!

Our flying became more varied and interesting: I visited Duxford in early 59 to take Javelin crews to El Adem for gunnery training. I remember this visit well because on the morning of departure, my flight plan, unknown to me, had been mislaid before it could be passed on to West Drayton Air Traffic Control; so we appeared on their radar close to Bookmans Park Beacon at 8,000ft, very large, very slow, and very unwanted. Apart from normal training we flew the Berlin Corridor at the lowest level (I think that was 3,000ft) to uphold the right of the West to use the Corridor at a time of disturbed relations with the Russians. What they thought of the Beverley I do not know but we often had the odd Mig trying to formate on us. The Middle East featured mainly in our overseas support flying including Malta. Then we started detachments to Aden. Our route took us: Orange, Luqa (night stop), El Adem, and Khartoum, over Asmara and into Aden. The heat and turbulence over the El Adem - Khartoum sector (seven hours) was very uncomfortable as we could not climb higher than about 8,000ft and often had to settle (!) for lower with overheating engines. Asmara is 7,000ft above sea level and I once managed to clear it with 1,000ft to spare. Once past Asmara the terrain fell steeply to the Red Sea and one could at last reduce power and watch the cylinder head temperature gauge needles come out of the red. Then down to the Perin Islands and into Khormaksar. On one return flight I had an engine fail some 20 minutes after leaving Khartoum. With full power on the remaining three we managed to return to Khartoum in a continuous descent for a straight in down wind landing! To repair our aircraft a couple of ground crew had to be flown in from Fayid with necessary tool kits to repair number three engine on site. What had happened was that a cylinder had blown its way through the cowling but luckily had not damaged much else. So in effect we had some new cowling to put on and a replacement cylinder and sleeve. This took about three days, I say days because we really worked at night. During this period there was a coup in progress and it was thought wise by the Embassy that we should not appear in uniform and only slink about at night and do our work on the airfield then. We were accommodated at the house of the BOAC Station Manager; a chap called Don Levy whom I had known well when I was working at Airways Terminal many years previously. Of course being Jewish he had changed his name to something else and they looked after us extremely well and despite the heat and the dust and the night time working we got the airplane together again in about three days and set off again for El Adem.

In September 1958 there came a notice from Headquarters asking for a volunteer pilot to fly the Embassy Heron in Washington D.C. I put in a bid for it but did not get it: I must have upset someone somewhere. I did have a friend in "Postings", Eric Reeves who commiserated with me and offered to put me on a list as a volunteer for an exchange post. Six months later a United States Air Force exchange post came up for grabs – two years with Strategic Air Command in Southern California flying KC-97's with a possibility of going on to the KC-135, just then coming into service. This is for me I thought so I put my bid in and much to my surprise and to the astonishment of my boss and no doubt others, I got the job. It was then that I did one of the few smart things I have done in my life; I took the exam (after much swotting) and flight test for a US Commercial Licence. This would at least cover me for gliding (should I be lucky to find a gliding club nearby) and perhaps some light aircraft flying for fun.

June found me at RAF Strubby near Skegness for a Jet refresher on Meteor 7's and 8's. My instructor, Chris Doggett was an old friend from Harvard days and a brave lad too. The instant transition from Beverleys to Meteors for me was quite a challenge and I owe Chris a debt of gratitude for keeping cool and calm in the rear seat while this idiot cavorted round the circuit. The course lasted seven weeks and was great fun. It was good to be back doing aerobatics, formation flying and generally misbehaving in the Mk 8. The flight departure routing from Strubby to our exercise area in the North Sea was eastwards to the Lincolnshire coast, only a couple of miles, and then a sharp turn southwards along the coast for two minutes all at 500ft, to avoid air to air firing ranges above and finally a turning climb eastwards out to sea. If one poured on the coals on the two-minute leg southwards, one could arrive over the beaches of Skegness, where all sorts of naughties were going on, very fast, very low, and very noisy before the two minutes were up. Of course someone had to spoil it by flying over the sea front below pier level saying his watch had stopped and we then had to behave ourselves again. From Strubby I went to 233 O.C.U. at Basingbourne for a Canberra course; there seemed to be no limit to the depths of the public purse of the Treasury to provide one young Flight Lieutenant with so much enjoyable flying. Ground school was followed by "runs" in a decompression chamber including an explosive decompression (not nice) and a ride in the Martin Baker bang-seat trainer. I liked the Canberra very much, the two Navigators were not so enthusiastic being crammed in behind the pilot in a very small space. I was attached to B Flight being run by a Squadron Leader Laing with whom I did my asymmetric flying: little did I know that I would meet him again many years later. If the Canberra had any vices it was in the single engine flying configuration. There was a 45 knot gap between take off speed and safety speed; the Meteor was similar as were many twin engine aircraft of the period. The Americans cured this very quickly on there own version of the Canberra by fitting a power assisted rudder. However at Basingbourne a student pilot had to be specifically cleared for single engine flying and a certificate to that effect inserted in his logbook. This, of course, meant that if things went wrong it was always your fault. The main problem was the single engine overshoot in the landing configuration when 300ft could be lost in cleaning the aeroplane up and increasing speed from 125 knots to 150 knots to climb away. I completed the course and stayed on a couple of weeks, mainly doing navigation exercises until it was time to return to Abingdon, say our farewells and embark on the Mauritania on the 28th September for New York.

Saying goodbye to 53 was hard, it had been an exceptionally good squadron with a boss who was both respected and liked. It says much for the personnel both flying and ground crew that we still meet at the odd reunion and remember the good times and the mighty Beverley. We are often joined by many wartime members and our real pride was having the Squadron Commander of 53 Squadron of 1937 as our first President for a short while. It was a real wrench to leave after 18 months of quite hectic flying but remembered with much pleasure. However, a thought of two or more years with the United Stated Airforce was a huge compensation – and California sounded so much better than Aden! Coupled with the privilege of being a part of SAC (as an alien) added to the excitement of going. SAC maintained the great deterrent at this time in conjunction with Bomber Command. Make no mistake without that deterrent I would not be writing this now. It was maintained by having bombed up B47's and B52's and later the B-58, aircraft on 3 minutes states of readiness 24 hours a day. The Tanker fleet would be on the same high state of readiness to either rendezvous with the bombers in the event of war or in the case of the 135 to fly with them topping up tanks as required. In the 60s as the cold war got warmer came the Airborne Alert (Operation Chrome Dome) which had B52's always airborne on roughly a 20 hour flight on tracks close to the presumed threat. I did many re-fuellings on this system in fact I think the B52's were refuelled at least twice. The whole thing hinged on early warning radar stations feeding in information to North American Air Defense Command at Cheyenne Mountain in Colorado (Norad). So that is what I was going to see and hopefully play a part. I looked forward to it.

8. U.S.A.F Exchange

The voyage across the Atlantic in the *Mauritania* was an experience of a lifetime for all four of us, only to be bettered by returning 3½ years later in the *Queen Mary*. It was, without doubt, the only way to travel and my wife, two children and I all considered ourselves very fortunate. I spent a good deal of time exploring the ship and made friends with the Third Engineer, who explained the mysteries of his department. The weather was reasonably kind too.

On the first night out one could come to dinner in a casual jacket and tie, but from then on, even in cabin class, it was DJs and long dresses. I sometimes look at film footage of cruise liners today and shudder. The final two hours of the voyage were spent on deck, watching the famous skyline of New York slowly rising above the horizon, the tops of the skyscrapers appearing long before any land; a never to be forgotten sight. I was also amazed at the mass of cars on the ring-road round Manhattan; they were all colours of the rainbow, so different from the uniform black of our cars back in England.

We spent a couple of days with my family in Connecticut; it had been five years since they had all left England for their new home. Then to Washington DC by train, a briefing at the Embassy by those who looked after all exchange officers and by air to Los Angeles and March AFB. The journey from LA to Riverside was by helicopter, over what seemed an endless vista of roads and houses, all shrouded in the infamous Los Angeles smog, which reduced visibility to about three miles. Suddenly we burst out into brilliant sunshine over the Chino Hills, about twenty miles west of Riverside, the terrain becoming more rural (it was 45 years ago) and we finally landed to be welcomed by the chap I was going to replace, Flt Lt Tommy Thompson, and were whisked away to our new home on the base.

I remember asking Tommy if the smog posed problems at March. He said that it rarely extended to Riverside and quite often the line of demarcation between "smog" and "clear" was a well defined vertical line of smog, rather like an advancing dust storm, although it was almost stationary.

Riverside is some seventy miles east of LA just South of San Bernardino which straddles two passes through the Sierra Nevada mountain to the high desert; the Cajon to the north and Banning to the east. Down these the Santa Anna wind blows whenever there is a high pressure system off the California Coast inducing a hot dry easterly wind off the desert into the Los Angeles basin, leading to an ideal situation for forest fires to start, as we soon found out. To my delight outside San Bernardino railway station there was a monument to steam; one of the largest steam engines ever built (240 tons of it) on a short length of track.

My first administrative chore was the purchasing of a car in the shape of a 1949 Pontiac 2-door Sedan. Our first trip out into the wilderness was to Lake Arrowhead, some 5000ft up in the mountains. I happily drove on the wrong side of the road for some five miles until approaching a hair-pin bend Pam yelled, "You're on the wrong side!" I wrenched the wheel over to the right just as a Highway patrol car slid by.

There was just one more thing that made life here a little different from the sleepy Berkshire village we had just left; Riverside is on the San Andreas Fault. California is riddled with geological faults and we now happened to live very close to the biggest of them all. Once or twice we heard a subdued rumble and felt a slight tremor; rather like a train running deep underground.

I joined 320th Air Refueling Squadron (Colonel Charles B Lockhart commanding) on the 25th September 1959. We were part of 22nd Bomb Wing, consisting of about forty B47 and sixteen KC-97 tankers. The 97 [or Boeing 377] was really a B29 with a double fuselage, giving it two decks. After a few days of introduction by my predecessor Tommy Thompson, I settled down to ground school and the conversion, which was done on the squadron. My first day caused much amusement; I parked my car, a second hand 1949 Pontiac, behind the flight line fence and close to the parked KC-97s. There seemed plenty of room. While in the squadron headquarters one of these aircraft started its engines; it was then that I discovered that the Pratt & Whitney R4360 was a bit of an oil burner, like the Centaurus on the Beverley and I returned at the end of the day to find my car covered in oil. At least it never went rusty!

Tommy Thompson went home at the end of my first week and I was now on my own in a very different air force. Never before had I been treated with such consideration and made to feel so at home. The wives took over Pam, my wife and helped us through the pro-curement of base housing, furniture, etc. I had an officer assigned to me as a 'minder', who was a great help in steering me through matters administrative. I said I very much appreciated his help, to which he replied that it was standard procedure to do this for any newcomer!

I also began to realise what an important part wives of exchange officers played. We were both amused at the Squadron's insignia [which had been designed, I was told, by someone in Walt Disney Inc] worn on our flight suits. It consisted of a circular white cloth patch bordered by a green edge, the whole patch being some five inches in diameter: Green was, of course, the colour of our baseball hats – the bomber crews wore red ones. In the centre of the patch was an embroidered Dumbo the Elephant with a fuel drum in his trunk, Mickey Mouse sitting on his back and with Dumbo's tail shaped like a refuelling boom!

The 97 was Boeing's first major adventure in air refuelling with a flying boom system. This device was a long tube attached under the rear of the aircraft containing a fuel pipe with a telescopic end which could be extended to mate with a receptacle in the bomber. The end of the boom had two movable aerofoils with which the boom opera-tor, who had a position under the tail of the tanker, could "fly the boom" into a suitable position for inserting the last bit into the bombers receptacle, hopefully in the correct place! The system worked extremely well. During the operation of this aircraft it was called upon to carry more and more fuel as the B47s gave way to the much larger eight-engined B-52s. BOAC operated the 377 at about 142,000lbs gross weight; by the time I left the 320th we are flying off at nearer 175,000lbs. Engine failures were more frequent than I would have wished, partly due to relatively long periods at high power (METO or Maximum Except Take Off) during refuelling to get up speeds compatible to a bombers requirements. The combo once joined, also required a descending flight path. Landing, especially with a forward C-of-G, could well result in the nose wheels hitting the runway ahead of its associates, but the fix for this was simple using a maximum of 80% wing flap and a minimum of 15lb of manifold pressure on touchdown. Flight Engineers, who handled the power and were renowned for a desire for longevity, would put big hairy fists behind the throttles, thus ensuring that no pilot would ever be tempted to use less than the 15lb. In fact the Flight Engineer really was the kingpin of our six-man crew.

The Pratt & Whitney R4360 gave out some 3,500 brake horsepower. It was an air-cooled radial with 28 cylinders in 4 banks, manual spark and mixture controls and turbo superchargers. Cooling was a problem, especially after take off and during prolonged climbs in high ambient temperatures. In arctic conditions the engines had to be continuously heated when the aircraft was on the ground and oil dilution after a flight was a must, and possibly contributed to reduced engine life. For all its difficulties SAC's 500+ tankers fulfilled a vital role before the KC135 came into service and I thoroughly enjoyed flying it. The view from the cockpit was magnificent and one could sit five abreast facing the front, the two pilots having observer seats outboard of their own positions and, of course, the indispensable flight engineer sat in the middle. I was astonished at ground school, when I learned that each Flight Engineer's position was fitted with an ignition analyzer. This was a modified cathode-ray oscilloscope which provided a means of detecting, identifying and locating any ignition fault whilst in flight. A single dud spark plug could then be identified and then changed when on the ground. The only option we had in the RAF, on all the large piston aircraft that I flew was to change every spark plug in the event of ignition trouble, a costly and time consuming business. I thoroughly enjoyed my time on the '97. (I think it is my favourite of its type), it was the last of the gentlemen's aeroplanes; and so onto flying again.

The departure routing from March was invariably to the north towards Riverside and entailed an immediate left turn to the west, very gentle (about rate half in instrument flying parlance) because at the weights we operated at our rate of climb was about four hundred feet a minute straight and level! We now skirted the San Bernardino Mountains that form the northern rim to the LA Basin, then another gentle left turn tot he south. We were now climbing (just) quite close to the Santa Anna Mountains on our right and still below their peaks and eventually passing Mount Palomar and its observatory (5000ft) on our left at the same height. It was a long drawn out climb and by the time we came abeam San Diego on our right we might have clawed our way up to 8000ft: The Flight Engineer was a busy lad, constantly adjusting throttles, mixture, ignition, timing to keep the engines running at best mean effective power (BMEP) derived from his library of graphs, and, of course, when we were high enough (around 10,000ft) bringing the turbo-superchargers on line! The upshot of all this (!) is that on a clear day (no smog) one had quite the most magnificent and unique view of the Los Angeles area and at night the sight was quite breathtaking; the vast acreage of lights below being strong enough to illuminate the flight deck and to read a check-list. On these occasions the slow grind upwards was well worth enduring.

Once I had checked out and had my own crew I was put to task as any other squadron Captain in the flying programme. We did a lot of practice refuellings with B47s in our local area usually west of the Santa Catalina Island, we had one area further away called the Dead-wood area over the Grand Canyon, not really a good spot as it could brew up some enormous thunderstorms. Returning one night from this area I saw what looked liked a shower of meteorites or space debris fall through the atmosphere about 30 miles ahead. Several other aircraft reported seeing them as well. After landing at March we learnt that the display had been the remains of a large Russian satellite, breaking up over Hawaii some 3,000 miles away!

We also operated to Edmonton in Canada for two week alert stand-by's which reminds me that in Christmas '59 I won two cases of Carling Black Label in the Mess draw, but forgot to collect them. I wonder if...! In winter the Chinook wind would often blow across the Rockies. This wind descends on the eastern slopes, is heated by adiabatic compression and if it does ever reach the ground usually some hundred miles east of the Rockies it is often warm enough to melt the surface snow. On one occasion we had taken off from Edmonton to return to March at maximum all out weight the temperature at the time being -20° Fahrenheit. Climbing away to the east at about 9,000ft we encountered the warmer air of the Chinook the aeroplane ceased to climb in fact it lost a bit of height at times. The situation remained static until we entered the cold blast of the arctic air yet again and continued our climb.

I like the mountainous north west of the U.S.A. and Canada with it's pine forests and rivers but I suppose what attracts me most is the sparseness of population: after the Los Angeles basin it was always a joy to go to Edmonton and smell the pine woods instead of the smog! My one visit in December 1959, to the KC-97 Simulator School at Malmstrom A.F.B. afforded me a golden opportunity to see some of the northwest. Malmstrom was close to Great Falls, Montana; a state that brings to mind names like Custer, The Little Big Horn, Sitting Bull and the remarkable Chief Joseph of the Nez Perce tribe who outwitted the whole U.S. Army for nearly a year in 1877 in a desperate attempt to seek sanctuary in Canada for his people.

There were six of us, four pilots and two flight engineers scheduled for a week "in the box" and since the weather looked promising we elected to drive the 1200 miles in a large Ford Station Wagon; indeed the weather remained cold, crisp and cloudless until we returned to March some ten days later. This was my first encounter with a flight simulator and although it was static and lacked a visual display through the flight deck windows, it was an effective training machine.

Today, modern simulators completely convince their "victims" that they really are flying.

One of a tanker driver's worst fear is fire in the fuselage and this was well demonstrated by the training staff by igniting some oily rags close to the Simulator's air-conditioning intake. Half way through one detail smoke duly poured into the flight deck and I called for the "Smoke Clearance Drill" and put on my oxygen mask. The smoke thickened and no one responded to my calls. Looking over my right shoulder I could see Flight Engineer's empty seat and then realised that I was alone and bathed in a dull red glow coming through the flight deck windows – I left. Outside, the nose was ablaze and fire extinguishers were going off in all directions. Another way was found to simulate smoke!

We finished the course ahead of schedule and took a day off to see Glacier National Park and Watterton Lake just inside the Canadian border. Returning to the U.S.A. using the same border post that we had used two hours earlier, I was denied entry on my R.A.F. I.D card – no passport no visa equals no entry! This caused much merriment among my colleagues who also denied all knowledge of me until discovering that Immigration officials the world over are utterly without humour. It took a call to H.Q. 15th Air Force at March to get me re-admitted to the U.S.A. Great Falls was the home of the artist Charles M. Russell whose work is considered on a par with that of Remington when it comes to depicting the Old West. We paid a visit to Charlie's house and gallery and later stopped by at a bar called the Mint. This pub has been kept just as it was in the 1880s, and it is the only place where I have ever seen a barman send full tankards of beer sliding down the bar to stop in front of a customer: and yes, it still had sawdust on the floor! We took three days to return to California, passing through Yellowstone Park, Bryce and Zion Canyons and Las Vegas for one last night stop: a short one! We all shared rooms. About four in the morning my cellmate reached out from his bed for the light switch to find it activated a pulsating vibrator pad: every motel should have them!

Back to work. We were on occasions involved in refuelling B-47 squadrons on their non-stop three monthly rotations between their Pacific Alert bases and the continental USA. This brought us welcome TDY (temporary duty) in Honolulu from where we would catch the bombers near French Frigate Shoals at the extreme northwestern end of the Hawaiian Islands. Guam in the Marianas was another base (Anderson AFB) where we flew similar missions. Guam is an interesting island geologically speaking, it has a central plateau and escarpment which is in fact an ancient seabed raised eons ago. This gives one a fascinating insight of the earth's crust when exploring the 1000ft high escarpment, and attracts "rock-hounds" from all over the world.

Swimming was our main recreation and beaches designated "safe" were quite handy to the base; swells and sharks being the main problems. As always there were some idiots who swam beyond the reef and got drowned or eaten – contrary to Base Standing Orders! I was one of those and one day two of us ventured past the coral heads into the crystal clear deep water beyond. Here one could see the bottom a hundred feet down. This was the first (and last) occasion that I saw a large shark some forty feet below me. We broke all Olympic records in one mad swim for the reef and flopped gratefully, still intact, on top of it!

I made several trips to Yokota and Tachikawa with B-47 crews on short leave. Our tract took us past many islands made famous during the Pacific War. Saipan, with its many runways once full of B-29s. Tinian from where Captain Paul Tibbets and crew flew their B-29 Enola Gay on the Hiroshima bombing raid. Then past Iwo Jima still looking battered after the endless fighting to wrest it from The Japs, and Mount Suribachi still dominating the south of the island and famous for the photograph of the US Marines raising the Stars and Stripes, on its capture. We had little time in Japan leaving the next day with returning crews. There was a notice in the Flight Briefing Room at Yokota which read "Don't go near the mountain"! This referred to the severe turbulence to be expected near the crest of Mt. Fujiama, especially on the lee side, a phenomenon regrettably forgotten by the crew of a BOAC aircraft that ventured too close many years later, resulting in its disintegration.

On one return flight to March we had collected all the B47's crew's Christmas gifts (there was little room in the B47 for such stuff). Among the presents were pieces of ironwood to be made into coffee tables. This was so hard that it required a diamond dusted saw to cut it but it polished up beautifully. It was also extremely heavy, 10 times that of Oak and it was only to be found in the swamps of Guam apparently. With a direct flight to Hickham planned (17 hours) we were at maximum weight. Take off on runway 09 at Anderson Airforce Base ended over a 200ft cliff, which was to be a lifesaver, for just as I lifted the old 97 off the ground we lost an engine with an almighty bang. The drill now was to dump fuel first, feather, pull the fire bottles and hope for the best. I used most of that 200ft to the surface of the sea to build up a little speed and slowly; ever so slowly we clawed our way back to a 500ft circuit and landed. The B47 guys watched all this, their thoughts on their "goodies" perhaps never to be seen again! Anyway, they treated us well in the club that night as we waited for a new engine. The following day we set sail again for Hickham but had to land at Johnson Island about 800 nautical miles west of Hawaii to replenish engine oil. Johnson was a long narrow strip of coral on which some enterprising engineers had built a runway during the war; it was now on a care and maintenance basis under a Warrant Officer and six airmen. Anyway, we re-oiled and prepared to go. "Keep away from Mag Drop Charlie" said the Warrant Officer. "Who" I asked, "Yeah" he said "it's a shark that listens to your run up at the take off point and if you have a rough motor, swims to the other end and hopes that you will fall in the sea"! I think he really believed this story, he must have been on Johnson Island for a very long time!

As a R.A.F. Exchange Officer I was expected to set a good example of such a person as befitted the post. However one day I was arrested by two plain clothes Officers of the Law, not a good advertisement for the Royal Air Force. The charge? Drinking in a public place, viz Laguna Beach. Bill Constantine, then a young Second Lieutenant, and his family had invited us to a beach barbecue one lovely sunny Californian day, when halfway through our first beers, two cops turned up clad only in swimming trunks, emptied our beer cans in the sand and arrested us. Despite protesting that I could not speak the language and had been led astray by Bill, the court fined me $40 – a lot of money in 1959, Bill got the same, that's democracy for you. He went on to become a Brigadier General in his 25 years of service – I remained a convicted felon. Bill is now, would you believe, a very successful male model (no, not one of those) and his good looks have appeared in many a Marks and Spencer catalogue. For recreation I joined a gliding club at El Mirage (elevation 2,000ft) in the Mojave Dessert and flew the Schweitzer 1-22 for solo pleasure and instructed on the TG-6. Neither sailplane had a great performance but the thermals were strong and narrow and 6 – 8,000ft above the desert floor was an easily attainable height. I also did some glider towing in an ancient PT-23 trainer. El Mirage was run by one Gus Breigleb – an American version of James Robinson Justice, a wonderful character. One day we were all watching some skydivers, a relatively new sport, when one pulled open his parachute at about 3,000ft to find that it was not attached to his harness. We watched spellbound and at no more than 1000ft he managed to get his emergency chute open. He was easily recognisable for the rest of the day by his somewhat pale complexion.

Bill Constantine used to rib me about my gliding activities so I invited him for a ride in our two-seater. After his usual healthy American breakfast of Orange Juice, stack of hot cakes with Maple Syrup, bacon and fried eggs we were off in the Scweitzer behind a tow plane. The days thermals were very strong, small and very turbulent. After 30 minutes of tight turns I levelled off at 8,000ft above the ground to the sounds of much retching and groaning from the front seat – Bill never ribbed me again.

SAC was very good to me. I had a couple of flights in B47's at March, the first Boeing Jet Bomber and when I got to Mather A.F.B. and the 904th I got another in the B52, on one of the very early low level mission profiles using terrain following radar coupled to the auto-pilot: fascinating stuff. I also qualified as a Dry Martini maker (first class honours) and hamburger cook.

Soon after I first joined the 320th I went to pay a courtesy call to the Commanding General, General R.T.J. Olds, commander of the 15th Air Force whose headquarters happened to be at March Air Force Base as well. He was an old buddy of General Le May from the 8th Airforce days in England during the war and had been a distinguished B17 pilot. After the exchange of a few pleasantries he asked me to form a cricket team – he had played a bit in England. I had to say that I had never played cricket in my life – or football or rugby for that matter. This astounded him and I was dismissed somewhat abruptly. However, he must have relented for a message arrived from him via underlings that an opening on the KC135 programme was now available for me. After much correspondence with Washington and my minder at the Embassy there, a Wing Commander Fear who looked after us extremely well, it was agreed to extend me for another year and enter the then fairly new KC135 programme. It may be remembered that the Boeing prototype for the 707 series of aircraft was the famous "Dash 80", and was intended as demonstration for a military jet transport and tanker. On it's seventh flight it conducted air-refuelling rendezvous (without the boom fitted) with a B-52 bomber. A boom was fitted later and more tests were flown. Although the early civil version looked very much like its military counterpart, the KC-135A, the essential difference was that the tanker had a huge belly tank in place of the luggage holds and a much strengthened wing: This aircraft had to be able to stand for days fully laden with fuel at maximum weight and then fly!

In early '61 I prepared to leave March, the 320th and many friends (40 years later we still have the odd reunion in the USA) for Castle Air Force Base and KC135 School. Castle was situated in the Central Valley of California near the town of Merced. The course was extremely well run and I was paired up with another aircraft commander for the flying and simulator phase. The navigator and boom operator joined us later. We did not carry a Flight engineer: there was no position for him and the Navigator sat in his place behind the pilots facing the starboard side. Years later I was astounded to find when I flew civil 707's with British European Airways, that they carried a Flight Engineer. If ever there was an aeroplane that really did not need a Flight Engineer it was the 707, but I suppose the Flight Engineers have a very powerful lobby.

The course went well for both of us but my colleague had some considerable difficulty in coping with the aircraft's Dutch roll. The 135 flying controls were all manually operated; a power assisted rudder and fin extension came (much needed) later. Consequently, she Dutch rolled badly once the yaw damper (part of the auto-pilot) was taken out. So to cater for the event of a failed auto-pilot we practiced our counter measures for the Dutch roll. Once the roll had been induced it could wind up rapidly to angles of bank of 40° with the nose swinging wildly from side to side so that one could hear the change of airflow over the flight deck. The cure – a quick stab of rudder and a sudden input of opposite aileron, immediately centralising both. After a couple of stabs the roll usually stopped. My friend was often behind the "eight ball" in this and took umpteen stabs to stop the sickening oscillations. More on the 135 later. Two weeks from the end of the course the postings came through: I was assigned to Moses Lake AFB (Moses hole) near Spokane, Washington State. It was in a pretty desolate part of the world and when my colleague (a Colonel) got to hear about it he said "I think you all deserve something better". Ten days later my new posting came in, California again!

The course ended and I was posted to the 904th Air Refuelling Squadron at Mather Air Force Base on the eastern edge of Sacramento, under Colonel Le Francis. There I acquired another crew Fred Holgrave Co-pilot, Charlie Martin Navigator and Jim Watland, Boomer. Mather was primarily a SAC base which had a Navigators Training Wing as a lodger unit flying Convaor T-29's, similar to the Varsity. There was another RAF type attached to the training wing, Don Wright a navigator whom I got to know quite well and helped me a great deal in the early days since I was the first exchange pilot the 904th had seen. Mather was on the eastern edge of Sacramento, the

Capital of California. Not far away was Sutters Mill where Sutter, a Swiss immigrant first found gold in 1849 in the millrace. The subsequent gold rush is history. We did quite often explore the old mining towns along the gold reef and panned for it ourselves: nearly two years later we had found enough to put on a pinhead! Just east of the airfield was a vast gravel plain on which a huge dredger worked away night and day, floating in its own lake as it worked its way along. Rumour had it that it yielded 10,000 dollars of gold a day! Back to work.

Life was very similar on the 904th to the one that I had become used to at March except that the aircraft was a lot quicker. I had several temporary duties in Honolulu which involved me in extensive refuelling operations and also at Eilsen Airforce Base in Alaska. Sometimes we struck lucky on our visits to Honolulu and had several days off in a row during which time we moved out of the Hickham Air Force Base and had a few days off at Fort Derussy on Waikiki Beach. This was an old coastal battery from the war, and now was an R and R establishment for the armed forces. I think it cost us $1 a night. Several attempts had been made by developers to buy it (real estate on Waikiki Beach was astronomically expensive) but I think to this day that the Defense Department has been able to resist all bids. Time spent here was very pleasant and I do remember the local laundromat (laundry) which had a big sign above it which said "dunk your duds in spuds suds". Waikiki Beach at this time was still relatively unspoiled, the Royal Hawaiian (all pink) and the Moana Loa Hotels being the only two on the seafront of any size. Elsewhere it was palm trees, cafés and restaurants, including the famous Bare Foot Bar where you could attempt to eat a 54oz steak and all the trimmings for free providing you finished it! Diamond Head still had its famous outline and the road over the Central Mountains (the Pali) was just a two lane one. On the eastern side of the Mountain lay Bellows Field, a coral strip in use before the war and home of the Hawaiian Gliding Club and I enjoyed soaring along the mountain ranges in the reliable and strong easterly trade wind. It was from Bellows Field that two P-40s took off during the Pearl Harbour raid and managed to shoot down several Japanese planes. On one of our sojourns at Hickham we bought an old car for $25, it was cheaper than using taxis. One evening we sallied forth to an Army Officers Club behind Diamond Head. Handing over the keys to the Major Domo outside who organised parking we started to go into the club. This chap summoned a driver who got into the car to park it. After about 100yds the whole car collapsed, the rear wheels came off and it sat on its tank. We made a hurried retreat into the club forthwith. Pearl Harbor was also a must to see the remains of the USS Arizona, which was a grim reminder of the Pearl Harbor attack. The battleship is of course a war grave and now so many years later I believe much of it has disintegrated but the Memorial is still there over the Hulk.

On one detachment to Hickham we returned via Eilsen Airforce Base, Fairbanks, Alaska rather unexpectedly: where the temperature being November, was 20° below zero Fahrenheit, Hickham being a pleasant 80°. All SAC crews carried Arctic gear as well as Tropical on all their flights no matter how short so we started to put on layers of woolies and parkas etc. long before we landed and allowed the aircraft to cool off. Opening the crew door on the ground was still a shock as 50 degrees of frost hit us like a hammer in the chest.

As an Exchange Officer I was expected to promote good feeling between our two services: not a difficult task since the bonds between us forged during the war had continued to grow stronger. To help, the Treasury had been persuaded to grant us Duty Free Liquor obtainable from the local Consulate or Embassy to further the good will and we were thus able to entertain on a pretty good scale, and not always officially. My source of supply at March had been Los Angeles now it was the Consulate at San Francisco where, thankfully there had been a change of leadership since my brush with Sir Edward 5 years previously.

My favourite tipple when I can afford it and apart from Gin, was Pimms No.1 and at 4/6d a bottle for once in my life I could afford to indulge a little. Pimms No.1 was also a favourite with my guests to whom it was quite possibly something new. One colleague watched me make it, the usual bottle of Pimms to three of 7UP, ice, cucumber and if possible mint. I occasionally added a little Vodka for good measure. Some weeks later my friend threw a party and produced Pimms No.1 – American-style. My first taste told me that something was not quite right and I noticed Pam topping hers up with copious amounts of 7UP. Half an hour later only about a dozen of us remained standing, about another dozen were sitting and at least that number were stretched out on the grass sound asleep.

I asked my chum what he had put in the mixture.

"Oh," he said. "Three bottles of Pimms, three bottles of 7UP, three of gin … and lots of ice!"

One day I received an invitation from the Consulate to celebrate Princess Margaret's wedding. The other types on exchange in the area were also invited; two Navy, one Marine and Don Wright, the navigator on the training wing at Mather, and one pilot from Nellis Airforce Base, Las Vegas. We all met at the appointed hour of 11 o'clock; we were, of course, the first guests to arrive. The head man made us very welcome and had assembled a good number of American dignitaries, including the mayor and senior United States Service Officers, as well as ourselves. He proved to be an excellent host. My estimation of the Foreign Office went up. There was one young lady, a daughter of one of the guests, who sported the latest 'beehive' hairstyle. This had been lacquered so that it fitted like a helmet, apart from the back, which stuck out a bit. She was standing by the empty fireplace, arm on the mantelpiece, when lunch was called. In turning her head her hair swiped three delicate Chinese figurines off the mantelpiece to utter destruction. Our host was really charming about it and put her at ease. Madam host was not quite so happy. An aged retainer swept away the debris and we went into the garden for an excellent buffet lunch. Afterwards we saw a 15-minute film of the wedding ceremony and then after some tea and "stickies" it was time to go. Our host made a short speech and asked us to join him in honouring her Majesty the Queen, followed by the President of the United States. I was now aware that the aged retainer had returned and was moving towards a suitcase lying on top of the table. I then realised what it was a gramophone, circa 1935, complete with the picture of that little dog

(His Master's Voice) and wind-up handle. This he proceeded to crank, looking balefully at his boss. We all stood up and the Ambassador called "Ladies and Gentlemen, Her Majesty the Queen!" The aged retainer placed the heavy pick-up arm with a steel needle on the 78 record – and out came 'The Star Spangled Banner'! A fun day.

Prior to my arriving on the 904th the squadron was already involved in refuelling B52s on the airborne alert circuit. Coinciding with my arrival I received a letter from Washington saying that I was not to get involved. Why, I cannot think. Perhaps some political row would develop if I were shot down in a United States Airforce aircraft as a member of the RAF and the Russians had my corpse on view in Moscow. Restrictions were also imposed on refuelling the RB47s, whose crews, with considerable courage, penetrated the edges of Soviet airspace for various reasons. I acknowledged this miserable letter and saw my boss.

"Well," said the Colonel, looking me straight in the eye. "I had a copy of that letter too. I put it in the waste basket".

"Thank you sir. Allow me to put mine in the same place".

I suppose that after over 40 years I am safe from a court-martial!

Most of my American colleagues on the squadron spent many years on B50s and B36s before coming to Mather, and quite a few had seen service in the Mighty 8th. It seemed that once you became a SAC man (!) you could never escape. I enjoyed my time with the 904th immensely.

The 135 was a fast ship; we refuelled the B58 Hustler at .9 mach and the aircraft's red line limit was .95 mach. We could fly 2,000 nautical miles, offload more than 50,000 lbs of JP4 and return to our point of departure. Fuel tanks were in the wings, under the fuselage floor and behind the rear pressure bulkhead, leaving the entire fuselage deck available for freight or seats. It could carry roughly twice its basic weight in fuel, 202,000 lbs, all of which could be used or offloaded to another aircraft. In fact, in a war situation we were expected to offload all our fuel and then bail out! We had a formula in the flight manual to work out our gliding range – 160 into the square root of the aircraft weight over 100,000lbs. I am glad to say I never had to work it out – square roots were always a mystery to me at school. However, getting the beast into the air was another story. The Pratt + Whitney J57 engines gave you 12,000lbs of thrust with water injection up to about 100° Fahrenheit outside air temperature. They used 5,500lbs of water (to augment thrust in high ambient temperatures) in two minutes on take-off; not a lot of power for an aircraft with a maximum of 301,500lbs. A small reserve of power was available on "wet" take-offs and was obtained by moving the throttles fully forward of the wet setting, otherwise known as 'firewalling' – a time-honoured practice. There were other small engine deficiencies. The J57 was not fitted with thrust reversers; landing on icy runways required the shutdown of the inboard engines to reduce the landing roll. Engine fire extinguishers were not fitted: pulling the cockpit fire switch merely shut off fuel, oil and hydraulic power and electrics from the offending engine leaving it happily to burn itself out on the pylon. Flying at 280 knots plus would hopefully keep the fire off the wing. However on the few engine fires that were experienced this did not really happen and years later fire extinguishers were fitted. There were no wing or tail anti-ice systems although the engine intakes were heated. However, we had little or no trouble with airframe icing, strange as it may seem, even in the North American winter.

The aircraft was equipped with conventional aileron, elevators and rudder, actuated by cables from the cockpit control column, which moved tabs in the appropriate control surface. The resultant displacement of the tab moved the larger control surface. Additional lateral control was by hydraulically-operated wing spoilers-cum-air brakes, acting in conjunction with the ailerons (in a left turn the left aileron came "up" with the left spoiler rising, to assist the bank and therefore the turning moment) but the rudder lacked any power assistance. Cross winds did pose a problem on take-off because in trying to keep the into-wind wing (remember, this aircraft had a 35° sweepback) down and therefore the wings level, too much aileron input bought the spoilers up causing more drag on that side thus adding to the pilots difficulties to keep straight, as well as extending the take-off run due to the extra drag. On slippery runways the minimum speed for controlling the beast on the ground could exceed the stop/go speed! The introduction of a hydraulically powered rudder soon cured this problem but until that time (long after I had left) the technique on all take-offs was to hold the control column fully forward right to take-off speed in order to try and prevent the nose wheels from skidding!

The first 250 aircraft had no leading edge flaps at all but after number 251 two small Kruger flaps were fitted between the engines. Rotation on a 135 had to be a precise 8° body angle – or else. Once airborne the bird was climbed at V2 (take off speed) + 10, gear raised and the aircraft levelled off at 500ft to accelerate and retract the flaps. Since one could spend nearly 50 seconds on the ground, roll and flap retraction had to be completed before water run-out (after 2 minutes) the water augmentation was timed by the navigator, who called 110 seconds, at which time the aircraft was immediately levelled off and accelerated, whatever the height! Noise abatement was not heard of (!) in those days and running out of water in a climb of V2 plus 10 was not conducive to longevity. With the aircraft clean it was accelerated in level flight to 285 knots and then en-route climb commenced. Once this magical state of affairs was achieved the ship became transformed and leapt skywards as if a great weight had been removed. Indeed it had – the weight of the take-off fuel and water used prior to en-route climb amounted to about 7,000lbs.

One more little quirk, the aircraft were fitted with wire treaded tyres, called ice tyres, with a maximum ground speed of either 199 or 190 stamped on the sides. This was initially assumed to be in knots, and could on a tail wind take-off impose a limit to take-off speeds. After some spectacular tyre bursts, sometimes accompanied by fire, some bright spark found out the tyre placards were in miles per hour. My aged Dalton shows that 199 miles per hour equals 174 knots a figure often 15 knots below take off speed. Amended performance charts were rapidly introduced.

SAC had a unique way, devised I believe by General Le May, of keeping the force on its toes. It was aimed at everyone not only flight crews but entire bases from the Base Commander downwards. It was called the Operational Readiness Inspection (ORI) and it was a no-notice total evaluation of a selected Airforce Base. I experienced one such inspection during my time at Mather. We were on alert duty one night blissfully asleep and unaware of the drama taking place above the underground alert facility. We slept in flying suits with zip up boots handy, ready to be in the aircraft and taxiing within the statutory 3 minutes from the Klaxon sounding. We were always allocated the same room to facilitate our rapid exit to the aircraft. However I do remember once we were given another room about 50 yards away from the one we normally occupied, and the door of course was in a different position. We had a practice alert one night and Charlie Martin my Navigator was up and running before any of us, unfortunately he headed where he thought the door should be and came to a grinding halt on the wall. I digress. Fred and Jim the boomer were silent sleepers but Charlie's snore had to be heard to be believed. I too was a silent sleeper in those days and that night I became aware of someone leaning over my bunk. I shot up in bed and the figure let out a squawk. It was Fred, he said he was just making sure that I had not died! At 02.00 hours, a shiny C97 from Omaha (SAC Headquarters SACHQ) had just called up without any prior warning for an immediate landing, containing the main element of the ORI team, which on landing quickly dispersed to assigned areas like to the Station Base Headquarters, Operations Room, Line Maintenance and alert facility. At the same time an ORI convoy of vehicles drew up at the main gate and immediately entered the base and sealed it off from the outside world – no telephone calls, no wandering off to the married quarters, no movement at all until the ORI teams were in position. Then the Klaxon sounded for an alert reaction. Flinging boots on and grabbing jackets we all pounded up the ramp to the flight line. Ground crews had already removed engine blanks and chocks; Fred fired up the engines, No.4 first then 3 then 1 and 2 together. Charlie and I took down the coded broadcast from the Command Post, authenticated it individually, realising that it was a practice involving taxiing out to the runway and awaiting in the planned sequence; B-52's first, followed by the tankers. After 5 minutes the alert was cancelled and we all taxied back to refuel. Here the penny dropped and we were greeted by the ORI teams. Individually, then as a crew, we were grilled on our EOW (Event of War) mission mostly without references. The first half-hour of such a flight was very much a memory item. After this came the technical paper on the aircraft and our escape and evasion plans. After two hours of this we then planned a mission which contained two air refuellings. B52 crews had a similar grilling and then planned an integrated flight involving us and some simulated bombing runs on radar targets. Quick nosh and then out to the aircraft which had to be accepted as they stood – no snags to be rectified unless it was a major no-go item in which case the Wing Commander tore his hair out and the aircraft remained on the ground. This was to be a MITO take-off (Minimal Interval Take Off). The first two bombers lined up in a staggered pair on the runway the leader wound up the power and rolled, followed by the second 15 seconds later and the rest of us at the same interval. There was no wind on this particular morning (dawn just breaking) and the smoke generated by 60 plus J57 engines at full power with water injection made the field pretty well fogged out. With three aircraft on the runway at any one time (one just rolling, one at about V1 and one lifting off) it fell to air traffic to relay any abort call if an aircraft failed to get off – to ensure that those behind stopped their take-offs in good time. One had to be prepared to take to grass in this unhappy situation to avoid a collision. In war this was a requirement to let the rest of the force get off the ground. Once in the air we fanned out a bit and tried to avoid wake turbulence. The whole procedure got a lot of aircraft into the air in a very short space of time but the toll on one's blood pressure and heartbeat must have been quite something. About six hours later, back on the ground, de-briefing, more questions and then collapse. Next morning the ORI team gave it's verdict at the mass briefing, outlining any areas to be looked at and improved, and gave us a pass: the sigh of relief was quite audible. The base was then put back on an operational footing. Today over 40 years later, I think I could still do a credible briefing on that EWO mission of ours from memory.

Air refuelling on the 135 with the boom system was quite simple. We used the autopilot, hand throttling the engines. All the receiver had to do was to formate on our two rows of under belly lights colored red, amber and green. Providing he kept in the green all was well and the boomer had the responsibility of effecting the hook-up. Should the bomber get out of the refuelling envelope then the boom auto-disconnected and retracted with an audible thump and if the situation looked hairy then the boomer would call "break-away" usually in a very high pitched voice. I had only two such incidents in three years. One occurred when a B52 lost part of its hydraulics when hooked up. I think this resulted in the spoilers (usually up two notches to allow a high rpm on the engines) slamming down and the aircraft starting forward. Jim shouted "break-away", Fred rammed the throttles forward and I disconnected the autopilot and started to climb. Just as the VSI showed a slight rise, we were very heavy, I saw the tail fin of the B-52 some 30ft in front of me; Fred says he saw the gunners chalk white face. SAC bomber crews were pretty good at refuelling and anyone could always tell just how good by listening to their engine handling when taking on fuel; small changes in noise no problems, whilst vigorous and frequent changes in power, then you knew you had a potential boom snatcher "stuck on your tail". We of course had the use of a simulator to not only practice run of the mill engine failures and other catastrophes but also the full range of refuelling problems. Unfortunately this was still the era of static simulation but it was a pretty sophisticated "box". We shared the one simulator with the two other SAC bases in the area, Travis and Beale, the simulator being fitted onto two railroad box-cars and shunted from base to base: Easily recognisable as it was painted in full SAC aircraft colours, badges and blue star-studded encircling band!

An episode I do recall most vividly also occurred when I was on alert duty at Mather. It was again in the early hours of the morning and I was trying to sleep despite Charlie's snores. The Klaxon sounded. Boots on, up the ramp to the aircraft at the double. As usual, Fred fired up, Charlie and I took down the broadcast and then looked at each other in sheer disbelief. It was not a practice. Charlie passed the message to Fred for him to authenticate just as the first B-52 taxied past the nose. I said (I think) "this is for real Charlie, tell Jim". We taxied out in turn behind the last tanker, Charlie swears to this day that Fred's hair stood on end. Me? I felt numb for a moment then I went into the drill and confirmed tracks, reporting points, heights to fly with Charlie – at least I like to think I did! Over 40 years have passed but I think we did the right things. I said something to the effect that the base would take care of the families, but not with much conviction. I stopped the aircraft at the end of the taxiway and looked ahead at the other six tankers and then at the two leading B-52's at the runway opposite me, trying to see if they had power going up. It dawned on me later that similar operations had not just been confined to our base. We remained stationary for some 15 minutes waiting for the launch order. It never came. The alert was then downgraded and we returned to our parking area, topped up with fuel one at a time and waited until the alert was cancelled. A de-briefing followed but no explanation and we ordered in no uncertain terms to pass off this incident as another practice.

It was many months later when I was in England that I learned NORAD (North American Air Defense Command) hidden in Cheyenne Mountain in Colorado, had picked up a radar signal for what seemed to be a mass launch of missiles from Uncle Joe. There was a Canadian Air Marshal on duty at the time who certainly earned his pay that night. As the launch was tracked he was aware that the predicted impact areas saturated the whole of North America. The urge to launch must have been nearly irresistible, and no doubt there were hurried consultations with Omaha and the White House. Armed with the updated knowledge of the Soviet missile capability he reasoned that a total saturation of North America was not possible so he alerted the SAC force to the very highest degree of readiness and not for the actual launch. I believe that he had about a minute or two at the most to assess this situation, which speaks volumes for his courage and coolness. A few minutes later the radar missile predictions began to reduce and eventually vanish completely from the screen. One can imagine the consternation all round and the frenzied search for an explanation. It later became known that a Ballistic Early Warning Station had picked up a rising moon on its ultra high powered radar and interpreted it as a hostile launch. I read this account in the Readers Digest! My conclusion with hindsight was that thorough training would always get you through a situation like this and this was proved by the clockwork precision with which SAC met this challenge. As for the explanation, well, I feel that this may not have been the full story.

Which brings me at long last to a warm wet afternoon in Alaska in the fall of 1961. A grey day with clouds at 500ft, damp but still warm enough to support voracious swarms of king-size mosquitoes. We were setting out to refuel a B-52 far to the north of us who was part of the airborne alert fleet. Taxiing out at an all out weight of 300,500lbs allowed us to get airborne at the maximum structural weight of 297,000lbs: our bomber would need all the fuel we could give it. I taxied slowly, any manoeuvre over 2g whilst on the ground or in the air could seriously damage the aircraft's health. I parked carefully on the entry lane to the 14,000ft runway, the aircraft lurching gently as the fuel in the under floor tanks settled again.

On the "go" from the Command Post and release from the Tower confirming a 14-knot crosswind we started to roll. Fred set "dry thrust E.P.R (exhaust pressure ratio), I called "water" the E.P.R. registered the expected increase on all four engines confirmed by a deafening high-pitched roar and clouds of black exhaust smoke. A rolling start onto the runway, starting my stop watch (what else) and we were on our way, one hand on the tiller and one holding the control column fully forward against the forward stop. At 70 knots Charlie started his acceleration check – we had to have 120 knots in 17 seconds. Check OK, V1 at 135 knots was followed by VMCG at 150 knots. 40 seconds into the take-off roll a feint thud followed by a lurch to the left, easily held on tiller and rudder. Fred said "we are slowing down" and at the same time I realised that we were definitely not accelerating, as we should be. I called for full thrust, I noticed the 4,000ft remaining marker flash by – we should be rotating here. I opened my mouth (somewhat dry by now) to call for fuel dumping, when the aircraft once again lurched to the left and then began to pick up speed. I said to anyone, who cared to listen, it's the left main gear. I raised the left the wing a little with the Ailerons and sure enough we quickly accelerated. V2 was 179 knots and at the 1,000ft remaining marker I started rotation as Fred called "170 knots". We used some of the overrun, Asphalt at this airfield thank heavens, and cleared the pines on the airfield boundary and levelled off rather low, to get at least V2 before climbing. I called "gear up". Fred lifted the handle, it remained locked down. He said "the trucks not level" just as Charlie called in a rather flat calm voice "110 seconds". Jim the boomer saved the day by immediately tripping the left main gear circuit breaker, Fred pulled the gear lever up and the nose and right main retracted and we started to accelerate. The outskirts of Fairbanks whistled by almost level with my side window as we reached flaps up speed of 220 knots, and slowly cleaned up. The water ran out on one and three engines causing the usual swing and then two and four ran dry. Meanwhile Jim had re-instated the left main gear circuit breaker hoping that the truck would level itself. It did, and the left main gear slowly retracted. I told Jim to take a look and he came up on intercom to say that most of the left rear tyre had departed leaving bits of itself wrapped round the axle of its next door neighbour which looked flat. There was some smoke so he kept an eye on it for half an hour and then returned to his seat. Meanwhile, I had at last achieved 285 knots still very low and sweating profusely and with a mouth as dry as the bottom of a birdcage I left the treetops and started to climb. Command post offered us a choice by saying we could return to base, but the crew said "no way" and I could sense the relief in the controller's voice! The Tower sounded equally relieved that we had not joined the bears in the forest.

We made our rendezvous on time having seen the trail of our receiver over 100 miles away in the clear arctic air. We flew in total radio silence towards him head on at .78 mach while he in turn started his descent 80 nautical miles away from us. He then offset his track to ours to the right by a mile. At 21 miles from each other we turned 180° onto his track ahead of him reducing to .75 mach n. And there he was, two miles behind us, 1000ft below just as the good book said. As we approached the planned air refuelling point (the point at start of transfer), we felt the bombers bow wave tipping the nose dose down, the autopilot trim coping well with this intrusion. The roar of his engines could now be heard as he positioned underneath our belly on the refuelling lights. As Jim called "contact" there followed a slight thud as the boom locked on to the bombers receptacle right on time. Fred began the transfer at the rate of 6,000lbs per minute, the throttles being continually retarded as we got lighter. I think we gave him about 100,000lbs of fuel. His final gesture before disconnecting was to hold a sheet of paper on his windscreen, which read "holes in left inner flap". With that cheerful message he dropped behind and continued his deterring mission. We turned for Fairbanks just under two hours away.

20 miles out and we were cleared for an immediate approach over the non-directional beacon outbound into the teardrop pattern onto the I.L.S. We left 35,000ft, flight idled all around, airbrakes at 60°, crossing the N.D.B outbound at 25,000ft, gear down, airbrakes still out and maintaining a decent rate of 4,000ft a minute. At 3,000ft, speed brakes 'in' and speed bleeding off to 210 knots in a level turn on to finals and the I.L.S. Now running through the flap lowering schedule, at 10 miles from threshold I did my best to make my usual (?) smooth touchdown and for once succeeded, I was thankful that the bull Moose that had crossed the runway a couple of days earlier and had caused us to overshoot had not appeared. But the day was not quite over as yet. That evening we had an intelligence briefing given by a Colonel from Omaha on the general world situation as it affected us. Starting his briefing with the words "I assume there are no Foreign Nationals here" a friend of mine behind me "yes we have, we have a spy from England here" at which time I had to get up and made as if to leave. My Wing Commander came to the rescue and all was well but I am afraid the representative from Omaha did not have much of a sense of humour.

I commended Jim the boomer on his awareness and prompt action that day. He went on to bigger and better things. After transferring to the Army he became a chopper pilot and spent 100 hours a month for a year flying Hueys in Vietnam, most of the time being shot at – sometimes by his own side! He retired in 1999 as a much respected Senior Training Captain on Boeing 747 400s with Northwest Orient Airlines. Me, I retired from a similar post – on a Short 360! Our biggest reward was of course that we had avoided the wrath of our illustrious chief General Power and also General LeMay plus cigar. My crew split up just after I left; Fred having decided, as I did later, to go Civil and take his chances with Pan American at just the wrong time. The last I heard of him he was flying for some Arab Sheik in the Middle East. Charlie made Bird Colonel and retired and lives in Merced. We see each other every other year and frequently correspond and talk.

My tour drew to a close all too quickly, I completed my end of tour report (20 copies) endured many wonderful leaving parties, packed my new duty free right hand drive Rambler Station Wagon and with the family set forth to drive across America. Near the Grand Canyon I was nearly arrested again! Pam had been reading a newspaper in the left-hand seat, when with lights flashing and sirens screaming we were brought to a halt by the Highway Patrol. A six foot Policeman complete with the regulation Stetson, dark glasses and large calibre hand-gun poked his nose into the car and drawled "well Ma'am, I have seen everything now, reading a newspaper and driving, how do you do it?" Then he saw the steering wheel!

We visited my family in Connecticut for a short stay, then drove to New York and embarked on the *Queen Mary* on the 30th October. Our car came too, in the forward hold, which had never been designed for large cars and I had to watch my pride and joy being lowered through the hatchway at an angle of 70°. Still it was insured and by that I mean I left the statutory two bottles of whisky on the front seat for the crane driver. And so we left America for fog bound Britain with many happy thoughts and memories. It was not until now that I could relax after a hectic three years and look back, that I realised what an important part wives of Exchange officers played in the success (or otherwise!) of their husbands' work.

Pam had had a few misgivings about going in the first place, one of which was not having a driving licence. On arrival at March AFB she learned to drive and passed the stringent Californian driving test at the first attempt: no mean feat in a foreign country in a car twice the size of an old 8HP Morris! It began to dawn on me at last, that she had made an enormous contribution on behalf of the Royal Air Force with little thanks from officialdom, and I fear I must have taken quite a lot of it for granted.

9. On The Ground

The voyage home was another never to be forgotten experience and without doubt the only way to travel; I was so fortunate at being able to return by sea. Home on the 5th November to the Air House, enjoying one of the last pea-green London smogs, to learn of my posting to Marham was not to fly Valiant Tankers but a desk as Station Adjutant! Doom and gloom descended. A de-brief followed on my tour, a mild rebuke for extolling the virtues of the KC 135 especially its range and carrying capability – nearly twice its basic weight in fuel. "Tankers do not have to be large," said this Group Captain. I remembered his words so well years later after the Falklands war when it took umpteen Victor Tankers to refuel each other in order for one to refuel the Vulcan that bombed Fort Stanley airfield and then missed most of it. The RAF then got its VC10 and Tri-Star Tankers – better late than never.

Before I got to Marham I had to do the OATS course. I believe it stood for Officer Administrative Training Course or something like that, and passing it was a pre-requisite for those aspiring to air rank. By now in January 1963 I knew that I could not expect another flying tour should I be promoted to Squadron Leader; it was time to fly a desk, possibly forever. I decided to look at the feasibility of "going civil". To do this a window of opportunity would open at what was called the 38-16 point; age 38 and –or 16 years of service, whichever came first. In my case this would occur in January 1968. I think I decided there and then that this would be my goal and I would work to have the necessary ATPL (Airline Transport Pilot's License etc) in my pocket by December 1967 – this I achieved. Anyway, I resolved to make the best of my last 5 years and duly turned up at South Cerney for the dreaded course, in the middle of one of the coldest winters since 1941. To be fair, the two months at South Cerney gave the young aspiring Air Marshals an excellent grounding in matters administrative but I must admit that I was not a willing pupil. By the end of the course I knew my decision to eventually go Civil was the right one for me.

So to Marham, a brief hand over from the outgoing adjutant who was off to fly Canberra's (again) and a formal interview with my new Station Commander, a formidable Scot with a DFC. Unfortunately he had a bad stutter which came to the fore when he was displeased. In the air this disappeared completely. I was determined this time to do my best and not upset the boss as I had done to others in the past, for he was my only hope for a return to flying at the end of my two year sentence. After the interview I sat down at my desk and viewed the next two years with some trepidation, and wished that I was back in the USA, or knocking over policemen in the Beverley, or screeching towards Skegness in a 'meat box' emitting that familiar blue note at low level! Never mind, one day!

The first day in command of the desk was a Friday; the Group Captain was away flying a Valiant to El Adem. I made my acquaintance with the Station Warrant Officer at the guard room, for one of my duties was to keep my eye on prisoners and to arrange for them to be arraigned in front of the Station Commander, a process known as Commanding Officers Orderly Room. This involved the wretch being marched in front of the CO's desk escorted by two burly RAF policemen and made to stand to attention whilst his fate was decided. No doubt in today's nanny state it would all be dealt with over a cup of tea! This W.O. had been a bomber pilot in the war, a jolly chap with a DFM and seemed very out of place in his present assignment. In this we had something in common. Anyway he had one airman in the cells, and asked for an early Orderly Room with the Station Commander. I suggested Monday at 9 o'clock. I remember he gave me a questioning look but said nothing. Monday arrived, and the CO had turned up at SHQ at his usual time, 08.45 and I asked him if he could hear a charge at 9.00. "What", he yelled "I never hear charges or anything else before 10.00", seeing my rather crest fallen face he eventually agreed. On time the accused was marched in, a small unhappy looking airman. After much stamping of large boots by the two policemen the SWO read the charges and, as was the custom, the CO asked him his number, rank and name in his worst stutter. "Y-yes s-sir s-sir I a-a-am" came the reply. Oh god I thought I am not hearing this. We could be here all morning and in any case I bet the old man thinks I did this on purpose! As I stood next to the CO's desk holding the airman's records of service, my eyes strayed and focused on the SWO's shining brass belt buckle. To my horror it started to heave, ever so gently, gradually gathering speed. Unfortunately, our eyes met and we both choked as one does trying to suppress laughter. It was a very short hearing with the charge being dismissed, and as the SWO and escort left the room I awaited the wrath of the CO. After a pregnant silence he looked at me and said quietly "never before 10.00 o'clock FitzRoy": there was just a hint of a smile on his face and he went up 100% in my estimation. We got on famously after that.

Apart from supervising the guard room and other mundane duties, the complaints from the inhabitants of the married quarters; the Sergeant's Mess, accounting, station parades *ad nauseam*, I held the keys for all the buildings on the camp. These were in an awful state when I took over: I had enough keys for three times the number of buildings, some looked as though they belonged to the original 1915 airfield, the remains of which were still visible on the northern boundary. I had a large carton of surplus openers in my office, not once did I require any of these so I ditched them before handing over to my successor! The Ministry of Works and Bricks was another chore: this strange organisation of semi civilians looked after the maintenance of all the buildings from hangers to drains; this led to my sobriquet of Officer I-C bogs and drains. Chaps can be very cruel at times. To help me I acquired a Station bicycle from my friend the SWO. RAF bikes in the 1960s were at least 50 years old, coloured grey contraptions that took an immense amount of energy to get going fast enough for momentum to play its part. Once moving they required a fair distance to be brought to a halt. The bicycle was cheaper to run than my Rambler.

There were two new building projects in progress when I arrived at Marham. One was a new 6-hole bog (lavatory) sited on a gentle slope for the use of Senior NCOs and airmen only, near the station workshops. I visited this site one-day to formerly take it over onto RAF strength from Works and Bricks. After accepting the privy, the works Forman said, "it will never work, guv", "why" I asked? "Because the drawing office has put the cesspit above the pans!" was the reply. They never did work at least not in a hygienic way and I was never able to find the genius responsible, perhaps he later had something to do with the millennium footbridge. The other project was a freshwater pipeline to connect the camp reservoir located near my quarters (ideal for drowning children playing with boats) on the west side of the airfield and main runway. The quick reaction alert facility was on the extreme eastern boundary. The QRA was a hutted camp enclosed by wire and included 6 concrete pans for the Valiant bombers on standby; these were still Cold War days. The QRA was very different to the underground bunkers of SAC. The cost of this pipeline was astronomical. Another genius in the Air House had decreed that it had to be heat proof, radiation proof and bomb proof in order to ensure that the lads on QRA would have an abundant supply of water at all times, war or peace. The pipe was therefore buried deep underground for its entire mile and a half-length leaving the destination and origin open to the four winds above ground!

There was a Bloodhound missile unit next to the QRA. This was for airfield defence. Its commander was a squadron leader whose name I have unfortunately forgotten. However he had also been on exchange in SAC at Westover Airforce Base in Massachusetts, flying KC-97's just before my arrival in California. He was the chap who, while refuelling a B-47 near Thule, Greenland in the depth of winter, suffered a rupture of the main 3-inch refuelling pipe in the fuselage of his aeroplane. The navigator just had time to get a bearing on Thule before all electrical power had to be switched off. With a crew on 100% oxygen he managed to find Thule an hour later, successfully baled his crew out and landed the KC-97 with the help of the Flight Engineer. When the fire crews arrived at the aircraft and opened the lower door a torrent of JP4 flooded onto the runway – about 100 gallons! JP4 is almost as volatile as petrol and I once saw a basin of the stuff placed 50ft in front of a B-52 and ignited it by the aircraft radar. For this effort my friend was awarded the American DFC; the RAF awarded him two years on a missile site. Needless to say he soon pursued a more rewarding career in Civil Aviation.

I had been at my desk for 6 months when the Officer IC Station Flight was posted and the Station Master (bless him) gave me the job. The flight consisted of two Ansons (a Mk 19 and a Mk 21) for communication work and a couple of Chipmunks. I unashamedly hogged the Ansons and in my last 18 months at Marham managed nearly 400 hours of Anson flying. Not bad for a ground tour. I got very fond of the Annie and at SHQ where my desk was hangared, the Station Master was often heard to yell, "where's FitzRoy – off in the bloody Anson again?"

I returned to gliding whilst at Marham. The RAF GSA club at Feltwell was a flourishing one and I was able to get up to speed again for the 1964 National Gliding Championships in a KA-6. It was in this sailplane that I made my last bid for the elusive 500-km distance, Watton to Ouston on Hadrian's Wall, 50 km short. I also did some flying with the Norfolk and Norwich flying club at Swanton Morley, mainly instructing. The main camp at Swanton Morley was still RAF but the airfield was a joint Civil – RAF affair. It was here that a club member asked me to do the maiden voyage in his Luton Minor which he had just finished rebuilding over a period of 6 years. One fine day, I got into (or rather put it on) this superbly rebuilt little aeroplane, started up the 2 cylinder Jap engine and after a few low hops to check the controls etc. got airborne. As luck would have it, I found the biggest thermal of all time, throttled back and soared this little gem of an aeroplane to 7,000ft. An hour later I thought I had better land, to find the owner beside himself with rage, having assumed the worst. On reflection I think he was justified.

Taffy Rich who some may remember, was CFI of the flying club and in '64 was doing film work in the Exeter Mosquitoes for "633 Squadron". He had also just acquired a contract to ferry two Messerschmidts 108's to the USA, would I like to take one? I did an hour's dual with him in this delightful aeroplane and we started to plan our route – Iceland, Greenland, Novo Scotia and Maine – a dream come true. Unfortunately the RAF had other ideas and I could not get the required permission to take leave and ferry a civil aircraft out of the country. Taffy found another willing pilot and they set off. Taffy got through OK but "my aircraft" I believe is still on the Greenland Icecap where it forced landed with engine failure.

My Anson flying proved remarkably free of drama – I never got lost again (never took a navigator) and suffered only one engine failure. A piston came through the cowling in the left engine and I spent a happy two days at Boscombe Down while awaiting a spare donk. Chipmunk flying abounded at weekends at Marshall's of Cambridge with the ATC Air Experience Flight and of course I still got my hands on the two Chipmunks at Marham. It was one of these WD-373, now often seen at Duxford, which let me down over R.A.F. Alconbury on May 1st 1965, resulting in a GCA radar approach in thick fog. I was flying WD-373 from Marham to Bicester on a bright sunny morning. I routed myself by Molesworth airfield and then direct to Bicester for some glider towing. The weather was gin clear, with a lovely great high over the U.K. The only snag was a band of fog some 30 miles wide, which stretched from the Wash to Duxford. Climbing to about 4,000ft I set course and was soon over the fog just past Downham Market. Some 20 minutes into the flight my feeling of well being (I had even done a couple of barrel rolls along the way) was shattered by several backfires and much rough running on my Gypsy Major engine. Plugs, I thought, quickly into lean, open the throttle. No luck, the rough running got worse and the engine would only "run" at idle. Fog all round with no way of reaching a clear area. I set up a minimum rate of descent at about 65 knots and then the engine stopped.

It seemed time to leave the aircraft, but I gave a call on RAF common 117.9, someone replied and said "its Sunday try 121.5" – bright lad that one. So to the distress frequency and a May Day call, passing 3,500ft with the hood open (this can't be happening to me). West

Drayton came up immediately with the triangulation fix which put me overhead Upwood, invisible below.

Then a strong American Texan drawl came through my radio "RAFAIR are you in trouble? Steer 250° this is Alconbury ground control approach". "I am the maintenance man, but I am going to get a guy from the Tower to talk to you". The Tower came up and asked my rate of descent, air speed and height now passing 2,500ft. This was followed by a rather breathless GCA controller who took over and talked me down onto that lovely wide long runway which I saw just as the wheels hit, bounced into the fog again and then fluttered down for good. I sat there, and waited, thinking this has been my lucky day; it takes at least 20 minutes to warm up GCA equipment and here was one up and running because some maintenance man decided to service it. In the rush they did not even have time to put the runway lights on. I suppose I could have saved my neck and jumped out but the resulting paperwork would have probably finished me off. By a strange coincidence my former boom operator from my KC-97 days, with the United States Airforce at March Airforce Base was stationed on the base so I was well looked after. Marham sent a team down to fix the engine: the plugs were the cause after all; they were of a new type and had been incorrectly gapped, resulting in welding of the electrodes. New plugs, profuse thanks to the maintenance man a tech-sergeant and to the USAF in general, and I resumed my journey this time in brilliant sunshine. They say that things come in three's, so I am not due another stoppage. But if I am, it had better be soon or I will have escaped and departed elsewhere.

Marham being a frontline V-Force station had three funk holes or dispersal airfields; Middleton St. George, Tarrant Rushton and Manston. At each there were hard standings for the bombers and a hutted domestic site for the air and ground crews with provisions for about a month. One of my jobs was to visit these every 3 months or so and do a stock-take with a supply wallah who checked for out of date cans etc. The Anson came in handy for these visits and with clever manipulation for the paperwork I managed to increase the visitations to one a month.

And so life progressed at Marham: it would have been a lot worse without the Anson flight, and a year ago I ran into my old Station Master and was able to thank him properly. "Oh" he said, "not at all, things went more smoothly with you out of the way".

My friend from Flying Training School days in Southern Rhodesia, John Cheesbrough, was now a Flight Commander on No. 49 squadron flying Valiants. He claimed he was a better dry Martini maker than I, a challenge I could not ignore. Mess life was also very good, dining in nights, boisterous with much rivalry between the squadrons. High Cockalorum and other crazy games were played with great enthusiasm. I once had a joust with the Station Master playing knights in armour – station bicycles and broomsticks, no armour. He won and I have a dent in my shin to prove it. Sadly the Mess life of old has long since disappeared and political correctness now reigns supreme. I know I saw the last great years of Service life.

In 1965 the RAF, in conjunction with the British Gliding Association, hosted the World Gliding Championships at South Cerney near Cirencester and I got a temporary posting there to become Chief Marshal; i.e. organising the glider launching system, checking out pilots for the 20 Chipmunks that the RAF had loaned for towing purposes and generally helping the foreign teams to settle down. The competition was a great success; we achieved a launch rate of two every three minutes and we had some 90 sailplanes to launch. The Russians brought their K-19 all metal sail plane, one of which demolished a plywood one in a mid-air collision (pilot baled out), and emerged unscathed. Charles Brown, the doyen of aerial photographers was there with his famous Palmos camera with which he had started his photographic career long before the war. I took him on several sorties in an Auster which for him must have been very painful: he was suffering from severe arthritis and we had to carry him to the Auster and place him gently in the rearward-facing seat. A great man with much courage.

One evening during the practice fortnight, I attended the Russian team's cocktail party (each country gave one, and if so minded, one could attend an average of three a night). This was a jolly affair; an opportunity to meet the five pilots, their retrieving crews and the female Political Commissar, a femme formidable of generous proportions – I think she had been a tank commander in the Great Patriotic War. Also present was the Russian Air Attaché, one Colonel Valantin Elistratov. On being introduced to the Colonel he asked me what I thought of the KC-135 and if I had enjoyed my three years with SAC! I passed this information on to Special Branch later. We had a long chat about more mundane matters and he asked me to dinner the following night at his hotel in Cirencester: "bring a friend if you wish, we have plenty of Vodka". I was intrigued by this and accepted, and fearing that I might be persuaded to talk too much I asked an old ex Airforce friend along to act as Chaperone. It was a great party, the Russians as always very hospitable. Much Vodka was drunk; many toasts proposed Churchill, Stalin and Roosevelt honoured by much rhetoric. We sat down to dinner, Roger Neaves; my Chaperone immediately fell asleep and was laid out on a settee. He took no further interest in my welfare. The landlord fell over, absolutely rigid, rather like John Cleese at his best and I did my utmost to uphold the good name of the Airforce. The high spot of the evening was the sing-song of patriotic Russian songs (and others) to the accompaniment of a squeeze box, topped only by the Commissar who performed a traditional Cossack dance, all medals jingling on her heaving chests with the grace and agility of a gazelle. I took my leave of the Colonel at about 1.00 a.m. together we carried Roger, still asleep, over the inert body of the landlord, still rigid, and poured him into my Rambler. I had to promise to take the good Colonel flying in our Blanik in the morning!

It was a short night and when I woke the last thing I felt like doing was to go flying. However, honour had to be maintained and I had the Blanik out and ready at 7.00 a.m., a tug pilot and Chipmunk hooked up and with the Colonel strapped in the front seat we took off. Although he had once been an ace fighter pilot, the Colonel had never flown a glider and I do not wish to dwell on the manoeuvres we attempted once free of the tug, for my head and stomach rebelled at every lurch. However, he insisted on doing some aeros and since the

Blanik was all metal and stressed for limited inverted flight there was no holding him. This is Bill Constantine's revenge I thought. Valantin pulled off a very creditable landing with little help from me. After we got out he roared with laughter and said, "come we both need some Vodka". My health improved as we pushed the Blanik back into the hangar and said our good-byes "you come and see me in London – or better still in Moscow", and roared again with laughter. He then gave me several of his official cards, his Moscow address and slapping me on the back said, "until we meet again". Needless to say we did not meet again, more is the pity because he was great fun to be with. A year later I took a Britannia into Waddington to pick up some V-Force crews for cold weather Training in Winnipeg. I stayed in the Mess overnight, and it was the custom (I hope it still is) for a visitor to leave his card in the tray in the Mess foyer as a courtesy to the Officers and the Mess President. This time I left one of Valantin's cards as well; I later heard that it had created quite a major stir!

The Blanik I flew that day belonged to the R.A.F GSA at Bicester. It must have done thousands of launches and hundreds of hours of flying; most of us had instructed in it for years. However, it eventually took the life of Andy Gough, who headed the GSA at Bicester, on his last air show display before retiring from the R.A.F. An old rusty, Czech spanner, entombed in the metal fuselage since assembly, came loose and jammed the elevator cables. It was a cruel end for a man who had done so much for gliding in the Service and indeed for the sport as a whole.

It was nearly July before we had cleared up after the competition, returned all the Chipmunks to their rightful owners, etc, and left South Cerney in peace. The time came to return to my neglected desk. When I got back to Marham I found the Station Master had been made an Air Commodore, he richly deserved it, and had left for the Air House, recommending me for a return to flying. I immediately applied under a very old rule in Queen's Regulations to return to my old Squadron, 511 at Lyneham. With a little help from old mates in high places I started a Britannia course at Lyneham in late 1965.

10. Britannias Over Wiltshire

I left Marham in October having handed over to an enthusiastic young man who was obviously destined for high places. He was very keen to make an empire for himself and I feared for my old friend the Station Warrant Officer who liked things as they were! I was not sorry to leave. The Ansons were doomed: corrosion had been found inside the tubular steel structures of the fuselages and this coupled with the high cost of maintaining the aged Cheetah engines brought to a close the long career of this remarkable aircraft. Someone said that the Annie could transport eight passengers at 120kts and do five miles to the gallon! Twenty years were to pass before I would wield power again behind a desk. But I now looked forward to rejoining my old Squadron, No 511, at Lyneham to fly again. There was, of course, another family move to organise and there were now five of us, Rosemary having been born at Marham. Initially I rented a house while I struggled with the conversion course, but we soon decided to build a house based on the American Cape Cod design. This was achieved a year later at Wootton Bassett.

I spent the first week at Lyneham on a short indoctrination course and aircraft visits, then it was off to Bristol for the maker's ground school. I will not dwell too much on the eccentricities of the Britannia, however I will pass comment, en passant, on various aspects. Although the aircraft was already in airline service when the RAF chose to buy it, many modifications were needed viz: a strengthened cargo floor, roller conveyor tracks, a large cargo door and a seat for the Flight Engineer. It is also worth mentioning that two Brits had crashed in the early days of development; one, G-ANCA, was put down to a run-away autopilot, which the pilots were unable to override. Later an A/P master isolation switch was fitted. The crew was killed. The second accident resulted in the forced landing of G-ALRX on the Severn estuary mud flats following a turbine over speed and failure, which ignited an oil tank. The Proteus engine was of the "free turbine" type; i.e. the compressor turbine and propeller turbine were entirely independent of each other (one shaft turned inside the other). It follows that an overspeeding propeller could cause havoc to its turbine before it could be detected and identified. To stop this various devices (limiters) were fitted which were supposed to act on the turbine's first fleeting desire to over speed and, would shut the engine down. As a matter of interest it was possible to operate an engine for a limited time with the prop feathered! One other modification that the aircraft needed was an APU; this was turned down by some noddy in the Air House on the grounds that the Brit would never operate off Transport Command routes! Woolly thinking to say the least...

Entering the Bristol Ground School one was confronted by a 6' x 6' diagram of the aircraft's electrical system, which caused much dismay among the pilots most of whom, myself included, were mystified by the workings of an electric light bulb. We already knew that the aircraft relied almost entirely on electrical control of all systems, from throttles, HP cocks, pitch control, fuel pumps, etc, etc, to operation of the windscreen heat! I have given my aircraft manuals to the Duxford Britannia Society, so I have to rely on my failing memory for details, but I do remember it required at least three sources of electrical power to start the brute. In other words a special ground power unit was really essential and often one had to be carried on board to "off Transport Command" stations which seemed to be most of the time. Once, at Winnipeg in winter, umpteen battery "Trolley-Accs" were plugged into each other to make up 112V DC for start up. The button was pressed and the trolly-accs started to explode rather like a giant firecracker! Anyway, somewhat depressed by the sight of this awesome diagram we trooped into the classroom for our first lecture – electrics, and the welcoming words of the instructor "never mind, gentlemen, you will be able to draw this diagram from memory when you leave here"! The course lasted seven weeks, and a more demanding seven weeks I have yet to experience. Still, it stood me in good stead when I took my CAA Flight Engineers exams in 1972 – electrics were no longer quite such a mystery.

We also spent another two weeks on the Proteus engine and all its quirks. Perhaps a few words on this contraption might be of interest. It was originally designed to replace the eight wing-mounted Centaurus on the Brabazon. When this project died the inevitable death of all Jurassic monsters, ten were fitted into the Princess flying boat wings, but this leviathan also became extinct. To be wing mounted the Proteus was made short and fat and this was achieved by ducting the intake-air to the rear of the engine, then through a 180° turn in the plumbing (trouble here!) forwards into the 12 stage axial compressor, then through another 180° turn to the rear through the flame cans and eventually through two compressor turbines and two propeller turbines, then exhausted (!) through the tail pipe giving about 1000 PSI of thrust. That first u-bend caused major problems when ice formed on the curve. You did not have to be in wet cloud to get it; at the right temperature and the right amount of moisture, ice would inevitably form restricting the airflow. Unfortunately in areas of high humidity (Far East) these conditions were found at the exact altitudes at which the aircraft was most efficient. It follows that ice on the bend = flameout! The fix for this was called Cowl Heat and consisted of a labyrinth of pipes taking tapped hot (very) engine air to the outside of the engine air intake as well as to the rear wall of the dreaded u-bend. All this took a lot of power out of the engine but it was essential to prevent ice forming, becoming detached, whirling into the engine and thus causing a flameout. It was, of course, a preventative system not a de-ice system. To prevent flameouts, some flame-cans had glow plugs which automatically relit the fire within one eighth of a second of it going out. Up front you might get a slight fluctuation on the dials and hear a light "thump" when relight occurred (after a certain number of relights the engine compressors had to be examined using a special shufti-scope). Further aft in the cabin, any passengers gazing out at the night sky would hear a loud "thump" and see, with some trepidation a tongue of flame stretching from the tail pipe to the tail-plane! One had to avoid indicated outside air temperatures between +2°c and + 12°c (about 18000ft in the Tropics) and between +2° and + 6° speed had to be reduced to 200kts which in turn altered your indicated OAT reading!!! Inside this band of 10° anti-ice procedures were essential, and from all this evolved the High-Low" technique of initially flying at about 12000ft then climbing, when the weight had reduced, to an altitude where the OAT was below +2°c. Years ago I used to think that crossing the Bay of Bengal in a Hastings without radar was pretty hairy, but I can recall some Brit operations in that area that were just as interesting! Suffice to say the correct use of anti-icing on the engine was essential for ones well being but it was expensive on fuel. A badly planned flight and unlucky encounters with clouds would have you watching the fuel "Howgozit" with eyes on stalks. Enough I think!

The course complete, back to Lyneham where we got stuck into the simulator programme, starting, yes, with electrics. It was an early sim – no visual or motion, but a very good procedure trainer for its day. The drill involving the ""OMC" lever always amused me. The Brit had 4 x 24V batteries plus two more in parallel. These two had but one role in life: to re-excite the alternators in the event of all four coming off line (it could really happen and then you were in schtuck). When this occurred everything went black, especially at night and the most appropriate crewmember, with a shout of "Oh my Christ" hit the "OMC" lever and with luck and a little help from upstairs this would bring the alternators into the electrical family circuitry again.

Sim over and I started with conversion flying in December. The Brit was pleasant to fly, though it took a little time to get used to the "free-floating control surfaces", i.e. movement of the control column resulted in a small trailing edge tab moving in the opposite direction, thus moving the elevator, rudder, etc. in the desired one, a sort of poor man's power control system. On take off, until about 60kts had been reached, all the surfaces hung down (except the rudder which just swung around). This often caused consternation among other aircraft crew waiting to take off who where not familiar with our weird system. Needless to say, indicators were provided in the flight deck to make sure that "all surfaces were flying" before rotation! In really cold upper air temperatures the complicated gearboxes in the control runs (which transferred push-pull motion to rotary and back again!) could become cold-soaked and gradually stiffen which was very disconcerting. Heaters were later fitted to these devices.

Then it was time for the round-the-World route trainer. We set off from Lyneham on 28th January with three trainee crews and a staff crew on board, on an east-about route: Akrotiri, Bahrain ("Muhuraq-on-Sea"), Gan, Cocos, Singapore (Changi), Hong Kong, Guam, Honolulu ("Hickalulu"), San Francisco, Gander and so to Lyneham on 11th of February. Cocos was a fascinating place, once a "private" colony with a history that could fill a book. At Perth in Western Oz, the customs man found a couple of *Playboy* magazines amongst our ground crews' luggage (Aircrew **never** read this sort of stuff!!) and threatened to have us arrested for smuggling in porno. We all found this a bit of a joke and were having our legs pulled. Not so; with beer-bellies heaving Customs made it very clear that they were not amused and, to prove it, impounded the aircraft for a thorough search, which gave us an unexpected but very pleasant night-stop in Perth! Things went pretty smoothly after that until between Guam and Honolulu we picked up a Mayday call from a USAF C-124 flying (?) on two engines (and one dud would not feather). Remembering from my SAC days that most large USAF aircraft were fitted with UHF/VHF D/F (Direction Finding Equipment) we got him to "home" us to him. He was at 4000ft and getting lower by the minute but we stayed with him to Wake Island where we both landed safely. After a very convivial evening at Wake, refuelled and refreshed, we pressed on to the next day to Honolulu and Hickam AFB. Not having been here since 1962 I was appalled at the concrete jungle of high-rise hotels that had replaced the beautiful Waikiki beach in four short years. Even the famous headland of Diamond Head had not been spared. Back at base, a final check or two and I was on the line with a "C" category (passenger carrying). I see my first trip was to Aden; it was going to be a very busy tour.

In March '65 Ian Smith had declared "UDI" for Southern Rhodesia in a vain attempt to protect his country from the inevitable decent into civil war and anarchy that seems to be the lot of most African countries. This resulted in the UN oil embargo of Southern Rhodesia which in turn totally deprived land-locked Zambia (ex Northern Rhodesia) of her oil too: an inevitable knock-on effect which one would have thought that UN strategists might have anticipated with even a fourth-formers knowledge of geography! All Zambia's oil came through Livingstone via Bulawayo by rail and now the frontier was closed! And so a re-supply of oil by air to Zambia was put into effect in December. Harold Wilson decided that the RAF would bear the brunt of this oil airlift with Britannias, aided by sundry civilian cargo companies. The RAF Brits flew over 10000 hours in the next 10 months, all paid for by the taxpayer. In all I spent March, April, August and October based in Nairobi, flying almost daily into Lusaka and N'dola carrying fifty six 44 gallon drums of highly volatile fuels, all chained together on a metal cargo floor, happily rattling, swaying and gurgling in unison to the tune of four Proteus engines! The cost of this futile effort must have been enormous; all our aircraft required new cargo floors at the end of the operation and this was only a small part of the taxpayers' burden. As for the effectiveness of the airlift, well, we never ceased to be amazed seeing the Zambians filling up the Air Rhodesia civil Viscounts on their daily flight from Salisbury, with our "hand flown" fuel.

To start with chaos reigned supreme, so much so that one wag named the operation "Mushroom Airways – kept in the dark and covered ......!" I remember in May the day before our C in C the famous "Bing" Cross – visited the detachment someone (still un-known) stuck large red day-glow mushrooms right at the top of each Britannia fin 36 feet up. When an irate Wing Commander ordered them to be removed it proved impossible – there was no equipment at Eastleigh capable of reaching the offending insignia!

Eventually a pattern of flying emerged; each of the six Brits doing two round trips a day about 7 hours per sortie, one at 0500 and the second at 1430. We routed direct to M'Beya, whose NDB still pooped off the largest thunderstorms in the area, and then to two Zambian destinations, N'dola and Lusaka, but not before getting clearance from

Salisbury to enter what was Rhodesian controlled air space. Much friendly banter often took place on the R/T! Some way south of Nairobi lies Lake Natron, a soda lake, and Mt L'Engai, the Mountain of God. This is an active volcano with a record of getting angry every seven years or so. We were fortunate to see it erupt, happily ignorant (at the time) of the effect of volcanic dust on aeroplanes. L'Engai was always a fascinating sight, not so much an eruption but lots of lava flows and a cloud of ash that rarely exceeded 12,000ft.

Of the two destinations, old Lusaka Airport was the most demanding and the most important because six RAF Javelins and a mobile Radar unit were based there, plus a squadron of RAF Regiment to "defend" them – against what I never found out! The 5000ft single runway at 4000ft above sea level was not much for a fully laden Brit with return fuel; and in fact we were over the WAT (Weight, Altitude, Temperature) limit for landing, i.e. hit the ground, bounce and, no, you cannot go round again! There were no taxiways and the runway was too narrow to do a 180° turn other than at the three enlarged turning points. BOAC VC-10s used to go in (very light) about twice a week. This leads me to one of two memorable exhibitions of total lack of airmanship that I saw in forty years of flying (the second involved an Alitalia 747 at Kai Tak many years later which caused the inhabitants of the ATC tower to desert their posts in unseemly haste). I had just completed my landing and was turning at the end to backtrack when I came face to face with a VC-10 cockpit some 400ft away and still moving. The aircraft stopped and the pilot began his 180° at the next turning circle with the cheerful words "don't worry, old chap, we have good brakes". He got more than a flea in his ear on returning to London!

In Nairobi we were accommodated in a watering hole known as the Spread Eagle, which probably rated one star. Later in the year we got more realistic allowances and were able to move to the Norfolk, which was an excellent hotel and very civilized. This almost unknown largesse by the paymasters was prompted by reports in the press (bless 'em) that civilian crews were earning huge wads of danger money, on top of everything else, every time they came within ten feet of a barrel of fuel, either on the ground or in the air!

Nairobi in those days was still a good place to visit. The nightlife was fun; Laverini's Restaurant produced the finest Lobster Thermidor I have ever eaten and old man Laverini would cash our UK cheques – he was never let down. The Long Bar at the Stanley still attracted real old Africa hands and sitting outside at the Thorntree Café one could see everyone who was anyone in Africa walk by. One could still send a girlfriend home at night in an Archers' taxi alone, and know she would reach some outlying farm in safety – don't try it now, not even in daytime! On one's rare free days I would hire a large station wagon and as a crew we would visit Thika Falls, Lake Naivasha of the pink flamingos, the foothills of Mt Kenya, not to mention the Nairobi game park. Which reminds me that driving in the crew bus to the airport early one morning, the driver had to do an emergency stop as a pride of lions trotted by just in front: Mum, Dad, three cubs and Granny. I think that was the morning I had an aborted sortie. I had just started No.3 when I caught a movement out of the corner of my eye; a driverless forklift truck used in loading was advancing towards us, prongs up like a praying mantis. Gathering momentum it pierced the skin just below the freight-floor to a depth of three feet!

Departure times had to be adhered to on an operation like this; very little ATC control existed once south of Nairobi and we made position reports in the clear on (I think) 126.30 for the benefit of other aircraft. Maybe this still has to be done! This leads me to the departure one evening of Flt Lt Micky Martin, an ebullient character who liked to sport a gold watch chain across his uniform tunic much to the annoyance of the boss, and was never enthusiastic about getting his hair cut. A good friend, a very competent pilot and in a previous life he may well have been a buccaneer. Anyway, Micky and I were parked on the ramp at Lusaka one evening waiting to return to Nairobi at 1800 and 1830 respectively. Micky had been warned that he would be taking the British Consul and several important (?) Foreign Office dignitaries on his aircraft. At 1755 there was no sign of the VIPs and I saw a small tongue of flame come from Micky's No.3

engine as he began to fire up. At 1800 with all four turning, the chocks were pulled and just as he started to taxi the cavalcade arrived. A flunkey dashed out in front of the Brit frantically waving his arms. The Captain's side window opened, an arm appeared, the hand revealing two fingers in the air, the arm retracted, the window closed and Micky took off: the perfect squelch! I am glad to say that "Bing" Cross backed him all the way. A week later Micky started with Caledonian! I, of course, had the task to fly the abandoned VIPs back north. Inevitably they wanted to take-off immediately: we left on schedule!

I think that it was in August that the Secretary of State for something or other, one Arthur Bottomley arrived to review the troops on the front line in Lusaka, accompanied by an unbelievable number of sycophants, press and general hangers-on. Arthur did not seem to have much of a grasp of geography for at his address to Zambian government officials, us troops and general public who were watching; in front of the world press and media he welcomed all of us to the Gambia. Unstoppable and not content with that he consistently referred to "Rhodesia" as Southern Rhodesia which to any red-blooded Zambian was like a red rag to a bull, Zambia having originally been Northern Rhodesia. Ah well, with cameras rewound dear old Arthur managed to get it right at the second attempt.

The airlift came to an end in October '66. It had been a fascinating experience. The views of Mt Killimunjaro against a dawn sky, so different from seeing it in the rays of the setting sun were sights that I remember today. Flying over Africa again reminded me of many happy hours in Harvards at Thornhill, Southern Rhodesia in my training days. It would be another nine years before I returned to Africa, to fly refugees from Angola and Mozambique to Lisbon in 707s, quite a different experience.

In between Africa detachments I had been busy flying routine trips to Aden (due to be de-colonised" in Jan '68), re-supply trips to the Far East and frequently to North America. In my two years on 511 I put in some 1500 hours on the old Brit. It was a time of tremendous variety and hugely enjoyable; the sort of flying that only comes once in a career. But constantly in my thoughts was the decision I had made to leave the service in Jan '68 and go civil. In every spare moment I studied for my ALTP, Instrument Rating, etc, and here I had some luck. John Cragg, a navigator and old friend, also had similar intentions and we tried to crew together whenever possible and study "en-route". It was a good arrangement. We had one trip together to Barbados and Bermuda in late '66. Someone in the Foreign Office had suddenly woken up to the fact that Barbados would be granted independence on 1st December and that there were some 200 British troops on the island and this was 27th November! So two Britannias were dispatched on 27th to hike them out. It so happened that on one of the sectors between Bermuda and Barbados, the Sun and Moon would be aloft together and a single position line could be obtained across track: a fairly rare occurrence I am told. I remember that at the right time John "shot" both bodies. I watched him plot it out and before I could say anything, he said on i/c for all to hear "No Commander, I am not going to explain it to you, it would take all day. This is Navigators' magic and you are a pilot. Go back to your chair, put your mind in neutral and your thumb in a warm place." John eventually joined Air Canada on DC-8s at the same time that I started with BEA. It was on this operation that the 120 troops that we embarked at Barbados came on board festooned with so much gear (small packs, I believe, is the Army term) that they could hardly sit in their seats and would never get through the over wing exits in an emergency. Through the Air Quartermaster (AQM) I got them to divest themselves of their accoutrements and had them lashed down on a freight pallet behind the flight deck. I had just begun our start-up drills when an irate Pongo Major stormed in demanding to know why his men had been separated from their Small Packs. "Did I not know" he roared "that British soldiers are NEVER parted from small packs". For once I was speechless, someone stifled a laugh and the Major departed in high dudgeon to write a full and damning report. Unfortunately he took the Captain's name from the previous crew list and I have always wanted to know who received the wrath of the War Office – it was not I!

In January I had a trip to Gander and Winnipeg taking V-force crews for winter training. The aircraft (and us) were required back at Lyneham ASAP so another crew flew 519 with us in the back (crew rest!), plus a Canadian delegation of MPs and sundry politicians. Over Prince Edward Island I was woken up by the AQM: the Captain wanted to see me. I wandered up front, mug of tea to the fore, to be told by the co-pilot that we had a "bomb threat". Now suddenly wide-awake, I learned that the RCAF hierarchy with whom the Captain was in contact was taking this very seriously: the aircraft number (519) and name (Capella) had been quoted, and some passengers identified from an anonymous source. We had a hurried conference: my crew and I would search the aircraft and I would talk to the passengers and tell them the truth; there was really no alternative. This left the operating crew to get us on the ground, hopefully intact, and keep in touch with ATC. Another message from the ground recommended an immediate landing: it was thought that the device would have a timing trigger and we were only an hour from Gander! Fredericton was close by, more chat followed and we started a steady descent. I did my brief in the cabin and considering this was at the height of the French separatists' hysteria everyone kept remarkably calm. It was twenty-five long minutes before we landed at Fredericton and no sooner had the aircraft stopped at the end of the runway, steps were at the doors, engines were shut down and we all left, very quickly. Twelve hours later we took off for Lyneham: nothing had been found. Despite a very thorough search I still had a slightly uncomfortable feeling over the Atlantic that maybe, just maybe the searchers had missed something.

We had a good thing going for us in Gander with the Airport Restaurant Manager who was a source of a supply of fresh salmon; real salmon, not the unhappy creatures that are "farmed" in Scotland today. Much business was done. It was here one night in the depths of winter that the benefits of "cloud and clonk" (weather) radar were brought home to a new co-pilot – straight from a Lightning Squadron. We were returning to Lyneham and it was blowing a blizzard. We gave the aircraft a final de-icing, quickly started the engines and taxied onto the runway. I lined up for take-off and did my usual mental check (clear right, clear left, right runway and radar), switching on the radar much to the amusement of the Co. About eight miles ahead the screen showed three of the largest thunder storm cells I had seen for a long time. It was, of course, the Arctic Front and we were looking at the build-ups in the Southern warm sector. "Point taken" said the Lad!

From then on most of my flying seemed to be eastward, and a couple of months later en-route to Akrotiri just north of Rhodes, again in the dead of night, I heard an Olympic Comet en-route for Nicosia make a position report very close to us but much higher! We had a quick chat with him on 123.45 about the two of us being the only real workers in the sky that night, and pressed on eastwards. Half an hour later Athens asked me to contact the Comet. I tried all frequencies without any luck; Athens then asked us to do a search of the area. With a sickening feeling I came down to 8,000ft just as the sun rose over the horizon. Within minutes a large patch of glistening water reflected the early sun's rays – fuel! Coming lower we could see objects in the water and some bright orange patches, probably life jackets. Sadly we headed for Akrotiri and reported the sighting to Athens: yet another terrorist tragedy.

Sometime that year, before the Comet incident, I had had a Changi "Slip", that is Lyneham to Bahrain, slipping for 12 hours, then to Gan and Changi. The aircraft I took over at Muhuraq-on-Sea (Bahrain) was full (no laughs please!) of ballet dancers! Had they been belly dancers then we could have had some light entertainment en route! No, this was part of the Royal Ballet complete with Prima Ballerina, Beryl Grey. How this charter came about I do not know but it was certainly different, yes, very different from the usual service personnel we carried. Anyway, Miss Grey proved to be a real charmer and spent some time on the Flight Deck regaling us with amusing and entertaining stories. Unfortunately we went u/s in Gan for twelve hours, which caused much amusement among the lads on Gan; I will not tell you what they dubbed me behind my back! We eventually made Changi and the lovely Miss Grey and her troupe departed.

Many years later, 32 to be precise, I bumped into Miss Grey in my village. There was no mistaking her; she looked just as lovely as ever. I had known for some time that she lived close by and this was my first chance to speak to her and reminisce a little. Bursting with enthusiasm I approached: "forgive me for asking but are you not Beryl Reid?" She drew herself up, glared at me in a way that only a Prima Ballerina can and said in an icy tone "NO I am NOT;" and that was the end of 32 years of waiting!

I have happy memories too of Gan; of course I was never there for more than just a few days unlike the staff, all without families, who could not escape until their year's tour was up. Which reminds me of another clanger made by Arthur Bottomley who, on one of his visits, asked a very senior Warrant Officer, who was nearing the end of his celibate year, if his wife had enjoyed the sunshine! The reply is unprintable. One could walk round the island in forty minutes and the swimming was great in the lagoon, which was home of the Wave Venture, a Fleet Auxiliary tanker that served as a floating fuel bunker. It really was a hulk and eventually I think it was towed away. It was manned by a Chief Petty Officer and a few ABs: no one seemed to know how long they had been there! There was also a tale about a Pig (Valetta) suffering an engine failure on take off and ditching about half a mile from the end of the runway. The crew hurriedly scrambled out onto the wing, inflated their Mae Wests and got into the dinghy, and began to row away from the sinking aircraft. After a few strokes they stopped when a voice said, "Where do you think your going?" Turning round, there was the Station Commander out fishing, standing in two feet of water! It was on one night-stop at Gan that the Air House decided that all Hastings were to be scrapped following yet another in flight failure of an elevator hinge bracket. All Hastings were to remain where they were and not fly again, and steps were taken to ensure that further flight would be impossible. And so it was that morning, getting ready to go on to Changi, that I saw the crew of Hastings 520 looking a bit bemused at their aircraft sitting on its belly, wheels up! So after some 20 years of loyal service the Hastings bowed out.

One of the strange requirements of Transport Command that no matter how much flying one did, and I often topped 100 hours a month, one had to do 2 hours of Continuation Training (CT) each month, circuits, let-downs, etc. and every three months Captains had to do a three engined take off with an outboard engine feathered! There was nothing difficult in this manoeuvre on the Britannia but to deliberately put oneself on three engines and then leap into the air seemed like pushing your luck. Perhaps some gung-ho type in the Air House thought it was worth the risk; perhaps it was the same chap who, in the early days of Meteors, insisted that all single engine flying would be for real, with one donk shut down. We lost a lot of pilots that way as I remember. The odd thing about three engine ferrying was that despite our diligent practice they were only to be done by QFIs on the OCU. We enjoyed CT but the cost of it…….! There was a plus side however. About a dozen of us were leaving in January '68 for civil flying; Bill Robinson, one of our QFIs, was also a CAA Type Rating examiner and we all managed to do our ratings with Bill during, and within, our monthly CT requirements. Thanks to Bill we all left with a marketable type on our licenses, which is why so many of us ended up in Caledonian and British Eagle.

During one of the Continuation details I paid a visit to Benson. Benson at that time was the home of the Royal Flight, an Argosy squadron and the odd Valetta. The thing that most of us remember about Benson was that the WAAF Officers quarters were on the ground floor of the south-east wing of the Mess, access to which via the windows posed no problem to any agile, fit young chap under 30 (I was well over 30)! Anyway, this particular visit was a rehearsal (sorry for the pun!) for the transporting of human remains, HUMs in today's yuk-speak, from Lyneham to Benson, and three or four crews were nominated for this task thus ensuring that at least one would be at Lyneham if the unhappy event occurred. The proposed HUM was obviously of high rank or a member of the Royal Family who, in the event of having the bad luck to expire overseas, would be immediately flown back to Lyneham in a VC-10, transferred to a suitably decked-out Brit with coffin compatible with rank, team of RAF Regiment pall-bearers and all the trappings of an important funeral and then flown to Benson where it would be officially "received" on Home Soil by a reception committee appropriate to the standing of the deceased. Timing was of the essence since the "welcoming" band would reach a crescendo at a certain time just as the Brit gently rolled to a halt in line with the red carpet with both port engines already shut down and the large cargo door open.

I left Lyneham at the appointed time with two other crews on board to watch and learn. Benson Radar did us no favours by confusing us with another aircraft for a few vital seconds and as a result I landed nearly a minute late. In the back the coffin had to be unlashed, put on a couple of trestles well hidden by a large Royal Blue blanket, the pall bearers positioned as well as the RAF Regiment escort party, all in double quick time. Benson's perimeter taxiway is a bit like a grand prix circuit with chicanes to trap the unwary. They did and on the last bend to the finishing line taken a little too fast, I heard a loud "thump", several in fact, and much subdued cursing. Braking to a halt as gently as I could there was another bang just as the cargo door reached its fully open position. Outside, an AVM, Station-Master Benson, Band, Hearse people and sundry other dignitaries viewed with horror the spectacle of the coffin on one trestle and on its side, four airmen tangling on the floor with the blue rug and the other two crews causing more havoc trying to put things right! A voice from the tower said "RAFAIR, taxi to threshold of RR/W 27 and take-off immediately!" Thankfully I never flew this mission for real, which was probably just as well!

We found ourselves going to Aden more frequently as the year wore on. Aden was becoming decidedly active as independence drew near. Gun battles in the streets of Crater were a regular and almost daily feature and it was time to get the families and their belongings out. One load I flew contained pets including some 200 budgies: we had a long discussion on the flight to Bahrain as to whether the aircraft's all up weight varied if they all got airborne in their cages at the same time! By July most "non-combs" had been evacuated and only essential RAF personnel remained together with a sizeable force of Army to maintain some semblance of law and order. It had been the biggest airlift since Berlin in 1948, the success of which was mainly due to the whole operation being run on the spot by an old friend Wing Commander Eric Reeves instead of from the remoteness of TC HQ at Upavon. Towards the end we flew troops out who had come straight off the street patrols, some with still warm rifles. In the interest of hygiene I had to insist that they kept their boots on otherwise the cabin temperature would be set a -10°! The troops took it very well. As I recall, landings were usually made to the west and take-offs to the east, thus offering less opportunity for trigger-happy Arabs to perfect their shooting. The aircraft parking areas were enclosed in revetments of large oil drums partially filled with sand, I think, and stacked in rows some eight feet high as protection against mortar splinters. Since one backed one's Brit into these spaces with reverse thrust one had to stop with just the minimum of forward thrust. I overstepped the mark one night and blew a whole row of barrels across the tarmac!

AVM J Johnson, the famous "Johnnie", was the Air Officer Commanding (AOC) Aden at this time and I had occasion to meet him one night…..! September 10th 1967: Brit XM520, Antarus, just south of Arak in Iran at 2300hrs and 19,000ft. Ahead lay the Zargosa Mountains, snow covered and brilliantly lit by the full moon. One hour to go to Bahrain. I left my seat for a coffee and a quick check of our load – two Centaurus engines for a Beverley. I stopped by the galley in the rear of the aircraft, had a coffee and a chat with the AQM and happed to glance out of the window. Instead of moonlit mountains I saw starlit sky with the stars moving rapidly upwards! I broke Roger Bannister's four-minute mile running to the Flight Deck. There, the Flight Engineer was filling in figures in his log (they always seem to be doing this), the Nav was busy with the Doppler, the Co Pilot – well, I don't really know where his mind was, and the auotpilot was busily winding the elevator trim forward. Outside the mountain range was at an angle of some 45° and disappearing upwards. The Brit was in a perfectly coordinated steep diving turn to starboard and no one had noticed! I yelled "autopilot!" jumped into my seat, hit the isolation switch and started to level the wings. By now we had lost 800ft and had an indicated rate of descent of some 2,000fpm! No one had noticed!! I leave my words of wisdom over the next five minutes to my reader's imagination.

We carried on to Bahrain where I sent off an SOR (Special Occurrence Report) to TC Upavon (Transport Command Headquarters) and with the Station Engineer's blessing continued on to Aden. We were very concerned about what we had experienced; autopilots had given trouble in the past and of course the demise of G-ANCA at Bristols many years earlier was in our minds. Still, we now had the A/P disconnected and no doubt a full engineering investigation would take place when Antarus returned home in three days time. Meanwhile it was "pole it by hand": the Brit did not have a conventional yoke but a bar rather like an old-fashioned motorcycle handlebar. I never got used to it. Landing at Aden in the early dawn I was looking forward to the usual large cold can of Tennants with pictures of lovely ladies on it, when the Wing Co Engineering came up to me and said "the AVM wants to see you – now!" Sure enough it was JJ himself, not exactly happy to be up so early, waving a telex in his hand. "Read this" he said. The telex was a reply from Upavon to my SOR, totally ignoring the near catastrophe and demanding that I be relieved of my command and sent home to explain why I had deliberately descended 2,000ft in Iranian controlled airspace without ATC approval! "Well?" said JJ. I offered to get my copy of the SOR but he said, "no, just tell me". So I did! The AVM said, "I thought as much – some stupid sod at TC can't read! I'll deal with this – you carry on as normal". Sad to relate it took TC ten days to get round checking our 23 Brits; seven were found to have the same problem – corrosion on the gyro stabilized platform in the auto-pilot. In the year 2000 while at Duxford during the Flying Legends Air Show, I saw A. M. Johnson in the VIP lounge. Unfortunately he had left by the time I could meet him but I asked his son to pass on my profound thanks for his support that night in Aden 35 years ago.

In October I made my last trip to Aden slipping in Bahrain, and handing over 638 to Len, another captain. I continued to Aden 12 hours later in 496 to find Len's aircraft belly deep in Aden creek mud some 500 yards off the west end of the runway, badly bent. The whys and wherefores have no place here, suffice to say that the Flight Engineer (new chap) had difficulty in getting reverse thrust. Len was maybe a little slow in appreciating this and they shot off the end of the runway at about 80kts into the stinking slime of the tidal creek. "There but for the grace of God go I" came to my mind, it was always a possibility to have a "bit of a horlicks" getting the props to change angle. Anyway, the nose wheel assembly broke off, ripped out all the crash switches (fire extinguishers, fuel cocks, etc, etc) in the nose wheel well before they could do their stuff, and entered the Flight Deck floor behind the Nav with both wheels intact! Consequently when the AQM opened the crew door he was greeted by numbers 1 and 2 engines still slowly turning flinging vast quantities of evil smelling slime everywhere. Eventually they stopped. Silence; mud everywhere, the Flight Deck full of it through a rent in the port side. The crew scrambled out of various exits; those that left via the crew door thought they were still fairly high off the ground (main wheels down), jumped, hit the mud six inches later and tipped head-first, one after the other, into the large water filled hole dug by the inboard engine. Reaching the side, they crawled and slithered out of the water. Len said, "where is the Judge?" This chap was the only passenger and had been standing behind Len for landing: he was to preside over a court-martial that day! A face appeared in the black maw of the door, or rather two eyes and teeth could just be seen. Everyone yelled, "don't jump" – too late! The Judge was the only casualty having broken his arm. In retrospect they were all very lucky to get away so lightly.

On my return slip from Aden I picked up a freighter at Bahrain that had come from Riyadh. The load was a fortune in used bank notes, mostly sterling and US dollars, lashed on eight freight pallets, and worth £11 million! This was a part-payment by the Saudis for their English Electric Lightnings. With the load came an aged Treasury official (unarmed) who promptly went to sleep in the air. We had much chat on how we could improve our pensions, and enter the Guinness Book of records for Theft, but sanity prevailed and we landed at Akrotiri to refuel. Leaving the aircraft on the ramp, no guards and with the elderly guard still asleep, we had a quick breakfast and flight-planned home. At Lyneham we were greeted by an armed escort, from touchdown to ramp, and a whole army of fully armed RAF Regiment. We were even searched to make sure the odd fiver had not escaped!

That year I had a welcome break from Aden; a trip to RAF Tengah, Singapore, with a two-week stand-by on base. Taking off from Akrotiri during heavy thunderstorm activity, I had just let go the brakes when it started to rain thick mud! The wipers could not shift it, so I shut down and had the aircraft towed back to the ramp to be inspected and cleaned of umpteen pounds of Sahara desert mud, not an uncommon occurrence apparently in that part of the world. When we finally reached Tengah I got my brief for our two-week stand-by. Relations with Red China were strained (what else is new!) and FEAF (Far East Air Force) required two Britannias on stand-by for as long as relations remained strained! I hesitate to put down the reasons for this for I found it utterly unbelievable at the time. Two Brits with a jeep and trailer in each and 60 RAF Regiment were to be ready at two hours notice to fly to Kai Tak, secure the airfield, evacuate the Governor and other important (?) Foreign Office worthies, should the 600 odd million screaming Chinese the other side of the border decide to grab the Colony. I have often wondered if this was the brainchild of dear old Arthur again! Anyway we had a very pleasant two weeks, two hours notice allowed us a little freedom to visit Changi Beach Club; Temple Hill Nurses Home was not too far away and there was always Ah Lim" mobile restaurant (one bicycle) in Changi Creek!

Two weeks later we left Tengah late at night and were just clearing Sabang and getting a radar fix off the coast when the radar screen showed two curved "lines" on the sea about 20 miles ahead and three miles apart, lying NE to SW. We watched for a few minutes and, thinking they might be tidal waves, reported them to Singapore. The lines then dissipated. Some years later I read in the National Geographic that this phenomenon was caused by cold water from the deep welling up to the surface following seismic disturbances on the ocean floor. This is what the radar had picked up – no wave, just very dense water. I wrote to the NG but regrettably never got a reply. Now it was my time to look to the future and do a final swot for my civil licences.

In the middle of October I took all the leave due to me and went to Sir John Cass College in London to brush-up for my ALTP exams, and also to do sundry ARB (Air Registration Board) tests as well as an instrument rating (IRT) for which I remember I was exempt from the asymmetric test, which saved a bit of dosh. The rating I took at Gatwick with Air London; little did I know that I would be with Air London for the next fifteen years. It was a carefully planned assault on the system and I managed all my goals. I was accompanied by Dennis Skidmore, an old friend in 511 which made studying much more pleasant. It was not entirely all work and no play. One evening we were invited to a party in Kensington, not far from our digs in Victoria, given by a bunch of BOAC girls! Trying to get a taxi home was proving difficult at 1.00 am so one girl offered us a lift. We got into this Mini with two other young ladies and set off. Somewhere near Sloane Square, Skid, who was navigating in spite of being distracted by one young lady, declared us uncertain of our position. We stopped and out of the shadows loomed a Bobby not unlike Jack Warner in *The Blue Lamp*.

"Ullo, ullo," he said, looking in. "Where do you think you are going? This is the second time you have passed me tonight!"

"We are trying to persuade these ladies to take us home – our home," said Skid.

"Do you know this young lady driving?" The Law then asked.

"No," said Skid.

"And you Sir (addressing me), do you?"

"No."

"Hmm… Do you know the other two young ladies in the back?"

"No," we said.

He looked at us again, deeply suspicious.

"It is late, I am tired. Please go and don't pass me again!"

Such justice is unlikely to be met in this day and age.

Having taken my ALTP, ARB (tech paper – turbo props) and IRT I now headed back to Lyneham hoping for an early result of the ALTP exams. Apart from one slight hiccup when the Board of Trade said I could not qualify for an ALTP because I had not done a triangular cross-country, solo, of legs not less than 47nm! This was quickly resolved! I was due to go to Singapore again on 25th November and on the morning of departure I still had not had my exam results. I rang the B of T to enquire and explained to a very kind lady that I would be all of a twitch in command of a Britannia unless I knew the result. "Stop twitching" she said, "you have and so has Skidmore". You may wonder why we had to take leave to prepare ourselves for civilian life: If I had wanted to be a bricklayer, or an estate agent, or – well, you name it, I could have had a fully paid course, nosh and accommodation thrown in. But to become a civil pilot....!! The irony of it all was that a few months later if you had a A + B Transport Command category (I had a B) and more than 5000 hours you were granted an exemption from the ALTP written exams! Ah well, it was good for the soul I suppose, but not the pocket. Skid, by the way, joined Monarch Airways in February 1968, then a brand new airline: his seniority number was ONE!

So now it was back to the squadron and work again. Lyneham still had a Maintenance Unit dating from a time before my earlier arrival in 1954. The Spitfires, Hurricanes and Tiger Moths had long since gone and maintenance of more modern types was now undertaken. One of these, a Lightning tried to escape, causing much havoc. The C.O. of the Maintenance Unit was a young chap, well qualified in engineering and had earned his RAF Wings on Piston Provosts. One day he was carrying out generator balancing (with both engines running) on a Lightning, on the southern end of runway 36. The aircraft had pretty well every access panel open, no canopy, u/c locked down and bang seat immobilised; but it was full of fuel. Whilst he operated the engines from the "open" cockpit, the engineers surrounded the aircraft. Somehow during a high power run the throttles became locked in re-heat. With a roar of after-burners and much flame from the jet-pipes the aircraft jumped the chocks, shot down the runway and into the air, just missing a crew-coach! I believe he reached 10,000 feet before he was able to reduce power. Clutching the control column to avoid being catapulted into space (no straps) he lowered the nose and managed to enter the circuit. After several hair raising (!) attempts to land he eventually got it onto the ground and stopped right at the end of the runway: A creditable achievement, I thought, but I do not know if they gave him an Air Force Cross or a rocket – perhaps both.

In December I had a final trip to North America and Honolulu, which took up the first two weeks. I routed back through Offutt AFB, Nebraska, SAC HQ, and saw several old friends from the 904th AREFS. This got me a couple of trips in a T-39 (Sabreliner), which was a fun aeroplane. My last trip in the service was to Singapore on 21st December, where we would spend Christmas and re-start the slip schedule on the 27th. It was a time of mixed feelings for me, with my inevitable departure from the RAF, which had been my home for nearly seventeen years, only days away. I had been lucky. I had had an immense variety of flying and I was now going to change all that and become 2nd Officer Fitz on a BEA Argosy freighter! I did not know that my luck would continue: I would have five changes of aircraft in BEA/BA in sixteen years (almost unheard of), Argosy, Comet, 707, Vanguard and 737 to say nothing of countless light twins in the air taxi world with Air London.

We had a very enjoyable Christmas in Changi with several other crews from other units but on the morning of our departure I got a call from Ops to say that we would be Aero Med on the return trip, with a full medical team and a bevy of nurses! It turned out to be a sad voyage: we had just one young patient, an airman who had dived into a swimming pool on Boxing Day to find out that it was empty. I remember the frightened look in his eyes when I first saw him on the aircraft. He was bolted to a "Striker" frame so that no part of him could move: he had broken his neck. The Doc's prognosis was not good. He said, "The only sign of life from that lad are his eyes and the flickering of his eyelids. He cannot talk but can hear we think. Please, no reverse thrust, no heavy braking, no turbulence and land like a feather. If we can achieve this we may be able to get him home.'"" I remember we could not risk a jerky tractor tow so we started engines tail into wind. Not a good idea in a Brit because as soon as you release the propeller brakes, the props rotate – backwards in this case. So it required an airman to hold on to the lower blade (they were only two feet off the ground) until the engine lit up and then release it! I had taken on extra fuel for Gan in order to dodge, if possible, the huge Cb in the Bay of Bengal. I see the trip took an hour longer than usual. Ops had radioed ahead for a ground power unit to be available at Gan and Bahrain; with the patient dependent on an electrically powered respirator and other gizmos we could not afford the slightest break in power supply. So off we went, gentle acceleration at Changi, picking our way through the storms on radar, wincing at every flash of lightning, constant request for smoother air, number four engine with a fault somewhere in the intake ducting heating, re-lighting itself with the usual thump and residual flame adding to those bolts of lightning!

The Service MO was a Flight Surgeon from Farnboro' and I had met him before; he had been doing research on pilots and crews on fatigue factors. He asked me before take off if I minded being wired up for pulse rate readings, to which I had agreed. In the cruise he had a coffee with us up front and remarked that my pulse had hardly increased on take-off. "Very unusual" he said, "either you're brain dead, singularly stupid, or completely at home up here; I hope it's the latter!" He was of course, quite right: I am at home in the air. In fact I often felt a sense of relief to leave earth behind and spend some hours in my chosen environment that somehow had a very soothing effect. Someone once said that flying was hours of boredom interspersed with a few minutes of sheer terror, to which I would more or less agree but I have never been bored in the air.

The weather at Gan was CAVOK and I managed a reasonably smooth landing for once. On the tarmac, GPU plugged in I shut down 1, 2 and 4 engines, checked the power supply and shut the HP cock on No 3 engine. At this moment Sod's law took over, the GPU stopped (run out of fuel). I snapped the HP cock open again and with a monumental thump and a gout of flame as the engine re-lit and we restored power.

I am told that I remained calm and quietly told the erk on the ground headset to get another GPU, like instantly. The doc burst in and asked if I was OK as my pulse rate had shot off the clock! Later we continued to Bahrain and slipped, having added another patient to our list, a WO with terminal cancer. It was a rather sad crew as we said goodbye to our patients and medics. Later I learned that our Brit has suffered a total brake failure at Lyneham but our patient had been transferred to a chopper at the end of the runway and was now in Stoke Mandeville hospital.

My last day of service ended at 23:59 on the 29th so we returned to Lyneham, as passengers on the next Britannia slip on the 30th. I was already a civilian! The next day I left the RAF. It felt very strange; I left behind many friends, though many I saw again in civil flying and with others I have kept in touch. I handed in my 1250 (I/D card) at the Guard Room and walked through the gates into a different world.

It is one of the advantages of putting pen to paper is that one can stop and reflect at any point, with 20/20 hindsight, of what has passed and how that past might have effected the future. My transition from Service to Civil flying was swift and I think now, 35 years later, I can take a look back in time and reminisce a little and perhaps find some answers for my decision to change careers in midstream.

There were many things that I was going to miss – free gliding for one! Motorless flight is as close to flying as a bird (apart from hang gliding) as one can get and it has always been my first love. I remember the opportunity the service gave me in South Africa and the thrill and challenge of my diamond climb. I would miss the comradeship of an operational station flying with a good Squadron, and the reverse, of watching others while I drove my desk! The security of service life was another plus: if one became ill in Civil flying and lost ones licence, things would be very different. I also would miss the large leather armchairs in the Mess where one could snooze happily for a while after lunch, until getting rudely awakened by some Senior Officer! But I think we all knew our life was changing: more and more civilianisation and the closing of overseas basis (our dwindling Empire) reduced the size of the RAF and indeed all armed forces, with a loss of many famous stations. And, of course, there was going to be less flying.

It was the overwhelming drive to continue flying that was my primary motivation to leave and I also knew at the time that an Officer with a permanent commission could expect no more than two or three flying tours: I had had six! Two years prior to leaving I had had the usual interview with the Air Secretary's Branch (personnel) with a Group Captain, following a letter from him that stated "Although I was not at the moment a strong contender for promotion, I was showing signs of improvement" (no escapades with Brian in the last 7 years)! The interview reflected this view. So I made my decision and opted out at the 38/16 point. Decision once made, there followed within days an acknowledgement from the same Group Captain in a letter in which he said "that my record clearly indicates the valuable service that you have rendered during your long (?) career in the Royal Air Force, and the high regard in which you have been held"! Nice to know!

My tour with the USAF was undoubtedly the high point and this had made me think very seriously of leaving the RAF whilst I was in America. There were several very distinct differences in the social side of life in the USAF compared to life in the RAF at the time. Life in the RAF was very much male orientated, a code on conduct in force that reflected the pre-war service. Bachelor Officers had to live in Mess and this made for a vibrant Mess life. Discipline was still there, when the C.O. came into the Mess ante-room everyone stood up. Ladies (wives) had their own drawing room. Dining in nights were formal affairs until dispersing to the ante-room after dinner when all hell would break loose! Times were changing and like it or not the Service had to change as well. One could argue the pro's and con's of this all day; as far as I am concerned I miss that post-war atmosphere and discipline and I find that now, on the rare occasions that I visit a Mess, having to queue up in a self-service dining room for lunch is not to my liking. Yet change had to take place.

~ *No Time on the Ground* ~

In the United States Air Force in 1959, the Mess was known as the Officers Club, and it was the centre of social life on the base. Wives participated in all sorts of projects and used the club at will. Bachelors lived either in the Bachelor Officers Quarters (BOQ's) or in apartments that they had bought outside the confines of the base. Most preferred this to the BOQ's. Of course, this gave them the chance to enter the housing market; an opportunity denied bachelors at home. There was formality, dining in nights did happen more or less on the lines of the RAF but not so boisterous, of course quite often wives were present. I thought the club was a good compromise between the old and the new. Living in a foreign (!) country, and as I explained to my American colleagues, at great risk, which really should still be flying the Union Jack, we had explored California as a family, from Crater Lake to the North to the end of Route 49 in the south, the Sierra Nevada's, panning for gold in "them thar hills", Virginia City and Las Vegas in Nevada and the beautiful Redwoods. The Grand Canyon and the Painted Dessert we took in on our drive to the East Coast and home at the end of my tour. This freedom to roam brought home the rather restricted life we led in the RAF, most of the time closeted in married quarters and very much separate from the local population: it got me thinking. Pretty well all my flying overseas, on Hastings, Beverleys and Britannias, our destinations were invariably military bases, run much like any other. As an example I went to Changi countless times yet never visited Singapore but remained in the confines of the camp. In the USAF things were very different: most bases had a pool of cars that could be hired out at very reasonable rates, water skis, snow skis and other sports equipment was all there to be used at very low cost. And so I was able to see most of the Island of Guam, then Oahu and a small part of Alaska around Fairbanks! Later at the end of my Britannia tour, I realised I had been all over the world and yet not seen it. It was very soon after I started Civil flying that I realised what a freedom it was to night-stop in places that were not homes from home, route flying became an even greater pleasure.

I had been very tempted to leave the RAF at the end of my exchange tour and return to the USA and Civil flying – I already had a US Commercial Licence type rated on the Boeing 377 and a Civil Instrument Rating. It is fortunate a friend dissuaded me on the grounds that when the Vietnam war ended, a lot of "foreign" pilots would probably lose their jobs to the returning veterans, a situation well forecast by my friend in good time. In any case, at the 38/16 point I would become eligible for a small pension, which now buys my Gin.

So, on the return to the UK on a dismal November 5th 1962 the seeds were sown for me to seek new pastures. I knew I would miss the Service that had done so much for me from the days in the V.R. at Redhill to my final flight. In fact today I consider myself more an ex-service than an ex-airline pilot.

11. Going Civil

A week after leaving the RAF at Lyneham I reported to the BEA training centre at Heston to begin an Argosy course as First Officer. At my acceptance interview I had been given a choice – Viscounts or Argosies. Roger Neaves (of Cirencester and Russians fame!) who had joined BEA some four years previously, advised me to take the Argosy course on the grounds that there were only four out of the original six still intact and that the type was bound to be withdrawn from service in the near future. This would leave me well placed to bid for a more interesting aircraft!

BEA at this time (January 1968) had a need for experienced air-crew to fill the F/O positions on their two-crew aircraft, viz. the Argosy, Viscount and BAC One Eleven. This left the Tridents, Van-guards and Comets to absorb the newly arriving Hamble Graduates. The "Hamsters" (many have now retired at 55!) were excellent drivers of airframes but lacked the experience to crew a two-crew aircraft. BEA impressed me; there was sound thinking in their approach to airline flying, the management that I met was friendly and I was quite happy with my lot – the money was not too bad either! It was the BEA "monitored approach" that has always remained in my memory – before the days of auto land and other gizmos. In this, one pilot, (usually the F/O) flew the let down while the other (Captain) moni-tored his flying. Near minimums the Captain looked ahead for the required visual reference for landing. The F/O would call "100 above" decision height and at minimums "Decide". The Captain would either say "I have control" or "Go around". If nothing was said the F/O went straight into the published go around procedure. The system worked like a charm because it did away with the operating pilot having to seek a visual reference in bad weather and at the same time fly the let down. Try it some time! BOAC, of course, would have none of it and many were the occasions when BEA was operating into claggy airfields where BOAC were busily overshooting!

In order to attract RAF types the Corporation offered us a year's jump on the seniority list (I didn't appreciate just how important this was until later in the Command bracket). By and large we had a good bunch of pilots on the Argosy; a lot of ex-wartime chaps as well as ex National Service pilots and, of course, peacetime warriors like me! Many of us were still on the RAF reserve.

I have lost my Argosy Flight Manual but I recall that the aircraft was a bit of a twin-boom oddball. In the RAF it was crewed by two pilots, Flight Engineer and Navigator – maybe a wireless operator as well! An old friend, Tony Hinds told me it was a bit under powered: he should know! He was once doing a base check at Gibraltar on an RAF Argosy when on a three-engined go-around the U/T pilot shut down the wrong engine, leaving them with two! This resulted in a large splash in Spanish waters and much swimming. Tony as training captain was held to blame and as he had displayed an affinity for water, he was posted to the Kipper Fleet.

The aircraft, I believe was designed around two Rolls Royce Tynes with 16' diameter props; thus the booms were positioned with this in mind. The Tynes did not materialise in time so four Darts took their place; consequently the two inner engines were well "out-board" putting the outers even further along the wing – not much help in an engine out case. The wing was very much the same as the Mk III Shackleton. The RAF aircraft had, on the insistence of the Army, been fitted with clamshell doors for the dropping of supplies and to facilitate easy loading of small vehicles among which was a small armoured scout car. Unfortunately the clamshell doors reduced the dimensions of the loading area so much that the scout car was denied entry!

Another problem was the mainplane de-icing system: 35% of the leading edge (between the inboard engines) was not de-iced. Icing posed a major problem and I recall many occasions when full power on all four engines in severe icing still resulted in a slow descent! Some boffin made an electrical ice detector, which merely confirmed that you had ice and were going downhill. Another bright idea was the gluing of a triangular piece of Perspex on the Captain's side window (prism) so he could see the ice build-up on the wing leading edge between the inboards during his enforced descent. I am told that one of the prisms iced up so badly that it left the aircraft together with part of the window.

We called the aircraft the "Noddy" because it did just that. If you were so inclined you could descend into the freight bay and watch the booms flex, usually in unison. Noddy did have some good points. The flight deck was well designed (for two) and the visibility excellent. It had nose and tail side-hinged doors which made for fast turn rounds with palletted freight. The nose door contained a loo and washbasin and I always wanted to get it opened with my Captain enthroned but never succeeded.

After three weeks of ground school we started Base Training (no simulator available). Unfortunately this was often interrupted by commercial demands as we only had four aircraft. Prior to my joining, BEA had lost two Argosies. One had hit the top of a hill near Milan Linate during an instrument letdown on the Non Directional Radio Beacon (NDB) in thundery weather. I do not know the ins and outs of the accident but I remember Ian the first officer telling me that they hit the hill so gently and had slithered to a halt before they realised anything was wrong. He remembered looking round and seeing grass protruding through the floor hatch to the freight bay. A rent in the starboard side of the flight deck offered a means of escape and they took it. A few months later Ian was doing an Instrument rating at Stansted when the Training Captain shut the starboard outer Dart on take-off (part of the IRT) with such enthusiasm that the prop went into reverse. The aircraft nearly cartwheeled and finally ground to a halt. Ian looked round, noted the familiar grass, saw the same rent in the flight deck and with a shout of "follow me, I know the way" they left!

Once on the line I quite enjoyed the flying. Tony Hinds was right; the aircraft lacked urge from the Darts. The first take off I did on training I thought the brakes had seized such was the lack of acceleration. "Patience" said the Captain! It was on the Argosy that I was reacquainted with Decca only this time we had a moving map display, forerunner of things to come. However, the system took a long time to set up with umpteen waypoints to be inserted. Changing chains was another obstacle and if you got it wrong the aircraft position indicator would retreat to the bottom right hand corner and sulk there for the rest of the flight. I think in the end we tended to stick to VOR/DME and left the Decca to sulk.

Our routes covered Scandinavia, Western Europe, Italy and Greece. There was a rather nice schedule which left the UK at 1600 daily, to Gothenburg (the old airfield with rock piles at either end of a shortish runway) and then to Stockholm Arlanda for a night stop. The Friday service returned on Sunday so one had a very pleasant weekend. I remember often taking a ferry to some of the outlying islands and of course visiting the Vasa, a three hundred year old Man-o-War that sank in Stockholm Harbour at the start of its maiden voyage – I think they got the Centre of Gravity wrong. That stretch of water is free of wood boring worms etc, and when the ship was raised (in 1966 I think) she presented the world with a brand new example of late 17th Century shipbuilding. At this time she was being sprayed with a formaldehyde solution 24 hours a day to preserve her.

Our runs to Milan (via Nice to avoid the Alps!) were entertaining as we invariably returned with a couple of highly expensive cars – Ferraris, Lamborghini's, etc. To return to the UK even with this light load one had to circle in the holding pattern of the Milan NDB until we had achieved 12000ft before setting course, still climbing, for the Alps and home. It was on one of these trips that the Captain thought he would try the driving seat of one such car for a few minutes and dream a little. Unfortunately he locked himself in; I guess the car must have had one of the first self-locking gadgets. After forty minutes the F/O, with the aircraft on autopilot, came down to seek his commander to find him purple in the face and yelling, "get me out!" Rumour (well founded) has it that the F/O knew very well how to release him but declined and returned upstairs. Having informed Air Traffic and Company of his Captain's incapacitation, he landed the aircraft. The unfortunate skipper was greeted on the tarmac, still entombed, by the Flight Manager and other worthies!

My favourite route was to Rome and on to Athens for a night-stop. It was a delightful flight when the weather was good, and Athens has been a favourite place ever since. Struggling against a strong head wind on the return leg over the French Massif could be very unpleasant especially in icing conditions. We had frequent trips to the Channel Islands: Guernsey, then Jersey and home – all in six hours. For the First Officer it was a race to keep up with the paper work but most Captains would help out on the shortest sector. It was a salutary experience to be a First Officer (sorry, Second Officer) after some years in the Left Hand Seat, indeed some of the newly made up Captains were younger and less experienced than I. All the same, I had a lot to learn about the civil way of doing things and I never flew with a Captain who was not both helpful and friendly.

In January 1970 the Flight finally folded and the aircraft were sold, just as Neaves had foreseen. By this time BEA Airtours, a charter subsidiary of BEA, was being formed at Gatwick with nine Comet IVs. Volunteers were called for a five-year stint with an option to return to BEA Mainline. Ground Engineers, cabin staff and administrative personnel were employed separately by Airtours instead of on loan like the pilots. So it was really a separate company. The best part was that it attracted pilots who welcomed a break from humdrum airline flying, and in any case everyone hated Heathrow! So ended my first "tour" in B.E.A. It had been a difficult time from a domestic viewpoint and I certainly missed Squadron life. Now I went to work, flew, and went home: There was no meeting of friends in the Mess later. I felt that I belonged to an anonymous organisation that I only saw during working hours, it was a strange feeling.

It was about now that I threw away any chance of a continued warm and stable home-life, my wife and I parted company. This was an act of monumental stupidity and selfishness on my part and it says much for her that we have been able to remain friends all these years, much to the relief of our children. This book is no place for the ramifications of such an event and I will therefore not dwell on them any longer. It was, however, an event I have regretted all my life.

I now threw myself into flying anything and everything, anywhere and at anytime as I started the Comet Course. It was during the ground school that I joined the Airways Aero Club at Booker, otherwise known as Wycombe Air Park, mainly doing aero tows for the gliding section. However, it was here that I met the third great lady in aviation Joan Hughes, another A.T.A. girl who was an instructor with the power section. In fact I think she had been with the Airways Aero Club ever since the demise of the Air Transport Auxiliary. I took to Joan immediately and we became the best of friends. In one of the many books published about the A.T.A. there is that famous photograph of Joan about to set off in a Stirling standing next to the main wheel which towered over her. It was Joan that gave me the impetus to take up instructing and indeed it was she who flew with me and taught me so well. I took my test with the redoubtable Alan Branson in late August, after that I spent a great deal of time at Booker instructing on the Cherokees.

One of the last endearing memories I have of Joan, just before she retired from Booker, was when I flew a Stearman up there. Joan came trundling across from the Clubhouse, peered into the rear cockpit at me and said, "What's a silly old fool like you doing in an aeroplane like this?"

Joan died some years ago from Cancer, a brilliant pilot and a very dear friend.

12. Air Taxis

I am going to digress a little and write about a "parallel career" in the air taxi world since this covers a span of thirteen years! I hope I will be forgiven for jumping around in time! In November 1967 I had taken my instrument rating with a Gatwick based company called Mack Airways Training, also known as Air London. I took the instrument rating on the Beagle 206 at a cost of £40.00 an hour. The 206 was an ideal instrument platform, very stable and nice to fly. Although £40.00 an hour was rather high in those days, pilots managed to pass their I.R's in far less time than on the twin Comanche or the Aztec.

I thought no more about Air London until I was posted to Gatwick, when I paid a courtesy visit to Tony Mack senior, who ran the company with his wife Joyce and Anthony (Junior). The upshot of all this is that he asked me if I would like to do some flying, mainly instrument rating instructing and I jumped at the chance. Thus began a very happy partnership that has lasted to this day. In 1983 the company ceased their air taxi operations as costs began to spiral and there was not quite the same demand for small light twin executive aircraft. Air London then entered the brokerage business becoming more international and changing its name to Air Partners, and under the guidance of Anthony Mack, it has never looked back and indeed today it is a highly successful company.

BEA, in company with most airlines, had a ban on its pilots flying for other companies for hire and reward. In order to get round this Tony Mack senior kindly made me a non-executive director of the company and this proved quite acceptable to BEA. I suppose that this really meant that I was working for my own private company as it were and lots of other pilots had similar schemes, some were farmers, some had small businesses which they ran with their wives, anyway it made life a lot easier from a legal point of view and BEA were quite happy with this arrangement. Of course I had to be careful not to overstep the CAA regulations as to flying and duty hours and I therefore kept a tally of my flying in both companies for inspection by their inspectors. This arrangement worked very well. In what spare time remained I maintained my flying at Booker instructing on the Cherokees and other aircraft right through to my compulsory retirement at 55. I was a busy little lad!

Gatwick at this time was not as busy as it is today and the company was able to do training sessions on the ILS and NDB's and also short instrument rating type cross-countries radiating from Gatwick often to Seaford and then back to the Mayfield non-directional beacon and then into Gatwick itself. We accepted the fact of course; that schedule airliners had right of way so to speak and quite often we were shunted off into a holding pattern somewhere. But this was good training for our students anyway. We also flew to Stansted, which was really at that time a training airfield and performed our cross-countries and letdowns with our students all day long if necessary. In a typical day we would take off with 3 students, flying right through the morning, land for lunch at either Gatwick or Stansted and continue on in the afternoon and early evening returning to Gatwick later: we had a backlog of students waiting for Instrument Ratings. However the examiners at Stansted with the Civil Aviation Flying Unit (CAFU) had a rule that one examiner would only do two students a day, that was one in the morning and one in the evening and nothing would budge them from this procedure. Additionally they had Monday mornings and Friday afternoons off for travelling to and from work! Occasionally we were fortunate and were able to persuade an examiner to come down to Gatwick for a week to ease our backlog but unfortunately the same rule prevailed, one examination in the morning and one in the evening. It is indeed hard to change the ways of Civil Servants. On the actual test, if the examiner was qualified on the type of aeroplane, he would sit in the right hand seat, otherwise we would sit next to the student whilst he did his flying test to keep a look out. At no time were we ever allowed to assist him for this was a test for single pilot operation and the student was expected to fly the aeroplane, to navigate it, do the R.T. (Radio) and generally manage the flight on his own. And this of course is the typical routine for any air taxi pilot on a light twin. It was interesting work and I thoroughly enjoyed it, I had a whole variety of students, a lot of ex-service people and a lot of students who had come up the hard way, getting their PPL's and doing some instruction at flying clubs building up the hours towards a commercial licence. It did have its lighter moments. On one occasion I had a Naval pilot and I had been flying with him in the Gatwick area when Tony Mack recalled us back to the general aviation terminal; he had a charter to go to Geneva. Since it was early in the day he suggested I do it and take the Naval pilot with me for some free flying to which he readily agreed. The passenger was a Mr. Maimone and two ladies; he called himself a film director. We took off in the afternoon for Geneva with the Naval pilot doing the flying and about somewhere over the French coast this gentleman, our passenger, came up the front and put his face close to my ear and said "I have just sold 200 taxis to the Emperor of Ethiopia". I thought, good heavens I don't think there is more than 10 miles of road in Ethiopia, however I went along with this. He said "yes, and I am also a pilot" at which point the Navy pilot turned to me and gave me a very funny look. "Yes", said our passenger "and I would like to fly the aeroplane if you would kindly vacate your seat". Well the upshot of it was that he did not fly the aeroplane but I was very thankful to have this very burly matelot next to me because otherwise things might have got very strange. I dropped him off in Geneva, I said I would wait the requisite time that we agreed, 3 hours, and if he did not turn up then I should be faced with a night stop and he would have come back the next day. Needless to say he turned up 4 hours later and we night-stopped, he was not a very happy chap. We returned to Gatwick the next day and I thought no more about it. It was in 1978 I think that Joyce Mack came into the office and said "look who is on the front page of the newspaper" we looked and it was Mr. Maimone, he was pictured standing in the passenger entrance of an aeroplane at Rome Ciampino airport, in his hand he had a cigar box which he claimed was a bomb. Having frightened the passengers rigid all the way down from Zurich where the aeroplane had originated, he now said that he was the Son of God and demanded to see the Pope, the Italian Carabinier had other ideas – I don't know what happened to him.

In early '71 we flew several pop groups, Status Quo I think was one but the one I remember better than the others was the Small Faces run by Rod Stewart. We took them to several places in the Continent and the pilots job was always to count the money that they had been given for their nights effort and to work out the exchange rate to make sure that they had not been diddled by whoever had hired them. They were a fun bunch to fly

Without wishing to name drop but over the years I flew a lot of interesting people, Walter Kronkite for one whom came up and sat beside me and chatted all the way from Manchester to London, a real gentleman. Other gentleman of course was Henry Cooper. Another customer was Barry Sheene: the motor cycle ace. Barry was rather prone to accidents and I think he had had nearly every bone in his body repaired at sometime or another. He used to live at Charlwood. On one occasion I took him to Brussels to have an arm repaired, I waited for him for about a couple of hours whilst he saw his favourite surgeon and he returned with this arm in a cast at a peculiar angle so I said to him "that's a bit odd isn't it, haven't you got a sling for it" he said "Oh no, no, I need it this way as I am riding tomorrow". Eventually Barry bought a helicopter and taught himself to fly, unfortunately his neighbours in Charlwood got upset so he said, "enough is enough" and went to Australia. On another occasion I was summoned to go to Exeter to pick up a Roger Whittaker. I had never heard of him but my daughter had and asked me to get his autograph. Anyway I trundled down in the Navajo to Exeter, went into the airport building and sure enough there was this rather smart gentleman in a suit carrying a guitar. I went up to him and I said "good morning Mr. Whittaker, I am from Air London and I am here to take you to Manchester" this chap looked at me and said "no, this is Mr. Whittaker" pointing to a small man in faded jeans, T-shirt and a rather unkempt beard. He had a baleful look in his eyes; I had obviously said the wrong thing. Anyway, I took them to Manchester, Roger Whittaker never said a word but just glared at me and I never got his autograph for my daughter.

Towards the end of 1971 the air taxi market was beginning to boom and we took onboard several pilots from the Hamble College of Training. These unfortunate chaps had been promised a job with BOAC or British Airways as it was then I believe, but unfortunately had no vacancies and although BA honoured their training costs they were left without a job so we took about 4or 5 of them and jolly good chaps they were too. Without exception they all did well once they had left us 5 or 6 years later. One is now a Senior Training Captain with Cathay Pacific another runs a small Jet Fleet on behalf of a major company in America and all to a man have said to me, you know we really enjoyed our time with Air London, which was nice. But of course, air taxi flying is probably the best training in the world for your average airline pilot. He has to be resourceful, he has to be the pilot, the navigator, the engineer, and the steward, and he has to clean the aeroplane, keep the passengers happy, and carry their bags at the end of the trip from the aircraft to the terminal. I think we all enjoyed it, I know I certainly did and I would not have missed it for the world.

By the middle of 1971 the company had sold most of the Beagles apart from one, GATHO. This one was privately owned and when the owners were not using it, it became available to the company. We kept instrument-rating training going on this aeroplane but gradually we re-equipped with Aztecs and twin Comanches and it was this type that became the primary instrument rating aircraft. The owners of GATHO had properties near Alicante and we did frequent trips down there taking them on visits. These were always welcome, the owners were nice people and the flying was different. We routed through Bordeaux, refuelled then round Prepignon to Alicante having to avoid the Pyrenees because the Beagle 206's single engine performance was too low. We stayed with Aztecs and twin Comanches until about the end of '78 as I remember when we acquired a Navajo to operate on behalf of a customer and another one which we leased ourselves and these were both Navajo Chieftains. The Chieftain was more economical to operate than the Beagle 206, it weighed 500lbs less (all up weight of 7,000lbs) it was faster by about 25 knots, it could carry seven or eight people against the Beagles five and it had a much better endurance, an all together more economical and viable aeroplane.

That year we gave a job to a pilot called Andrew, I took this young man one evening to Stavanger in Norway using, the Beagle, it was a 3 hour and 55 minute flight. I left Gatwick at about 4 o'clock in the afternoon. Returning the same night, we were about half way across the North Sea at 1.00 o'clock in the morning when young Andrew said to me "'ere what are we doing flying at this time of night, I should be in bed!" so I said "well, I think you will find things in the air taxi world are somewhat different to that that you have been used to". We had at that time, a contract to take a customer to Dublin about once every ten days over a period of 2 or 3 weeks. This was a nice run and we had a night stop in Dublin. On one of these Andrew who had been checked out in the Beagle and had taken our customer there. While he was on his stopover he had bought himself a long black leather coat, almost ankle length, reminiscent of the style the Gestapo seemed to favour during the war. Unfortunately he couldn't bring it back because it needed a slight alteration so on the next trip he asked me to collect it. There were just a few snags attached to this. He had forgotten the name of the shop, the name of the street and would I pay the money, and he would pay me back on return. I set off for Dublin, dropped my passenger off, checked into the hotel and went on a search for this coat which took me the whole afternoon and evening. I eventually located it, paid the bill and brought it home the next day. The only thing Andrew could say to me (not a word of thanks of course) was "60 quid, I could have paid less for it here"! Anyway he thought this coat was snazzy, so Snaz became his name.

Sometime in 1972 in the spring I believe there was an air Traffic Control strike in France which prohibited virtually any aircraft on instrument flight plans of crossing that country. I took 2 weeks leave from BEA and we were able to take full advantage of the strike flying

VFR across France to destinations such as Geneva, Zurich and the South of France. I think I went to Zurich at least 3 times that week and Geneva once. The weather was absolutely glorious. Young Andrew however had been given a trip to Paris which was foggy for most of that time, in fact the whole of the Seine Valley remained fairly misty for nearly a week. Snaz, not being able to get into Paris decided to divert to Jersey which he did and the following day he had another go at Paris and again failed because of the fog and returned to Jersey again. On the third attempt he managed to get in and then returned to Gatwick empty having probably spent all the company's profits on futile attempts to land. After this he left our employment. It was many months later when his name came up again, only this time it had nothing to do with aviation. It was all tied up with the Jeremy Thorpe case, and Mr Thorpe's involvement with a friend called Scott in Devon. Snaz had killed Mr Scott's dog. I don't recall the ins and outs of the case but I do know that Snaz went to jail, for two years I believe, from where we had frequent extraordinary letters on notepaper headed 'HM Prison Pentonville'. After this episode we lost track of him.

We had an agreement with CBS news, that should they require an aeroplane at short notice, either to transport their representatives or as a camera ship, we would endeavour to provide one. With CBS I covered two of the Tall Ship races which was tremendous fun and once the Fastnet Race. The most interesting one I did with them was the Echo Fisk Oil Rig Blow-out in the North Sea in April 1977. We had an Aztec with tip-tanks which gave it a very good range and I used this aeroplane for the charter. I flew from Biggin to Heathrow early one morning to pick up two cameramen plus an announcer, and we flew to Edinburgh. I did not know quite where Echo Fisk Oil Field was but I had been led to believe by CBS that it was some 50 miles to the east of St. Abbs Head. However, I realised when I got to Edinburgh that it was more like 190 miles east of St. Abbs Head and how on earth was I going to find it without any aids. However, we set off and climbed up to 7000ft, I had got a good wind from the Met Office, and set course from St. Abbs Head VOR on track for the field. I timed it as carefully as I could letting down about an hour and forty minutes later through eight-eights of strata cu. Breaking cloud at 2000 feet to my astonishment I saw that the rig was about 8 miles just left of the nose. The CBS people thought it was a miracle; I knew damn well it was a miracle, we had about 10 minutes of fuel to do a few circuits and take our pictures before we had to climb up and return to Edinburgh. By this time it was getting dark and I was nearing the end of my duty and flight time limitations. However, they desperately wanted to get back to London to send the pictures off to New York so having refuelled and a quick sandwich we set off for Heathrow where I had dropped them, and then pressed on to Biggin Hill and parked the aeroplane. I thought "oh my God, how am I going to talk my way out of this" because I had exceeded my duty time limitations by actual flying time. Anyway, I made a clean breast of things in a letter to the CAA and sure enough back came a rocket in no uncertain terms and quite right too. However, our inspector, Tony Trowbridge, who had initiated this missive had written in pencil at the bottom, he said "sorry Ken but had to say something!" There was indeed humanity in the CAA after all.

We also did a lot of transporting of Jockeys and their equipment to the various race tracks, Newmarket for one comes to mind and on one occasion I took the owner of a horse and his wife and a jockey plus saddles and things that jockeys have, to Newmarket. I waited until the end of the racing and then got into the aeroplane, tidied it up and waited for the passengers to come back. First in sight were the owner and his wife obviously incredibly angry; behind them tottered a pile of saddles and other bits and pieces supported by two little thin legs of the jockey. He had lost all his races. There was a most unhappy atmosphere in the aeroplane all the way back to Gatwick. On another occasion I sent one of our other pilots, one Giles to go in my place to Doncaster. He took a twin Comanche, there were only three passengers and this particular aeroplane was a four seater. So the owner and his wife sat behind and his companion sat next to Giles. All went well, he got them to Newmarket on time and they did very well at the races, returning to the aeroplane with a couple of bottles of champagne. Giles took off. It was a nice day so they flew at about 2,000 feet. They had been airborne for about half an hour when Giles felt a thump on his right shoulder, he found himself supporting the ladies left leg. Where the other leg went he declined to find out, but in the back the owner and his wife were having a rare old time. Giles was a bit horrified apparently and he looked at his companion in the right seat and said "what do we do" and he said "nothing of course". Anyway, Giles got to Gatwick and came to see me straight away, he was apparently still horrified at this performance, I suggested that it was unique and that he should approach the Guinness Book of Records. "After all" I said "the owner cannot aspire to the 'mile high club' but in a four seat twin Comanche that must at least merit a record of some kind". Giles did not agree and left the company.

Some time in 1975 we got a contract to fly Farnborough Scientists to Warton on a twice a week basis. Warton, of course, had been the home of many famous aircraft, Canberra, TSR2, Tornado and Jaguar to name but a few. The former Chief Test Pilot, Wing Commander 'Bee' Beaumont, was the Operations Director. Apart from his fame as a Test Pilot Bee had had a full and exciting war both in the operational field and Test flying types like the Typhoon. He was a man that had earned the respect of friend and foe alike. I was fortunate many years later to chat to him at Duxford on several occasions and I am so glad to have been able to get to know a small part of him. Anyway, this contract was quite lucrative and it gave us a day at Warton which was always interesting. I remember one afternoon sitting in the crew room and Bee came in and asked if anyone had flown a Varsity so I rashly said "yes, I have." He said "right, outside, get into our Varsity taxi it over the other side of the airfield for some engine runs for the CAA, if you don't mind that is" and I said "no of course not" and as I walked out to the aeroplane I realised that it was 20 years since I had seen a Varsity and I struggled in my mind as I got in as to how the hell you started it. But sitting down in the cockpit the drill came back very quickly and I got the thing started and we taxied out and did our engines run and Bee was very grateful.

They say that the aviation world is a small one; if that is the case then the Air Taxi world is even smaller! Everyone seems to know everyone else. I went into the office one day to find someone called Doug standing there whom I vaguely recognised, it took me a little while but I suddenly realised he was the pilot of the Catalina that did the weekly round-the-Islands flying from Tahiti and I had last seen him in Bora Bora in 1956. He came over here a couple of years running to renew his British Licence and Instrument rating. I envied him returning to that beautiful part of the world but I remember him saying that the building of the airport at Papeete would open the floodgates to tourists and the idyllic island life as he knew it would be lost for ever. How right he was. The reader must now realise that one of the main attractions of this sort of flying was the variety of passengers one carried, apart from the enormous satisfaction one gets from flying and managing every detail of a flight oneself. Many a time I thought of throwing away an airline career but the timely and sound advice from Tony Mack Senior assured me that if I did he would fire me on the spot! "Air Taxis", he said do not pay your mortgage!

In April a lady called Anne Lloyd-Bostock joined us, she had a commercial licence and instrument rating and had done some twin flying with a small company up North. Anyway, I did a check ride with her and she was very good indeed so we immediately put her to work and she proved a great asset to the company. If one could be critical, the habit of hanging her handbag on the mixture controls could be a little upsetting. She stayed with us quite a while and eventually joined British Caledonian. When she went to the interview for Calie, they asked her which type she would like to fly and she said "the 111" and apparently the interview board shook its head and said "that is a very complicated aeroplane" to which she replied, "I know, I have just passed the A.R.B. Technical" which rather floored them. Anyway, I believe she stayed with Caledonian quite a long time and became a Captain.

Most of the time that I was with Air London our headquarters were in the old terminal building, the Beehive, which I am glad to say, is now a listed building. Our offices were in the original kitchen and believe it or not but in the corner there stood the dumb waiter, still serviceable with access to the Restaurant over our heads. We had a small ops room, an alcove for the accounts and another much larger room in which we had two link trainers run by Mr. Robin Wheatley an ex-pilot of great age and skill and it was here that we used to get our students to practice let-downs for instrument ratings. These were the original D4 links quite a relic even in those days. I think what I remember most about the company was that everybody mucked in together and nothing was ever too much trouble, every body was willing to do anything and it made for a very happy atmosphere.

One day a trip came up to Tarbes to take pilot, co-pilot, and flight engineer of a 707 for American Airlines, where one of their aircraft had gone unserviceable. Now I knew Tarbes very well for it was a place we visited quite frequently flying Comets taking pilgrims to Lourdes. Anyway, I set off with this crew of three, I think it was in a Beagle 206, eventually landed at Tarbes and got a taxi into Lourdes where we night-stopped and met the other crew that had brought the 707 in. After quite a convivial evening at about 9 o'clock the Captain that I had brought down said, "well now is the time to suss out a night club" and I said "you have got to be joking, this is Lourdes" and he said "there isn't a place in Europe that hasn't got a night-club". Anyway, we set out that evening down the dark streets and believe me in Lourdes at night there is not a chink of light to be seen anywhere, everything is shuttered, it is black, very black indeed. I have never seen a more despondent bunch of people in all my life, than that crew! A more convivial destination was Cognac and here we took wine and brandy importers for frequent visits to the distillery of Monsieur Henri Martell. It was usually a weekend trip out on the Friday night and back on the Sunday afternoon and Monsieur Martell looked after us exceedingly well. Apart from the hospitality it was interesting to go round the distillery and see just how brandy was made.

From about 1976 onwards I made an arrangement with Tony Mack that I thought would suit us both. I would get "paid" in flying time by this I mean when I had accumulated enough cash owing to me I would hire out the Aztec and take friends or relatives off to Deauville or Le Touqet for lunch. This worked very well for the company and for me, I was able to take my wife on a couple of occasions for the weekend to Le Touquet. I also took my next door neighbour, one Bill James DFC. Bill had been a Mosquito pilot during the war and had had a pretty adventurous time. After the war he joined the Foreign Office and became the first Governor of Christmas Island, that's the one in the Indian Ocean. Years later when I was in Brunei; he wrote and told me he was visiting Christmas Island at the invitation of the present Governor. Royal Brunei that year had a contract for flying once a week from Singapore to Christmas Island so I arranged to do the trip with Bill and his wife Janet onboard. Bill unfortunately had mislaid his passport and there was quite an upheaval at the Island airport while the Aussie customs authorities and immigration authorities haggled as to whether a) he shouldn't be sent back to Singapore or b) be put in jail or c) just allowed to come in for the week. Eventually sanity prevailed and they let him in.

One of my last trips with Air London of any note was in 1981 when a colleague and friend Peter Westbury and I took our Navajo to Shannon with a greyhound on board called "High-Flight". From Shannon we were to fly to a small strip about 20 miles away, the home of a well known horse breeder. I had phoned this gentleman up before leaving Gatwick and found out that the strip consisted of a runway of about 800 yards, which was fine for us. When I got overhead of the strip I realised that what he called a landing strip was in fact a small tarmac road. Anyway, it happened to be into wind so I landed on it. The wheels of the Navajo have quite a wide track and I think we had about two feet to spare each side. I stopped and we parked and got out and I said to the owner "not much of a runway is it" he said "no, everyone else uses the grass!" oh well! Anyway, the dog was looked at by a vet for about an hour. Then vet and greyhound came back to the aeroplane, we got on board, fired up, back to Shannon, cleared customs, back to Gatwick. The handler was full of praises for the dog and promised that it was going to win at Harringay that night and beat all odds and make a lot of money. This got round the General Aviation Terminal and other places at Gatwick and we all foolishly put cash on it (there is a moral here) - the only dog it beat was one that fell over at the gate exiting onto the racetrack. I kept clear of the GAT for some time after that!

High Flight.

Before I finally leave the air taxi world I must mention that another of its problems is the lack of utilisation of aircraft, at times. However, the staff at Air London were expert at integrating charters and very often I would set off for Farnborough and then Warton and having dropped my passengers off there go off and do another three or four sector charter to get back hopefully in time to Warton and refuel before my original customers were ready to return to Farnborough. I did this on several occasions and more by luck than good judgement it all seemed to work out.

In 1983 we started to sell or return aircraft to leasors. We retained an Aztec (GPIED) which was owned by the company until November. I did my last Airtours 737 flight on 19th September, the 20th being my 55th birthday! I spent the last few weeks of September and October enjoying the saved up fruits of my labours taking family and friends on sorties to Le Touquet. Le Touquet particularly intrigued my children because the railway ran right across the airfield onto the aircraft parking ramp. Plane to train and Paris but a few steps away! As a parting present Anthony "gave" me the Aztec to fly to Guernsey (where the fog rolls across the airfield at 40kts!) with my wife to visit Tony Morgan, who had been with me in Khartoum with <u>that</u> Beverley. This would be our first meeting since 1959.

Now it is time to return to BEA!

13. Comets

I started the Airtours Comet ground school (2nd course) at Heston in January, completing the Simulator and ARB examinations in March and moved forthwith to Gatwick. I think I was the only one in the company who could say he had flown in and out of there in the late thirties (passenger) and also in the early fifties! There had been many changes; the race course had gone replaced by a new Terminal Building and of course the New Brighton Road now isolated the "Beehive" of 1936 from the main airfield.

The new crews were soon on their way to Prestwick, still in the depths of winter, for base training which proved a very pleasant experience. I think everyone liked the Comet despite it's' unfortunate early history: the Mk IV was a very different kind from the early marks. However, cockpit heating still posed a problem: the flight deck floor being the pressure hull over the nose-wheel bay so electrical "tootsy-pads" were fitted to prevent frost-bite of ones feet. The passengers sitting over the centre section also had a similar problem: their floor was also the pressure hull.

After flying the KC-135 I found the Comet pretty ancient in technological terms (as had been the Britannia!). The flying controls were, of course, hydraulically powered but the rest of the equipment was operated by what was known in those days, "as a suitable system of wheels, bell-cranks and levers"! The elevator trim wheels for instance were massive cast alloy affairs. The third pilot sat facing the starboard side (poor-mans flight engineer) looking at the large electrical and fuel control panels below which was a long array of levers that would not have been out of place in a railway signal box! But it all worked, and worked extremely well, except for a few quirks, mainly in the air conditioning and pressurisation systems. There were two air-conditioning "packs" under the fuselage flour, one near the leading edge of the wing and the other about fifteen feet further aft. Incorporated in the system was a humidifier which although made breathing more pleasant (unlike modern day aircraft), caused severe condensation when descending to warmer layers and this combined with the fumes (and nicotine) of cigarette smokers, caused havoc with the discharge valves: - one sight of a nicotine gummed-up valve would put you off smoking for life! It was not uncommon to have to manually shut off in-operative rear pack valves in order to bring the single emergency one into play in the front pack. To locate the valve one counted the number of windows and having arrived at the "right" one, looked down for the tell-tale join in the floor carpet which indicated the hidden pack cover. However, no one seemed to have explained the importance of all this to the aircraft furnishers and cleaners for many is the time I have grovelled on the floor at a passengers feet looking for the missing join muttering "it must be here somewhere"! Small electrical faults also required descending into the electrical bay under the galley floor, (sometimes induced by spillages). Care had to be taken in this bay as one pilot found out. Squatting down and trying to rectify a fault he lost his balance, his rear end made contact with some live terminals via the coins in his hip pocket, and he shot out of the hole with a wild shriek! Could have been worse!

Handling the aeroplane was a delight and it was probably one of the easiest to land with the huge flaps creating a cushion of air when but a foot or two off the ground, ensuring a really smooth touchdown. With the engines so close inboard an engine failure on take-off was easily controlled: pilots who had spent several years on Comets and then went onto 707's noticed the difference! I remember returning to Gatwick at the end of Base flying and thinking this is a big improvement on the Argosy! Within two days I was earning my keep again.

A lot of early charters were, of course, to Palma and the resorts on the southern Spanish coast. It was a time of transformation for this part of the world; that lovely coastline was steadily being transformed into the concrete jungle that now stretches from Gerona to Gibraltar. Gradually we went further afield and with the Comets' excellent range Israel in one hop was no problem. We had a spate, a short one thank heavens, of flying National Union of Student charters to Tel Aviv. In the past I had flown all sorts of odorous cargoes: horses, dogs, on one occasion Rhesus monkeys, but nothing prepared me for cabins full of the recipients of higher education whom we dubbed the "Great Unwashed", and for their bizarre and at times anti-social behaviour. Still, compared to some modern day travellers they were angelic! The company once inflicted upon us a week of football supporter charters to Milan, after which the Cabin Crew rebelled and quite rightly too; I don't think we ever did this work again. It says much for our Management that they would always listen to our views in those early days. In return I think we gave a fair days work and this good relationship was still there when I retired in 1983. It says much for all the staff that we still have well attended get-togethers at Christmas.

Talking of Christmas reminds me of food, airline food and in particular crew in-flight food. BEA had always fed us extremely well and on the Argosy the top of the range meals were the delicious Scandinavian open sandwiches out of Stockholm, hot meals out of Heathrow on our many night freighter runs and Greek delicacies from Athens, all accompanied, of course, by the famous Cheeseboard, the contents of which BEA can be justly proud. It is said that some Captains briefed a crewmember, when discussing ditching and crash-landing procedures, to be solely responsible for rescuing the Cheeseboard while others gathered the emergency radio, and life jackets etc. After experiencing in my Service flying the infamous Habbaniya meat pie as previously described, I thought I was in heaven as an increase in body weight confirmed.

It was a rude shock to all of us when the first Airtours lunch box was sampled. Hard-boiled eggs were back, covered in mayonnaise (?). The strange thing about these was that they were rectangular. Thinking about animal cruelty led me to the Catering Manager who allayed my fears. "No"! he said "the yolks and whites are separated, cooked, and then moulded into foot long hard boiled eggs". How exactly this was achieved was apparently a trade secret, but at least the chickens had not been harmed. The eggs were usually served with a concoction described as Quiche Lorraine, which was promptly renamed by Tim, an old friend, as PTV and I leave the reader to decipher that one! Tim, by the way, had been lucky and had joined Airtours directly from the RAF, where he had incurred the displeasure of his squadron commander by running off with his wife. When the meal was "afternoon tea" the mainstay was a brace of Lardy Cakes soon dubbed by Tim as Blue Bottle Buns (BBB). They were not popular, but we did have one stewardess who would collect uneaten cakes from our meal boxes (passengers and crew) for her horse. What effect it had on the horse I do not know. Things did improve and everyone appreciated the need to keep costs down, but we did miss that Cheeseboard!

In early 1971 we started to visit the Canary Islands, especially Tenerife: this was the old Santa Cruz airport on the north coast, sited on the side of a hill at an elevation of some 1800ft. Here, one could land in clear weather and by the time you had turned round at the end of the runway you would be enveloped in sea mist! Part of the taxiway on the coastal side had suffered from subsidence so taxiing for take-off on the westerly runway one had to leave the taxiway and enter the runway, back-track for several hundred feet and then rejoin the taxiway – often in fog or mist. It was an accident waiting to happen and happen it did in 1977 when two 747's collided head on with a huge loss of life. Eventually a new airport was built on the south coast but this, too, was not without its problems. Getting to the Canaries involved an over water leg from Lisbon of some 750nm and to keep on track we enlisted the help of the early wartime radio aid "CONSUL", using the Seville transmitter to maintain track. It was interesting to see then on visits to Las Palmas that the Spanish Air Force still had some ME 109's and Heinkel 111's – all powered with Rolls Royce Merlins! It was here that the makers of the film "Battle of Britain" (1969) came for their aircraft. On one trip we had to bring back a coffin (occupied): an elderly man had suffered a fatal heart attack. Try as we might there was no way that the rather large box was going to negotiate the Comets' small luggage hold doors, so it would have to go in the Dome Freight hold. This was a 135 cubic foot space between the rear pressure bulkhead and the passenger cabin. It had it's own door so there was no access problem. However, in the limited floor space available it would have to be secured more or less on end and long did the argument rage if "he" should be standing on his feet or his head! Just as the Spanish loaders got it half way in, there was a thump from inside the box – the loaders fled and it was left to us pilots to finish the job!

Our offices and hangars at Gatwick were on the south side of the airport in what had once been the area of the pre-war airfield. We had one very large hangar and a two-story office block. The lower regions housed the Engineering and Operations, and the crew reporting room. Upstairs were the offices of those who managed us and a large crew room. The company arranged this room to accommodate both cabin staff and flight crew and equipped it very comfortably with a TV set, arm chairs and tea bar. To ex-service types like myself it was rather like a Squadron crew room, but to some of our more Senior Captains (and First Officers) this was heresy! Cabin staff and flight crew had never been accommodated in this manner and one must remember in BOAC at this time it was customary for Captains to be accommodated in separate hotels away from their crews! By and large most of our senior gentlemen eventually accepted the arrangements: it made for a very happy atmosphere. Which reminds me that one day at about noon, two men in white coats waving a piece of paper said they had come for the TV set to exchange it for a larger model. They duly took it and were never seen again – neither was the TV set!

One evening in 1971 Barnes Wallis was due to give a lecture to the Gatwick branch of the Royal Aeronautical Society. Such was the interest that this generated that it was held, I think, in a hangar and the doors thrown open to all for a couple of pounds apiece. The talk was supposed to last an hour, three hours later he was still there! He dealt with the famous Dams raid bomb as well as the swing-wing designs he was working on at the time. It was without doubt one of the most memorable talks I have ever listened to.

The early seventies were plagued with air traffic control delays, the French, I believe, being pretty upset at being left out of the holiday destinations which now seemed mainly in Spain and the Med. They caused huge delays in "working to rule" – so what else is new! Operators of BAC 111 and other similar types had a hard time of it but with the Comet we could go out to sea and avoid French airspace though this was expensive on fuel – even then, it was not uncommon to have a six-hour delay in Palma!

One of the nice things about aviation in the seventies was that it was still full of real characters – mostly ex-wartime people. I frequently flew with a Captain called Panda Watson, always an enjoyable experience with a fund of stories of his time on Lancasters. He was a real gentleman and never failed to ask the First Officer which leg he would like to fly, a habit I later kept-up. If the First Officer was flying no sooner had the gear been retracted when Panda would extract the Times Crossword from his briefcase and invariably had it finished at top of climb some thirty minutes later. One day someone fished his crossword out of his briefcase to find that it had been duly completed but in utter gibberish! Panda merely smiled! Another Captain I remember well was called John. We were about the same age (Forty-ish) and he had been in the RAF on an eight-year short service commission; we got on well together. When he joined Airtours one could not but notice that he was completely bald (he told me that this made wearing a bone-dome flying Meteors very uncomfortable). One day he turned up for work with a new thatch, some unkind person referred to it as a rug. Flying that day, John left his seat to attend to the needs of nature, leaving his headset on the appropriate hook together with his rug. At this point a stewardess came on to the flight deck and gave a piercing shriek; I suppose she thought we had scalped old John; this of course brought more viewers to see John struggling to extract his thatch. He took it in good part!

One of my fellow new arrivals at Gatwick was a chap called Dennis. Dennis was an ex-Squadron Leader – a bit more up-market than us ex-Flying Officers and Flight Lieutenants, and inclined to be a bit pompous. On one of our trips together he crossed swords with Caroline, one of our stewardesses. Caroline was a true blue Cockney with all the sense of humour and fun that these people have, and a really nice person. She came into the flight deck to get orders for tea, coffee etc. Dennis was silent, sitting in the P3 seat on "the Panel". Caroline said "OK mate, what is it for you?" Dennis turned round and replied "you may call me Mr, or First Officer or Squadron Leader, but you may not call me Mate!" Caroline giggled "OK Mate, now we know - what do you want to drink"!

Anyway, Dennis was recently divorced too, and had bought a large Victorian house in South Holmwood, surrounded by National Trust land: it had at least seven bedrooms. These he rented out to Airtours staff and I gratefully accepted this offer to put a roof over my undeserving head. There were about five of us in this menage, "we" had our own small sitting room and shared the very large kitchen with Dennis. He, of course, had his own sitting room etc. downstairs and the master bedroom (en suite!) upstairs. When one realises that we all often worked at different times, day and night, the arrangements worked extremely smoothly. Dennis had priority in the kitchen (he was a really good cook) and "we" all followed suit. I must add that when Dennis entertained one of his girl friends we always had a pretty good idea who it would be. A top-notch young lady would be cooked Beef Bourguignonne the scale of food descending through less exotic menus to "bangers and mash"! Because Dennis and I were both in our forties some unkind person dubbed the house "Geriatric Towers"! I remained with Dennis for some five years before buying a small flat nearer to Gatwick. Lest the reader thinks I led a somewhat monastic life, one of our inmates in "the Towers" was an Airtours girl called Robina. We hit if off immediately and she became a very dear friend and constant companion: she was also a Cordon Bleu cook! Despite an age difference of 23 years we had a really good relationship but I guess I balked at taking the plunge again and making it more permanent; more fool me! So I eventually bought that flat and Bina found a small house near Holmwood. She later married and moved to New Zealand.

In that first year of operation the company obviously was prepared to accept anything that was on offer in the charter market, within reason – viz the football charters! One contract was a series of charters to Tarbes in France, flying pilgrims to Lourdes. A fair number of these passengers were severely disabled and we (and the Civil Aviation Authority) had to impose a maximum percentage of disabled people on each flight. The Comet had, by modern standards, very small passenger entrance doors and if I remember correctly, a pad had to be fitted to the top of each entrance when open to guard against head contact! The crew/galley access door on the starboard side of the nose was even smaller and required ducking quite low to avoid cranium damage. The entrance made access for the disabled very difficult indeed, even when using the Fork Lift Platforms that had to be used for wheelchair cases; the wheel chair remained outside. The chances in the event of an accident of evacuating such people in the statuary time (3 minutes comes to mind) would be impossible. This had to be made known to the passengers and I believe the Cabin crew were briefed that in the event of fire breaking out to get as many of the able bodied out first and then the disabled if possible. Looking back it was unfair on our crews to put them in this insidious position since we often had a dozen such passengers among our hundred on board. Over the last half century of flight a great many cabin crew have lost their lives in trying to rescue injured or disabled passengers. On the plus side the cheerfulness of these people is something I shall never forget, and not one on my few flights ever forgot to thank the girls for taking them!

I did several of these charters with a Captain called Ivor, who was easily recognisable as the only chap to go flying with a banana in one hand and a headset in the other, unlike the rest of us who invariably carried bulging briefcases full of non-essential items! Ivor was an enthusiastic rambler and towards the end of the Comet era we decided to go on a weeks walking in the Pennines. However, his wife insisted that he cut the grass before leaving and unfortunately lost some toes wrestling with his Flymo! I do recall one flight with him quite clearly. Halfway though the flight to Madrid a passenger became quite agitated at seeing a "snake on the wing"! I went back to calm her down and possibly remove her bottle of gin, on Ivor's instructions, to find an elderly lady staring out of the window. There was indeed a "snake on the wing"; a long grey line about two inches wide that started just outboard of the engines and ran to the tip, about a third of the way behind the leading edge. It moved continuously. Ivor came down and had a look, and we finally decided that it must be the boundary layer breaking away. We reduced speed a knot or two and it disappeared! I never got that walking holiday.

My first year on Comets was enlivened by experiencing two near misses. One was at Palma when Approach Control had two of us on finals for the same runway (in cloud) but on different radio frequencies. The first I saw of the other aircraft, also a Comet, was it's mainwheels above us as we broke cloud! The other was on a night take-off from Gatwick over the Dunsfold NDB. Over the beacon we heard for a few seconds the roar of engines underneath! It turned out to have been a VC-10. I remembered from my air refuelling days that one could just hear a B-52's engines when it was underneath ones tail and twenty-five feet lower. The VC-10's fin is about thirty-five feet high! I thought we deserved danger money!

The Comet era gradually drew to a close and the Company negotiated a deal with BOAC (now BA) for the purchase of seven Boeing 707-436's. My last Comet flight was to Faro and Alicante on 6th January 1973. And so ended the first phase of Airtours. It had been great fun flying for a brand new company; everyone from Management downwards wanted it to be a success and indeed it was. A lot of credit must go to Bill Bailey our first F.M. and to Peter J McKeown who later took over. 'PJ' was a bit like my old boss Bas Taylor of 53 Squadron, much liked, straight talking, and very much respected. He did us proud for a great many years.

14. Back to Boeings

By early January the 707 ground school was well under way at the British Airways Training Centre at Cranebank. It was there that I ran into Flint Poutney, who had been the Flight Engineer on my crew at St. Eval. The last time I had seen Flint was on 6th May 1959 when I flew an RAF GSA Skylark 3 from Dunsfold to St Mawgan for my declared goal diamond, during the run-up to the year's Gliding Championships at Lasham. Flint was the first person to greet me on landing. He was now one of the school's engineering instructors. My course did not start until late January and I see I spent the intervening three weeks busy flying students for Air London. During this period the first 707 arrived and I wanted to see how it compared to the KC-135, prior to starting ground school. I was sitting in the Captain's seat (a cardinal sin for a First Officer) when our Assistant Flight Manager came in and viewed me with considerable displeasure. He was known as the Red Baron only partly because of his red hair and had been in the Fleet Air Arm. I am sure he wanted to say "clear out FitzRoy" but he confined himself to asking when I was starting ground school! I could not resist it – I said "oh, I did mine thirteen years ago" and left. I think I got a zero for tact that day!

Anyway, we prepared for ground school, which for First Officers was extended to work for a Flight Engineers Licence and Flight Engineers Type rating in order to fulfil the CAA requirements. This was hard graft and I see that my Flight Engineers licence is numbered 1707. After operating the KC-135 with two pilots I thought that this really was an unnecessary piece of design. We completed our safety equipment and dinghy drills before leaving for Cranebank. I must say that dinghy drill with the cabin crew girls in a heated swimming pool was a great deal more enjoyable than the last drill I did, at Marham. There my Station Master decided (with a malicious smile) that since I flew a front line Bomber Command aircraft (Anson!), like the other (Valiant) pilots I should at least join them for some of their "activities". Believe me, sitting in a one-man dinghy six miles off Yarmouth in a howling January blizzard is not a load of laughs! And so I started my fourth type rating in the last five years, if I include the Britannia, where although the flying was done in the RAF the ground subjects were taken with the CAA at Redhill.

The course was run on a self-help basis. We were split up into groups of five and allocated a room with a slide projector. Each "lesson" (hydraulics, electric's etc) was covered by a box of slides so we could set our own pace. There was always a "competent instructor" on hand to clarify anything. It worked well. After the Britannia and Comet the 707 was a relatively simple aeroplane – manual controls, well thought out fuel and electrical systems, in fact very similar, not surprisingly, to the KC-135. It was of course much longer, and had a greater wingspan, but the main difference was that it now had a 36" fin extension and a much needed powered rudder. Under the tail was a small fin which prevented over rotation on take-off: - the 135, I remember, was very critical in this area. It also had full leading edge flaps, wing and tail anti-ice heating, engine fire extinguishers AND thrust reversers on the engines, all a huge improvement over the KC-135. The 707-436 was build especially for BOAC and had R-R Conway engines giving 21000lbs. of thrust. My old KC-135 had J-47s giving 12000 lbs. and yet the maximum take-off weights were almost the same!! The 707 was probably, at the time, Boeing's best.

We took our ARB (Pilots) examinations and completed the simulator course. The Captains went off to fly and we were turned over to the tender mercies of the engineering staff to work up for our Flight Engineer Licences. Most of the instructors were excellent but there were one or two ex-Flight Engineers who were not happy with pilots taking over their jobs! I think they had a case in point; I never found out why the company did not employ Flight Engineers but I expect costs came into it somewhere. We took our exams and like a few others, I had to re-sit "electric's" with an oral examination conducted by the CAA Flight Engineer. Yes, I can safely say it was quite a grilling.

At the end they passed me and one said, "I see you flew Britannia's, how did you find the electric's on that?" "Complete mystery, old boy, " I replied "I relied on the Flight Engineer", and shot out of the room in case they changed their minds. Sometimes my tactlessness seems to get the better of me!

I started the type rating (1179) in early April by flying up to Prestwick with half a dozen other First Officers and a very senior training Captain long since departed this planet. It was still the days of "Seniority before anything else" in the training world, and this chap, with whom I later became great friends, had only just converted from Comets. Now one part of the 707 flight envelope where someone new to the aircraft could find problems, was flying with the wing flaps down in the approach configuration, prior to landing. I must elaborate on my earlier description of lateral control on cross-wind takeoffs so please bear with me. Each wing had a manually controlled inboard and outboard aileron, and four hydraulically powered spoilers for lateral control. The outboard ailerons (conventionally sited) came into play with 23° or more of flap. This then gave you two ailerons and four spoilers to help you lower / raise the wing, depending on how much control wheel movement you used. In flight roll rates of 35° per second in the approach configuration, and 45° per second during cruise could be obtained without control forces exceeding 40 pounds at the control wheel. Phew!! It follows that the unwary could over control this bird like no other! It was this unique system of lateral control that enabled a KC-135 of my old Squadron (after I had left) to land safely following a mid-air collision with a B-52 whilst refueling. The tanker lost its No.4 engine pod and ten feet of the outer wing (including the aileron), while the B-52 lost it's entire fin and rudder: what the bombers' tail gunner thought of it, history does not say! One is also reminded of Tex Johnston, Boeings Chief Test pilot who ably demonstrated the lateral control of the aircraft by rolling the prototype 707; to be recorded for posterity by the Flight Engineer on film, showing the port wing upside down over Lake Washington!

Anyway, one of our number sat in the co-pilots seat; I was on the "panel" (Flight Engineer) and the rest crowded round to hear a dissertation on over controlling, otherwise known as "wing walking"! On finals at Prestwick it was extremely gusty and our senior gent gave a really frightening demonstration of "wing walking" right to touchdown which was a cruncher! Silence. He parked the aeroplane, looked round and said, "that is not how to do it, I think we all have something to learn, especially me"! It takes a unique man and courage to admit fault in a situation like that. I never let on that I already had two years experience on the aircraft until we flew together on the line; for once I was tactful. I did impart to the other four trainees that to guarantee a soft landing one just had to ever-so-gently relax the back pressure on the control wheel (almost a feather-like nudge forward) when flaring on touch-down; this lowered the rate of descent of the mainwheels (miles behind you) resulting in a "smoothie"!

I see my first commercial flight was to Corfu on the 19th April, swiftly followed by one to Rhodes – the new airport by the sea, a big improvement on the old one in amongst the hills! The rest of 1973 was spent mainly on Inclusive Tour Operation to the Med. and Iberia, but towards the end of the year we had quite a few Far East Charters, through Dubai to Bangkok and Hong Kong, with reasonable stopovers in both cities. On one to Bangkok I crewed up with Arthur Summers, another First Officer. (Sorry, we were Senior First Officers by now!). Arthur's brother had been killed by the Japs whilst a Prisoner of War working on the infamous Burma-Siam railway. Arthur was younger and like me he had escaped the war. However, he had traveled extensively in his early life in various occupations before settling down(!) as an Airline pilot. There were few places in the world that I visited with Arthur whilst with Airtours, that he did not know someone, who invariably greeted him like a long lost soul!

On this Bangkok stop-over I decided to spend a couple of days up country by the River Kwai Yai at Kanchanburi, some three miles from Tamarkan where the bridges were built at great cost of life and human suffering. It is not well known that the route the railway took had been surveyed before the war by the British and judged as being impossible to build and operate. Anyway, I tried to persuade Arthur to come but he declined and that is when I learned of his brothers' fate. He did ask me, however, to see if I could find his brothers "grave" in the Kanchanburi Military Cemetery, and take a photo. Five of us left in a mini-bus reaching our destination in about four hours. It was a fascinating experience and whilst on the surviving steel bridge a logging train, pulled by one of the original engines (No 713), chugged slowly across. We spent the night in the Bridge Hotel, an erie experience in a place that had seen so much death. The next day I walked down the line to the cemetery with one of the cabin crew. We entered the cemetery, immaculately kept by the War Graves Commission, and tried to find a grave location plan but there was none. There are over 7,000 graves here in neat rows with several long access paths running at right angles to the main one from the entrance. I had a very strange feeling as we passed the rows of stones with their bronze plates giving the details of the dead, number, rank, name and unit. I stopped three rows from the end of the path, turned right and stopped again at the fourth plaque; it read: "J.H. Summers, Sherwood Foresters, 4th June 1945." My friend asked me how I knew where to go? I could not explain it, I was just certain it was there. He went quite pale, maybe I did too, and as I write nearly thirty years later, looking at the photograph I took at the time, I still get a very odd feeling. After much thought I decided not to tell Arthur, and now it is too late. He was, however, very grateful for the photos.

The mid seventies gave aviation a spate of hi-jacking, one of the most notorious being the three aircraft flown to Dawsons Field in the Jordanian desert and then blown up. Sussex Police, in 1975, put on a seminar at Slougham Manor, a Police Training School: all Aircrew and cabin crew at Gatwick were invited. The subject was hi-jacking: how to prevent it, how to cope when it had happened etc. Quite a number of our cabin crew went along but I am ashamed to say I was the only pilot. The lecture was very informative and we had some of the (anonymous) negotiators offer some good advice: I was appalled at the apathy shown by my colleagues. At this time the company encouraged crew to allow visits to the Flight deck by passengers, a practice I detested and it always bothered me to fly with Captains who seemed to enjoy an audience – maybe Freud might have something to say on this! It was a dangerous practice, in my opinion, and as passenger behavior became more violent and unpredictable as the years went by, it ceased. This is not the vehicle to argue the best means of preventing hi-jacking but I have to say, after a life-time in the air, that the determined hi-jacker will always be able to board his chosen aircraft and that the last line of defense (and very effective too) is the provision of armed guards. One might reflect that EL AL have done this for the last thirty years – their record speaks for itself. I have tried to argue my point through correspondence in various journals but to no avail; I am afraid my colleagues seem to be unable to accept that they are in the front line up there, whether they like it or not, and that in the post September 11th world, to be hi-jacked is almost certainly to die. I digress again!

In February 1974 the company negotiated with a German firm for three round-the-world charters. The same crew would do each charter there being ample time for crew rest at the various destinations. I got lucky and was ""elected" for one of them – as Flight Engineer – so now I can say I have been round the world sidesaddle.

We had a great crew Captained by one Mike Hood, shortly due to retire, Ken Byatt another Captain me as Flight Engineer come First Officer, and another First Officer whose name I cannot remember, who came as Navigator for the overseas sectors: In a short while the Company would purchase an Inertial Guidance System from Honeywell, but that was still a few months away. Our cabin crew were excellent and included the F.M's daughter! It had all the makings of a splendid month away from base and indeed it was probably the high spot of my time on the 707. We left Gatwick for Shiraz with some 170 German Tourists and two tour guides, both very presentable and female. I could see that our "Navigator" was smitten with one of them even before we crossed the French Coast. More later. Into Shiraz in the evening and two days of culture among the ancient ruins: I am afraid I stayed by the pool! Next stop was Delhi. Here we had two clear days off and to a man (and woman) plus Gerda, our Navigators "betrothed", we hired a large limousine and headed for Agra and the Taj Mahal. The Taj is without doubt one of the most wonderful buildings in the world; one gets a sense of awe when seeing it for the first time; similar to seeing the Grand Canyon from the edge. That great aviator Ernest K. Gann first saw it during the war, and I am sure he would not have minded me mentioning it here. Taking off from Agra in overloaded C-87 (converted Liberator bomber) at a ground temperature well over 100° F he soon discovered that the aircraft could not be coaxed above the trees! Staggering along a knot or two above the stall they had just got the gear up when the Taj filled the windscreen. Turning was not an option and they were well below the Dome! Yelling for "full flap" the aircraft ballooned up over the dome with a few feet to spare and mushed downwards towards the river and flat land beyond. Slowly they climbed away: in our world experience can often save your neck! In his book, a Hostage to Fortune, he says that the incident and its potentially catastrophic end haunted him for years. Anyway, we saw the magnificent Taj, looked round the fort at Agra and headed back for Delhi, the road often running parallel to the railway and a constant wonderful spectacle of huge steam locomotives thundering along! The only blot on this day was the awful sight of a "dancing" bear, which filled me with a strong desire to put a ring through the nose of its owner.

Next stop Bangkok for four days and the opportunity for a crew party. Since this is a tale of many experiences, warts and all, I have to say that my memory of this event is not very long. With the party well under way I was persuaded to show off my party piece: in those days I could put a tumbler of water on my forehead whilst standing and lie down (and get up) without using my hands, AND, without spilling a drop. This I succeeded in doing, Alan the CSO bet me I could not do it again! How right he was. I fell over, cracked my head on the floor and took no further interest. I awoke in my room, in bed the next morning wearing only a pair of ladies knickers and I have yet to find the owner. I never did that trick again! That morning we booked a beach house at Pataya Beach and most of us left that afternoon for two days of R&R. Pataya then was still relatively unspoilt and two days of swimming and delicious Thai food soon "mended" my near shattered skull!

To Hong Kong on 5th (night); the whole area was free of cloud and made an impressive sight flying down the IGS to runway 13. We only had thirty six hours here but time enough to visit my old friend Mr. Bill Hon of Princeton Tailors: an expensive visit in the end in the shape of two suits to be mailed later. I took most of the crew up to the Peak for lunch and for once the weather remained clear.

Then to Tokyo where we dropped our passengers and flew to Nagoya to park the aircraft and ourselves, there being no space (not enough money for parking fees?) available at Tokyo. We had two days here and took the opportunity to visit Kyoto, the old capital of Japan. On the way back on the "Bullet train" we nearly lost our number two Captain. The Bullet train, apart from being very fast, sticks to its schedule and that usually means no more than a minute at the most at intermediate stops. Ken was a little slow, the doors started to close, someone grabbed him from the platform and pulled him out just as the doors hissed shut! Tokyo was the next stop! Back at the hotel someone (and I blame the FM's daughter) rang our rooms at 6.00 p.m. and said "come as you are party, my room, now!" We were all dressed ready for dinner apart from one or two of the ladies and Mike our illustrious Captain, who, bless him, fell into the spirit of the occasion and rose from his bath and "clothed" himself with a large bath towel and set off for the floor below, like a Roman Senator in his toga, where the cabin staff had their rooms. Unfortunately, he got into the express lift and went from our 12th floor to the hotel foyer in a split second; there to be an object of much amusement and astonishment. We quickly rescued him at the request of the hotel Manager!

The next afternoon we flew back to Tokyo, picked up our passengers and made a night flight of eight hours to Honolulu. Here I met up with my old boss of the 904, now in his last posting prior to retirement, and spent many happy hours reminiscing. The next time I saw him was ten years later on a visit to Stuart, Florida where my cousin lives and heard her talking to him on the telephone – he lived in the same street! I took the crew to Hanuama Bay, a small extinct volcanic crater that is open to the sea, a delightful retreat. We toured round the Island which I remembered so well and of course visited the Arizona Memorial in Pearl Harbour. The bit that sticks most in my mind was the sight of the concrete jungle that now was Waikiki Beach complete with imported sand! But I am afraid this is the lot of so many beautiful places.

Two days later we were in San Francisco and here I parted company with the crew and visited old friends (mostly retired) from my Mather days. I even went up to the foothills of the Sierra Nevada to a place called El Dorado, an old gold mining town and a pub called Poor Reds. The owner remembered me (and our crew parties) and brewed up the establishment's famous tipple – a Golden Cadillac! I returned here in 1983 with my two daughters as part of a holiday in California. They were quite astounded that I and their mother were so well remembered in this den of iniquity!

The last stop was New York for a couple of clear days and I took the opportunity to visit my stepfather and my sister in Darien, Connecticut. The last evening the two tour guides (one still hotly pursued by the Navigator without success) put on a farewell dinner-dance in the hotel. The Navigator informed us that tonight was the night, and that his reward for investing a fair amount of time and cash in his lady's welfare would be his for the taking. We watched the pair dance round the floor so close that you could not have got a playing card between them – never mind a hand! He was all smiles, she looked demure. Next time round the floor they were at arms length and by the look on his face things were going very wrong. They stopped dancing and left the room. "Ah" we all cried! Ten minutes later the Nav was back looking as if his whole world had collapsed. We waited. "She's gone to phone her lover" he said "she showed me a photograph: about 40, heavily built and female!" There is a moral here, if I can find it! We returned to Gatwick on the 16th March, said goodbye to our passengers whom we had got to know quite well: handed over to another crew who took them to Frankfurt, and went home. It had been a really great trip, never to be repeated.

~ No Time on the Ground ~

A week off was our due, and then I did a couple of trips to Athens after which we heard the news that the company had negotiated a years contract with Syrian Arab Airlines based in Damascus – volunteers please! The deal was to do ten-to-fourteen day detachments in Damascus; the flying was going to be pretty intensive right up CAA limitations with usually a break of two or three days in the middle. We would have two aircraft allocated for this jolly; both painted in Syrian Arab colours, through we kept our British registration (in small letters) on the fuselage. Cabin staff would be all Syrian apart from the "chiefy" who would be Airtours. The whole crew would remain together.

So two weeks after our round the world I was off again with Commander Ken Byatt to Munich and then Damascus for my first flight. I looked forward to this contract and the opportunity to see a part of the world one would normally not see, the border tensions between Israel and Syria being pretty high at this time. I was not disappointed, Syria proved to be a fascinating country, and contrary to popular belief we found the Syrians particularly friendly. Our route network took in Teheran, Cairo – Tripoli, Doha – Abu Dhabi – Karachi returning through Dubai (Duty free booze stop!) and Dhahran. Jeddah – San'a was an interesting run, the Capital of Yemen being 7000 ASL which severely restricted our take-off weight. Unfortunately there was no chance to night-stop. During Ramadan we flew numerous Hadj flights to Jeddah, invariably at night. Jeddah airport at Ramadan is an extraordinary sight. Aircraft parked everywhere, long lines of disembarking pilgrims being escorted in "crocodiles" all over the airfield towards the terminal Buildings and then herded into busses. By dawn all was quiet—nothing moved! It was quite a lesson in moving people quickly and without a fuss.

That first flight into Damascus had been at night. The airport is some fourteen miles north of the city, in the desert. Approaches had to be made from the north (take-offs too, if possible) to avoid going too near the City and, of course, the 1974 "frontier" with Israel was but thirty five miles to the South West. The airport had two staggered runways with ILS/VOR, but no approach lighting, and the runway lights at night would only be switched on when you were about ten miles out! I guess they didn't want to attract too much attention! Being in the middle of the desert without any background lighting from towns, roads or villages, gave one the feeling of landing on an aircraft carrier. The lights went out soon after landing. At the time we thought all this a bit strange. However, the next morning I woke up in the airport hotel to the sound of thunder; odd, at this time of the year. Going up on the flat roof I found the crew watching Israeli jets rocketing (very accurately) a fuel dump some ten miles away! We were now; it seemed, in the front line! Hasty phone calls to the British Consulate assured us that this was normal and that we should not worry. The thought occurred in our minds that there might come a time when we would like to remove ourselves from the area – quickly. What did the Consulate suggest? We were given the phone number of a "reliable" taxi-firm which would drive us all to Beirut in the event of the Israeli army charging down from the Golan Heights! Our spokesman asked how the Embassy staff would leave in this emergency? No reply was forthcoming.

A few weeks later I got very friendly with the Douglas Aircraft Company representative and we would often meet for a meal in town. One evening we bumped into a couple of his buddies from the US Consulate and the subject of the outcome of Israeli – Syrian relations came up. They were much amused by the British Consuls' suggestions. Afterwards, one of them took me aside and said "here is a number, any trouble call it, someone will get you all out, and not via Beirut! Years later I learned that he was with the CIA at the time, and got caught up in the US Embassy hostage taking in Tehran, but managed to remain under cover!

On the subject of Beirut, I had a wonderful weekend there with my Douglas friend (on the company!). We drove from Damascus following the Barada River into the hills and then paralleling the railway from Damascus. On the steeper parts of the line it becomes a "cog" railway, like a Swiss Mountain line. Beirut was a great place at this time; we stayed at the Saint George, the city at night was a blaze of light and colour, small cafés and restaurants everywhere; soon to be reduced to rubble. On the drive back to Damascus my friend said, "we are being watched, the Israelis are all along these hills to the South!" I am glad we never had to avail ourselves of our British Consul's taxi-company! Come to think of it I have often wondered if being the Douglas Rep was my friends' only job in life?

Once we started flying it became obvious that the schedules had no slack built into them to counteract delays, and penalties for late arrivals were heavy. We provided our own engineering coverage at stops in the shape of the Flight Engineer (!) and did our own refuel-ing. The worst schedule was to Karachi through the Gulf States where I calculated we would have to fly at Mach 1.5 to maintain schedule! Someone at Gatwick had planned it very badly. The longer sectors were not so tight but a delay of 15 minutes on departure from base could rarely be made up en route. It was eventually sorted out with the Syrian authorities. The crews rotated back to the UK on the twice a week schedule to Europe through Rome, Munich and sometimes Paris. Which reminds me that I got home to Gatwick off one of these two-week detachments, to be accused of having a dead body in my car! Opening the boot I discovered a plastic bag containing very dead mincemeat and many live maggots, a left over from shopping – the 'pong' was unbelievable!

In between our Syrian trips work was mainly flying the "bucket and spade" runs to the Med and Spain, but gradually more interesting contracts came up, filling the gaps. Los Angeles via Ottawa and sometimes Bangor, Maine was one of them and on one of these my services as Flight Engineer were asked for to retrieve a lady's false teeth from the loo. I felt justified in declining! On the way back from LA one time we had Deanna Durbin's mother (shows my age) and her friend Edwina Mackenzie. Mrs Mackenzie had survived the sinking of the Titanic at the age of seven and her recall was brilliant. I spent nearly an hour chatting to her – oh for a pocket tape recorder! She died at 104 years of age. By and large I hate cities, London being at the top of the list, but Ottawa is a place I would willingly visit again and again. Our stopovers there were always enjoyable; I especially liked walking by the ten or so locks on the Rideau Canal – in summer! This lock system was the work of Colonel Bye, Royal Engineers, (Ottawa was once called Byetown), who later built the Royal Military Canal across the Romney Marshes in Kent, as a defence against a Napoleonic invasion.

I did another Damascus trip and took the opportunity to do some sightseeing. In the city I visited the Hedjaz railway station and was lucky to see a train pull out on a line that crossed a main road (no gates) and down another street which no doubt led on to the desert. The ancient tank engine was now fuelled by oil instead of wood but it's age and that of the four-wheel carriages were straight out of Lawrence's day and were probably ancient then! The street called Straight was a must and some excavation had gone down fifteen feet to the original roadbed, and of course the Kaysan Gate made famous by St. Paul. The Great Mosque was an impressive sight, with the Tomb of St. John the Baptist in the Prayer Hall; the whole floor being covered with magnificent carpets. But there were two places a friend told me to visit: one was the Crusader Castle I had seen from the air near Hamma from a Hastings twenty years previously; the famous Castle of the Kraks. The other was the village of Maloula and five of us set off in a Mini-Bus early one morning to see it. I wanted in particular to see the Church of St. Tekla which sits on a cliff above the village and is reached by a gorge barely a yard wide. Malaloula is one of the few places where the language of the Bible is still spoken – Aramaic. Disembarking we started up the gorge, passing numerous graves (empty) carved out of the rock. We could hear voices coming down from the top of the gorge a hundred or so feet above our heads. We reached the top at last in brilliant sunshine again and were met by the priest who I think was Greek Catholic. He gave us a fascinating tour of the ancient Church, remarking that the dome was so perfect it would require a computer to copy it today. Later we sat down in his sitting room and sampled the most delicious red wine that I have ever tasted; his home brew! We returned to our mini-bus having walked through the village below feeling that today we had experienced something special: and so to Damascus some thirty miles to the southwest. We all dined out in a really good French restaurant that evening, being careful to eat only well cooked food. Some, in the past, had been tempted to sample the delicious mezzes these places had to offer: twenty or so dishes of cold salads, meats etc. To do so could give you a bad case of Montezuma's revenge; I "caught" it once and it took me three weeks before I was judged free! In fact crews were issued on leaving Gatwick with a large jar of "Guanamycin", a powerful antibiotic which the Captain doled out to those suffering from complete evacuation of the bowels! It was rather like been given medicine at boarding school!

The next day we left our hotel at dawn, again in the mini-bus, for a four hour journey northwards to Homs and Hamma, there to visit the ancient and gigantic water-wheels, each wheel being some forty or fifty feet in diameter. Then on to (for me long awaited) the castle, the Krak des Chevalier. This castle was described by Lawrence as "the most admirable in the world" a big understatement. Started by the Crusaders in 1110 and constantly added to over the next hundred years, it survived four earthquakes and numerous sieges intact until the defenders were "persuaded" to leave in 1271. I know this narrative is supposed to be about my flying but this place was really something and deserves a mention. It is vast and could hold 4000 men; built within two concentric walls and two moats; it stands nearly 2000ft above sea level. The wooden roofs have all gone but what remains is simply an intact 900-year-old fortress. To walk through the stables and see the marks on the walls where the horses were tethered was truly an evocative experience. So was the sixteen hole loo (4000 ÷ 16 = ?)! The village below the walls once housed the servants and those who administered the castle, and to walk through the streets today one can still catch a glimpse of the odd fair-haired child with blue eyes!

The Tripoli trips were interesting, the more so for having the occasional night-stop in Cairo, in fact I spent Christmas '74 in Shepherds Hotel. On one trip as we were climbing out of Tripoli, a new First Officer thought he would exercise his Arabic: when he cleared with Tripoli Radio, he said goodbye with "Shalom Shalom! We rapidly increased speed eastwards! I did another run with an ex-Mosquito

Pathfinder Captain and another ex RAF, but more youthful (like me) chum, which has remained dormant in my memory for these last 29 years. Our turnarounds in Tripoli were always at night, I suppose Gadaffi did not want "us" spying on his missile sites! On this occasion, as was the norm, we had a Libyan soldier sitting in the Flight Deck keeping an eye on us! Eventually he got bored and went for a walk round the aircraft. One of the cleaners came in, closed the door and said in a very soft English voice, "are you chaps prepared to help me as I am in a bit of trouble – I must get out of here tonight". To me he looked like an Arab but he assured us he was not, "look", he said, "I can't tell you who I am or what I have been doing but it is important, not only for me, that I get out tonight". The three of us looked at each other and our Commander said "well"? We all agreed. I took him down to the lower 41 section (next to the nose wheel bay under the flight deck), and hid him right next to the radar scanner under the tyre covers, with instructions to stay there as we had Syrian Cabin Crew. The soldier came back, looked around and left, and our pulse rates returned to normal. We took off, hopefully with not too much unseemly haste. I got him out of the lower 41 for some tea and sandwiches with our Airtours "Chiefty" keeping an eye on the Cabin staff. "Thanks chaps" he said "when you get to Cairo I will remain hidden until after the passengers and staff have gone, try to keep the Syrian girls down the back. I will be met, don't worry and thanks again". At Cairo he was duly met by a car with dark windows and no doubt CD Plates, and with a quick smile he left. We all breathed a sigh of relief and felt not a little pleased with ourselves. It had had all the atmosphere of the film Casablanca, but regrettably without an Ingrid Bergman!

On another Damascus Tour I crewed up with Dennis my landlord and a Captain called Tony. Tony smoked a pipe even on the Flight Deck, which was not welcome. He could be a bit irascible at times and was not my favourite person. We positioned to Munich and took over the aircraft and left about 2300 for Damascus. At about three in the morning their was much chattering among the Syrian girls and our "Chiefty" came in to say that we were about to have another passenger! Tony raised his eyebrows and clenched his pipe, Dennis in the Flight Engineers seat said "never mind, I have been through this before and took over the arranging of a bed made from cushions by the side of the galley, which gave the mother-to-be a bit of privacy. I stayed firmly in my seat! The birth got underway, our Chiefty had had some midwifery training and one of the other girls seemed pretty knowledgeable. "I'll keep you two informed", said Dennis to us and he cracked open the flight deck door, "I think I see the head appearing…" There was a thud and Dennis passed out on the Flight Deck floor! The birth went well, apparently, Mother and son (and young husband) were carried off to the ambulance at Damascus and we came with her to wish her well. To my astonishment the ambulance, quite a modern one, had no furnishings inside, not even a bed, and they laid the young woman on the floor!

That afternoon we were all sitting round the airport Hotel pool apart from Tony, who eventually arrived a little the worse for wear with a mate of his equally sozzled. Tony saw our "chiefty", Fiona, sunbathing topless (covered by a towel – this is Syria) and with a shout to his chum they grabbed her legs and arms and threw her in the pool; her head missing the concrete edge by a gnat's whisker. I was incensed and got up and shouted at Tony, and gave him a shove in the chest which sent him and his nice tropical suit into the deep end. The first sign of his recovery was a series of bubbles followed by the pipe. Dennis helped me get our girl out of the water as a spluttering Tony emerged from the depths. "I think you had better go," said Dennis "I'll calm him down". I left, thinking that assaulting a senior captain with my own command shortly coming up was not the brightest thing to do! However, Tony did apologise to the lady, he grunted a few words to me and we shook hands. Our flight home together had a somewhat cool atmosphere about it and I sat firmly in the Flight Engineers seat!

We occasionally stayed in the Omayed Palace Hotel in Damascus. Comfortable enough but had seen better days. But it gave us more opportunity to see the city and its many historic sites, and to shop in the famous Souk. The hotel plumbing could be a bit of a problem; I once had a room with a shower, the shower being installed in a corner on a carpeted floor! The hotel did not have a pool so we made use of an establishment some miles out of town which was the haunt of the diplomatic staff of the various embassies. I first sampled the water on an extremely hot day, leaping into the deep end of that crystal clear pool to discover that the temperature was just below 40° F. The shock to my circulation could have been fatal! The low temperature also explained the lack of any other swimmers! I learned later that the pool did not have a filtration system so water was taken from a mountain spring to fill the pool on Mondays which was then emptied on Sunday evenings by which time it was an opaque green colour and rather turgid – but much warmer! Waters from the pool was used in the local apricot orchards – which were exceptionally delicious. In fact the Damascus water system was fed by the Barada River upstream of the city where it was a clear rushing torrent. By the time it had wound through Damascus it was anything but! The residue just filtered its way through the fruit orchards until subsiding into the desert in a swampy area called Bahr el Aatreibe some twenty miles east of the city. So ended my last Syrian tour.

In August and for a period of about five months, we had another wet-lease for some five aircraft this time, to Portuguese East African (Beira and Lorenquo Marques). I must add that we now had an Inertial Guidance System (INS) in most of the aircraft. The job was to fly refugees from Portuguese East Africa and West Africa (Luanda) back to Lisbon prior to those two countries being granted their independence. All sectors outbound from Lisbon were empty which improved our range no end: our R-R Conways consumed 6000 kg an hour! Our routes varied especially after Portuguese West went independent and became a place to avoid at all costs. We touched Nairobi, Johannesburg, Libreville, Windhoek in Namibia and of course Beira + LM in Portuguese East. It was great to be back in Africa again – though a very different one to the one of 25 years ago. Johannesburg was still nice stopover through lawlessness had almost got out of hand even in 1975. The same applied to Nairobi; it was not an option to walk alone any more, even at mid-day, down Kenyatta Avenue. On one Johannesburg two-day stop I spent a night with my old gliding friend, Helli Lasche, who made possible my Diamond Height climb at Bloemspruit, and his wife Cilia. He told me then that he as going to pull out soon and retire to somewhere warm. He predicted then the end of the South Africa as we knew it and forecast the chaos and decline that would follow. It has.

I see from my logbook that I once positioned out to Nairobi with a crew to take over a 707 and fly to Johannesburg, to pick up a passenger load off another aircraft from Beira. Returning we would refuel at Libreville and then go direct to Lisbon. It was now that I remade my acquaintance with Peter, the co-pilot who had flown with me for a short time on Shackletons in 1956 and who I had recommended be chained to the ground! Peter was now my Captain and we made no mention of our previous encounter. We picked our load of tired and tearful people, many of whom had been badly treated by the "new" authorities for wishing to leave, but thankful to a man for our help; these flights were becoming more and more like Red Cross Missions. It was my leg into Libreville; Peter said he had not been there before (neither had I!). The weather was pretty foul at our destination, thunder storms up to 40 thousand plus and rain, rain, rain. The ILS worked OK and we got down; kept the passengers on board and refuelled. It was a place I would gladly not wish to visit again! We taxied out, the weather clearing a little and a few stars becoming visible. I got clearance to depart and Peter let the brakes off. I said, "what about the radar, don't you want to look?" "No need" he said and I put my feet on the brakes. "No look – no go" and switched the gizmo on. He didn't say anything, but we could sense he was seething. Up came the picture with a solid line of thunder cells across track some ten miles ahead. Silence. Eventually he said "once airborne give me a course to steer to avoid the worst". "Yes Captain", I said. Once in the cruise I thought he might have said something (!) but no. He had not improved in the last twenty years!

Right up to the time of the hand-over in Portuguese West, Luanda was our base. It was a beautiful city with a lovely palm tree waterfront lined with cafes, shops galore and our hotel, "The Tropico", quite four star. Over the weeks we slowly watched it die, shops closed, restaurants were boarded up, the streets became filthy, power and water sometimes in short supply. Towards the end there were mass gatherings of UNITA supporters (Pro West "Good Guys") and MPLA (Marxist) followers. Gradually the town became more under the control of the MPLA; frequent "marches" by loads of followers left one with a feeling of dread. Slip crews became more and more concerned; the local Consulate was no help, the brave Foreign Office wallahs had long since gone leaving a caretaker to feed the cat! The airfield was run by International Air Radio and they had all left bar one who was Angolan. Traffic staff became terrified by the many armed gangs that wandered round. Some aircraft had been shot at (and hit) on landing; fuel was dwindling despite the oil refinery nearby. At dinner one night in the lovely restaurant with the balcony opening to the sea, a band of MPLA came in and sat down demanding food. One let his AK47 fall on the marble floor; we all ducked. One thing you do not do with an AK47 is to drop it: how this one didn't fire off a few rounds I shall never know. We were then treated to the spectacle of the men shovelling food into their faces by hand. It was time to go. The Skipper had a large room and sitting room and the girls all slept there while we kept a watch system going. The tragedy of it all! In the early days we had enjoyed so much fun on the beaches, going shopping, visiting the little fishing harbour and enjoying fish straight out of the sea – and now!

We left two days later, the day before independence – that's pushing it, I thought! Sad farewell to the hotel staff, I hate to think what happened to them. Into the bus, through the MPLA checkpoint – all out, searched, through the UNITA checkpoint and onto the airfield. Skipper Frank carefully briefed the Purser that he would take-off without any lights; therefore no cabin lights until he gave the word. We climbed up the steps, again to see 189 sad and fearful faces almost imploring us to go. I have to say we had about half a dozen extras from amongst the ground engineers that never got onto the manifest, "Can't leave them", said Frank. Once airborne, the wheels on a 707 retreat into the belly with a double clonk. This awakened our idiot Purser to start his duties so ON came the cabin lights just over the gun pits! The roar that Frank gave must have been heard on the ground! Thereafter Windhoek became a base – an interesting part of Africa though we had little time to see it. I do remember one day driving in the bus to the airport when a huge Kudu bull leapt in front of the bus and brought it to an abrupt halt. And so my African adventures drew to a close. I had mixed feelings about seeing places that I knew years ago, change is rarely for the better. I would never return.

Back at Gatwick we were still busy. More welcome US charters via Bangor and the chance to see that lovely Maine coast. Again, flying over the so familiar San Bernardino Valley and March AFB where I had first joined SAC: seemed like another life. The Far East came up quite frequently but by January '76 things got remarkably quiet. It was the time to take our leave, a generous six weeks off and two weeks free of duty (what that meant I am uncertain!). Anyway I see that in January, February and March I spent most of my time with Air London! In fact, after a very intensive two years flying the 70-7, 1976 was an undemanding year. I only flew about four or five days a month. Our 707 fleet was being reduced to be replaced by some Tristars, or perhaps I should say supplemented. Air London saw a good deal of me, so did Booker and the Airways Flying Club so it was a rare day that I had my feet on the ground.

I renewed my acquaintance with John (of the Rug fame) albeit from a distance. Taxiing the AL Navajo out from the General Aviation Terminal one day I heard again the dulcet tones of John, on ground control frequency instead of on his Cabin Address. "Ladies and Gentlemen, girls and boys (I hated that!)" he said. "The reason we are late and have an hours delay is entirely due to Air Traffic", and so on! The truth was two passengers had got stuck in Duty Free and would not board without their bottles! When he had finished, about twenty transmit buttons were pressed, including mine, with many ribald comments "Gentlemen, Gentlemen", said the Senior Air Trafficer, Tim Barnaby, whom I knew well, "you have made your point. Capt. R_____ would you kindly see me on your return to justify your comments on the Control Centre! Wow! We have all made this blunder, one of the most famous was in New England many years ago where a chap flying a DC-3 had an engine fire which was reluctant to go out. He said to the local Air Traffic Centre "Ladies and Gentlemen" as you see we have a slight problem but we are landing at _____ very soon so please remain calm". To the passengers he said "for Christ's sake get this bucket on the ground before it explodes"! One night in a Vanguard I had been holding over Lambourne VOR for about twenty minutes (unusual at 3 a.m.) waiting to land at Heathrow when I said to the First Officer "If we do this much longer we will disappear up our own rear ends," but I was a little more crude than that. Back came a few unhelpful comments until London Airways said "Captain, that was an unacceptable and non standard transmission". I grovelled, oh did I grovel!

On 1ˢᵗ November, I was senior enough to bid for a Command on Vanguards (Merchantman Freighter) and started Simulator and ground school at Heston the next day. It was hard to leave Airtours but knowing that the Vanguard fleet was again only five in number, I hoped it would not last too long and I would be able to bid to return to Gatwick on some other aircraft. It worked out just like that!

Looking back now I know I should have spent a little more time sorting out my domestic affairs, reflect a little on what the future might hold and what I could do about it instead of following this headlong rush through life. As a pilot I was required to record my flying, as laid down by the Civil Aviation Authority, in a logbook. I was now on my fourth book and each time I made an entry I thought "another day gone – where?" I suppose I trusted to luck and thought something might turn up to alter this life pattern. In the meantime I enjoyed my flying tremendously and for that I am thankful.

An event occurred that year that renewed my ties with the RAF. No 53 Squadron on which I had served flying Beverleys was due to be disbanded, its fleet of Belfast freighters sold off to a company based at Southend, Heavy Lift. Peter Lewis rang me up about it and I was able to attend this sad ceremony at Brize Norton on 14ᵗʰ September 1976. It marked the end of sixty years of continuous service. The Parade was held in a hangar, the weather being awful and the most poignant thing I remember was that at the end of the ceremony a huge Russian

Antonov freighter taxied slowly by the open hangar entrance and someone said, "There goes the opposition!"

Going back a bit in time, Peter Lewis and other stalwarts formed the 53 Squadron Association on 1st September 1976 and we are still in being. We have had many reunions and visits to Guinness Park Royal and I must voice my thanks to Gerry Rickman, our host at Park Royal for the unstinted support and hospitality we received. On one visit (in 1980) I took my wife, Trish who was totally enthralled by it all. Even more so, when Gerry presented her with a birthday cake; how this came about I simply don't know, but it was her birthday! The Squadron Association got off to an auspicious start by having the good fortune to have as our first President Wing Commander A.P.C. Hannay MC who had commanded the Squadron in 1937.

15. Mostly Night Work

One occasionally gets exposed to an aircraft that leaves you with the impression that with a bit more effort it might have been developed into a really nice aeroplane. I have never disliked an aircraft, I have been wary of a few perhaps, but not disliked, for that is to admit defeat. There is one well known display pilot, who was quoted by an aeronautical magazine reporter, that he hated flying Tiger Moths; to which one wag was heard to comment, that, yes, The Tiger did need to be flown properly, at all times! The Vanguard / Merchantman was similar. Sitting on the ground it did not give the impression of wanting to fly like Concorde or the 707. I have all my Flight Manuals for the aircraft but there is little to warn the unsuspecting pilot of its peculiarities.

On a low overshoot, for instance, the book says that a firm smooth pull on the elevator control is required on the application of full power. What it does not say is that it is possible to experience fluctuations of the elevators as the tail (long way back) leaves ground – effect. In fact no one while I was flying Vanguards ever explained this occasional phenomenon (shades of the Varsity at Swinderby!). Further firm backward movement was needed during undercarriage and flap retraction. Failure at any time to keep the nose pointer above the horizon bar (i.e. climbing) would give the aeroplane the excuse it needed to return quickly earthwards.

The rudder trim wheel was conventional and had an electrical motor which could be used to move the trim wheel through a simple "left-right" switch. This brought a rapid response in Trim Movement. An auto-coarsening device was fitted to each engine which could sense a reversal of torque in the event of an engine failure and coarsened-off the propeller blades to the feathered position: a quick and cunning drag remover. The manual lays down the engine shut down drills but does not elaborate. If an engine failed after VI on take-off, you had better be quick in getting it identified, shut down and feathered, put in a bootfull of rudder in the correct direction to counter the swing, use large amounts of "wing up" ailerons on the failed side and switch <u>full</u> electrical rudder trim (in the correct sense) all at the same time AND keep that nose pointing upwards away from the ground! After the 707 this was quite a challenge and the first few goes in the simulator brought much sweat to ones' armpits. The Vanguard always reminded me of the Hastings!

I discovered the importance of the rudder trim in all phases of flight. Any changes in airspeed or in power settings demanded an instant adjustment of the rudder trim, even when flying the beast in turns one's right hand was never far from that wretched little wheel! The autopilot did not have a yaw-damper, consequently in auto-flight one kept a wary eye on the Rudder Trim Indicator on the captain's instrument panel, which gave you the amount and direction of the force being applied to the rudder which one then relieved with the trim wheel. I do not think I have flown another modern multi-engined aircraft quite like it, but it was a challenge, an enjoyable challenge.

I duly turned up for training at Heston in time to meet the course before starting work. I looked forward to regaining the left-hand seat but I must admit in the preceding years I had learned a lot and enjoyed every minute of it. In this job the day you think you know it all is the day to stay firmly on the ground. There was another perk that went with four stripes: - I got first go at the cheese board! My other budding Captains were all ex-service and our First Officer new-entry pilots from Hamble.

We were three to a crew the First Officer, rotating on the Flight Deck between the Co-pilot seat and the "third seat". This position had no particular function other than to provide bottom cover for the third pilot. From this position a new First Officer could watch and learn, keep an eye out and above all else, make the tea!

Ground School over and into the Sim. The Vanguard had a spacious cockpit similar to the VC-10 but I did miss the excellent

707/727/737 design, which I still think is one of the best. In the Sim we explored the areas of flight as already described and began to realise that this aircraft was of a bygone age like the Shackleton or Hastings in handling. The engine failure drills (on take-off) required work from all arms and legs and a session in this field left you weighing a pound or two less!

At last, type-rated apart from Base Flying, we presented ourselves at the BEA Cargo Flight Office on the South Side of Heathrow in late November 76, to be welcomed by Capt. Griffin our new boss who promptly presented us with the traditional brown leather briefcase (I still have mine) which came with a suggestion that we might care to join, and contribute, to ICARUS, the BEA Pilots Retirement Society – how could we refuse!

We began our short base flying in the early part of December and then straight on to line training. By early January I was on my tod again; it had been a long eight years! I soon found out that our route structure did not differ much from that of the Argosy days. The aircraft was a lot faster, consequently we did not need to night stop Athens or Stockholm (shame!). Dublin, Vienna, Alicante, Gibraltar, Copenhagen were regular routes and once I visited Dresden to pick up an art collection. The airport staff there (East Germans) were distinctly hostile when it came out in "friendly chat" with the BEA agent that I had been in the RAF and for once I managed to be tactful – but not too tactful!

The runs to Gibraltar were always fun: the Spanish at this time being particularly bloody-minded and tracking in and out of Gib, avoiding Spanish airspace was quite interesting, more later. We always took general cargo to Gib and then proceeded to Alicante empty to pick up shoes: left-hand shoes one day and right-hand shoes the next, apparently to discourage thieving! The farcical thing about this sector, and it says much for the uselessness of the Foreign Office, is that we had to fly to Tangier, keep engines running while an airport official stamped our flight plan thus enabling us to look the Spaniards square in the eye and say "yes, we have come from Tangier because Gibraltar does not exist"!

The Vanguard / Merchantman was a good work horse and capable of taking eight full size pallets plus cargo in the lower under-floor holds (previously baggage holds). It also had the unique ability to weigh itself through weight switches on the three undercarriage legs which gave one a good gross error check of the load sheet. So 1977 passed swiftly and the only "incident" that comes to mind was a temporary stoppage one October night when loading-up for Frankfurt. The loaders "downed tools" in a vehement protest for an extra hours' pay because that night the clocks would be put back one hour! It took an hour of much nonsensical arguing (oh for a tape recorder!) to get them back to work!

The New Year bought much of the same, a bit more night freighting as I recall. Old Griff retired and Mike Butterworth whom I remembered from the RAF took over and who eventually handed over to Rod Fulton whom I had last seen at Lyneham with 511 Squadron on Hastings; and who had caused such amusement in re-enacting that Ball / Red Baron dog fight in Chipmunks so realistically! It was his unfortunate job to be the last F.M. before the flight folded in early 1980, an unenviable task which he handled well. By the middle of 1978 our utilisation was rapidly going downhill but Rod was able to assure us that though we were really going spare at the moment, (in a charter company we would have all been sacked) we would be much in demand at the end of 1979! Looking through my logbook I see I flew about three or four trips a month; very frustrating. However, there was a bright side. While most of my colleagues were beavering away in their gardens in their generous spare time, I found much happy employment with Air London and at Booker with the Airways Aero Club! I found I was much in demand with the Club for night flying instruction; and since this could only be done in fine weather I was more than happy to do it thus relieving the full-time instructors to enjoy an evening off. Dear Joan Hughes, however, was always keen to fly. In those days we did quite a lot of night cross-country instruction which I enjoyed. There were very few other part-timers who made themselves available for night flying. I know some thought it foolhardy to set off at night with only one engine: - strange pilots indeed!

I really cannot find any out of the ordinary trips that I did on the Merchantman, it was all very routine enlivened only by the frequent runs to Gib which is always an interesting place to visit, depending on which way the wind blows: occasionally in two different directions at the same time! The thing about the wind at Gib was to avoid being on the lee side of the Rock itself, the turbulence or wind shear as it is known had to be felt to be believed. Sometimes the curl over from the top impinged on the water two or three miles away! There are times when Gib is closed to all traffic because of the wind. The Spanish did not help either by insisting we flew clear of their airspace. For instance landing to the west one approached the Rock from seaward at about a 15° angle to the runway heading, making a quick left turn when within half a mile of touchdown. Their procedure put us fair and square in a bad area of turbulence with any kind of a south-westerly wind blowing. Another factor about Gib is that the runway is at least double the width of a normal one thus making it difficult for a pilot to gauge his height above the touchdown point. I think most of us have landed at Gibraltar in a "firm manner" at some time or another.

The end of the year came and went with minimal flying for BEA, so I flew constantly with Air London. Early in the New Year we operated a brand new Navajo Chieftain for a Mr Reg Pycroft, founder of Jet Aviation. Reg was a delightful person and asked us to supervise the radio fit. It had an autopilot, capable of coupled ILS approaches, radar and full VOR.DME with an offset gizmo! Registered G-SAVE this aeroplane was a real beauty and I spent many happy hours in it.

In mid '77 AL had acquired a contract to support the air taxi fleet of Messrs. Elliots at Rochester. The Airfield Manager at Rochester was a famous Battle of Britain pilot called "Pinky" Starke and our association with Elliots was an extremely happy one. Unfortunately Rochester proved too short (grass airfield) for our Navajos which were, of course, on Public Transport tickets so it was the Aztecs that took the flying. Strangely enough Elliots operated their Navajos quite legally and safely but on a Private registration! I think there was only one "incident" which comes to mind. The airfield AVGAS (petrol) underground fuel tank was once filled up by some idiot tanker driver with JET-A1- paraffin. Eric Taylor, Elliots' chief pilot duly took-off that day in the Aero Commander, had a double engine failure (hardly surprising) but put the aircraft down intact on the Motorway! I hope he got a Green Endorsement for an incredible piece of flying.

Rochester was once closed for a couple of weeks, this was later in 1981. Pinky, on an airfield inspection, discovered a wooden box stuck in the ground and oozing some evil-smelling substance. This proved to be decomposing dynamite! In 1940 many grass airfields in the south of England were mined as part of the anti-invasion defences. After the war most were cleared; somehow Rochester was missed! I believe Hawkinge was found to be still 'live' when another check of all airfields was carried out.

I often flew to Walney Island, Barrow-in-Furness with senior staff of Bowater's. These were usually night-stops and I used to put up at a hotel in Barrow for the sum of about a fiver a night. The Hotel, the staff, the rooms and food reflected this low price but it was all that was available. One night a customer complained (with justification) of some unpalatable dish and demanded to see the Chef. Chef arrived, 180lbs of irate Chinaman wielding a meat cleaver – no guesses as to who came out on top. It was a situation worthy of Brian Rix and the Whitehall Theatre.

One more run is worth a mention (because it may be hard to believe!). I had to go to Aberdeen at very short notice – as in *now!* A famous West End store had shipped, by rail, a fashion show complete with mannequins, dressers, salespeople, clothes, in fact the whole shebang, to the Granite City for a show that evening! When told, I simply did not believe it! However, old man Mack eventually convinced me. "Your job", he said, "is to fly two thousand plastic coat hangers up there because some wally forgot to bring them!! Two thousand coat hangers in boxes would almost fill a large 125' pallet! Anyway, I got into G-SAVE, Tony and Co. took all the hangers out of their boxes and poured them inside; they just about filled the aeroplane up to the ceiling leaving the only means of exit the emergency hatch in the cockpit. It caused quite a stir at Aberdeen when the ground staff opened the cabin door to be met by an avalanche of plastic.

In mid 1979 we got wind of the introductions of the Boeing 737 into the company, and Air Tours would be taking an initial eight aircraft. By luck no one seemed keen in bidding for Air Tours and by December my return to Gatwick was assured. I did two trips on the Merchantman in November and my last in mid December – one of these was with a young chap called Angus Mundie whom years later I would meet again. He was a keen Hamble graduate and very disenchanted with the abysmal lack of flying that was our lot. Despite my words of wisdom that "The grass is not always greener" etc... he moved to Britannia Airways, preferring the "mine field" (in those days) of a charter company to the security of the state airline. I cannot say I blame him and, as it turned out, it was for the best. In his position I might have done the same, in fact, I came close to making the same choice when I left the RAF. The rest of December and early January were pretty hectic in Air London when I called a halt to my "fun" flying and returned to Airtours House to prepare for the 737 course Ground School at Cranebank. It was great to be back, PJ had unfortunately retired but otherwise things were just the same. Many of the staff were still with us and most of the Engineers too, I am glad to say. I pen these words exactly 24 years later and yesterday I bumped into one of our "Ginger Beers" in a supermarket. He was Mr. Choprah, "Chop" to his friends, and came from India. He is a remarkable man, only about 5' 4", with a beard, and huge sense of humour. His wife and three children are among the most charming people I have ever met. "Chop" was a superb engineer, he had more types on his engineering license than most of his colleagues and when he said, "She's fit to fly" it most certainly was. Anyway, we chatted for a long time clutching our trolleys and I reminded him of one particular occasion the Company had had to sub-charter from BOAC, a 707 to go to Faro. With the aircraft on-stand, Chop and the BP Tanker driver went in to get the fuel load. On the flight deck the crew were having their coffee, so Chop asked the Captain how much fuel he required. Without looking round the Captain said, "kindly address all such enquiries to the Flight Engineer". So Chop asked the Flight Engineer who turned round to the Captain and asked him. The First Officer then said something like six tonnes, the Captain agreed and said to the Flight Engineer "six tonnes it is". Looking up at Chop the Flight Engineer said "six tonnes please all in the wings". Chop was highly amused at this charade, the BP tanker driver too. Chop made a great show of writing it down in his notebook and with a twinkle in his eye said, "Thank you boys, now I got it in black and white"!

Ground School over and I struck lucky: my Simulator Training would be with Pacific Western Airways of Vancouver in mid February. Oh yes, as the reader may already have guessed, I got married again!

16. Gatwick and the 737

Following the ARB type exam eight of us presented ourselves to Terminal 4 together with two "Trainers" who would conduct the thirty odd hours of Simulator training in Vancouver. My newly found status (well, nearly,) put me in Business Class but in fact I seem to remember the aircraft was no way near full and I think we all piled into First! On long trips like this I eschew alcohol and too much fodder – you feel much better the other end. I also rarely watch the film / video and never listen to the audio channels. I am always astounded when I hear people complain that their "small screen is not working" and what are they supposed to do for eight hours? For me, this is a time for relaxation, to examine the inside of one's eyelids and let ones imagination and memories waft through your mind: some-one else can drive!

I settled down and thought what a lucky chap I was. I had just married Trish, a lovely bubbly girl and taken on board her two children. Deserted by her husband, with a baby of 18 months and an infant of six weeks, she had had a hard time. With amazing courage, and a little help from her family, she took a part-time job, got a grant and put herself through college reading History and English, and was now training to become a Teacher. When I returned from Vancouver, we would set up a permanent home near Gatwick, this being my last posting in BA prior to reaching the compulsory retirement age of 55. Until then we were both busy. Little did I know what a rare and very close relationship we would have; we never seemed to fail to know what the other was doing or thinking, even when separated by thousands of miles. I closed my eyes.

The first thing I did in Vancouver was to buy a Parka: it was bit-terly cold! I teamed up with Bill Young who had been on 8 course at Thornhill in Southern Rhodesia: that was the course that "welcomed" mine on arrival and I think Bill took the part of the "Padre"! The Simulator was one of the latest breed from Redifon in Crawley with the new (now commonplace) all-round visual screens and full motion; it was hard not to think that you were not glued to the ground! For once we did not wear uniforms in the Sim; a rule that BA at home always insisted upon, and rightly so. We finished the course in about four weeks and it says much for the quality of the device that our actual flying of the aircraft when we returned to UK was a mere 2 hr 30 min day and 30 min night base training.

Bill and I finished the course with about one hour to spare so the Simulator consul operator, (the man who works all the "failures and problems" from the rear) suggested we might like to engage in a bit of fun! He re-programmed the machine and we were off! Take-off from Vancouver, down the lake, under the huge suspension bridge seeing the cars flashing by overhead, up to the left full chat to climb over Whistler Mountain, just made it looking at the skiers on the chair lift! I did a barrel roll, Bill tried a loop, fell out at the top and we started to spin from 20,000ft! I yelled, "Bill, opposite rudder, pause, stick progressively forward". We spun the other way! A few seconds later the horizon came into view in a high-speed whirl and then 'CRUNCH' a very, very loud noise and everything went black! We were both dripping with perspiration. But it was not all work and no play. The Motel, which was our temporary home, had a Strip-Club and there were those trainees (no names) who took advantage of this facility before and after their Sim sessions! But not on Sundays, such a sin was not permitted in British Columbia in 1980!

Returning to Gatters, quick base training, line training and then I was off again, but this time in a brand new 737-200 (advanced!) aeroplane, and believe me this really was a delightful piece of kit, with auto-land! Omega-VLF Area Navigation system and auto-brakes. Sounds old hat now but twenty years ago this was all a big leap forward. We did have a few night stops, Corfu and Athens come to mind, and eventually we ran a service to Bathurst in the Gambia via Las Palmas, which was fun. But the days of wet leases were over, I am sorry to say.

One of my early trips was to Zurich at night "Chiefy" brought in our coffees soon after take-off and told me that there was an old friend of mine from my Air Force days in First and would like to renew my acquaintance. "OK at Top of the Climb" I said, having asked if the First Officer minded. As I levelled off a figure came into the darkened cockpit and settled in the jump seat. Then a voice whispered in my ear "I thought I told you that you were taking a serious risk riding in this bus"! Ye gods, that shot my memory back twenty plus years! I turned to greet Eddy Wiles, whom I had last seen in Cyprus in 1958 when I was riding in a Greek bus (though Turkish territory) from Nicosia to Kyrenia "disguised" in civvies as a Greek, strictly against the Security Forces "advice"! Eddie had been a Hastings Captain on 511 Squadron in '54 and I knew him well. I knew he spoke Greek and Turkish and a few more languages besides, and that he had joined the Security Forces in Cyprus on a temporary posting to go undercover! "Face the front", he continued, "don't look round but for your sake don't do this again. When I get off ignore me". When he did get off that bus I didn't even recognise him! Anyway, we made him welcome, turned up the lights and caught up with the last two decades. Before he left he said "you did that trip again, didn't you?" I had to own up; the lure of Lotty's' Bar had been too strong for a weakling like me to resist. Eddy said "I caught the same bus on your return journey; you were very lucky to get away unharmed!

My last four years in Airtours were extremely busy but I managed to take my wife flying on occasions if the charterer had a spare seat. It was with her that I first met John Voukalis our Manager at Heraklion, I am sure I could have sold her off for several camels: John was quite smitten! We came away with a bottle of his home made brandy (I still have some) delicious, smooth and it is the quickest way I know of getting stoned on one small glass!

Madrid and Bilbao were frequent destinations, usually with a night-stop in Bilbao; in fact I spent my last Christmas and Boxing Day there, the crew being entertained by the British Consul in his chalet in what is known as Spanish Switzerland, a delightful area. I remember the morning of departure that it had snowed in Bilbao (it never snows in Bilbao!) and there were no deicing facilities. It says much for the company spirit that the whole of my crew set to with brooms to sweep the wings aided by nearly all the airport staff! Health and Safety freaks of today would have been horrified!

In the spring we bought a house in Forest Row on Ashdown Forest land, well half a house really. It was part of a hundred year old Mansion which had been split into two at the end of the war – we had the old servants half! Surrounded by trees and off the beaten track it is a delightful spot and at last my life was beginning to enjoy some stability. It was a happy house. I did little flying at Booker and with Air London; Air Tours kept me pretty busy doing Line Training. In any case, there was Trish at the end of the day instead of an empty flat. However, flying still proceeded at a pace and on one trip from Madrid I learned of a hitherto unknown procedure for storing newspapers for the returning passengers. These were put in one of the ovens (rarely used). On this occasion we had hot breakfast for our happy punters. Ten minutes out of Madrid I smelt burning! I leapt out of my seat in time to slam shut the flaming oven door just as one of the girls opened it to check if the breakfast were done! No prizes for guessing what had occurred.

Tenerife now had a new airport, Tenerife – South, with an almost E-W runway of 10,000ft built on the southern tip of the island at about 200ft above sea level. It was in the lee of the extinct volcanic peak of some 10,000 feet twelve miles to the north in effect a gigantic "Gibraltar". I had been here several times without any problems. Today, in March '82 things were to change. Jeff Bunn was the First Officer and he flew the leg down. We landed towards the East with a 10k headwind, but on the approach the turbulence was quite severe. With hindsight I should have guessed that this might happen: we had had a strong northerly wind at height and on the let-down, of about forty knots and the forecast showed at least sixty knots from the north for the return journey. Two other aircraft landed and one reported moderate turbulence on the approach. When it came to leave the surface wind was still from the east at about 15 knots, both windsocks confirming this. Halfway down the runway just past V1 I saw clouds of dust at the end of the concrete and the airspeed remained at V1 plus about 5kts. Jeff put on full power and then realised from the dust that we now had a tail wind. We shot into the gravel overrun just as I lifted the nose wheel, quite a bit below the desired speed. Somehow we launched into the air, with the starboard wing dropping several times in quick succession. Wind shear! The effect of wind shear and the associated down drafts is something we practice in the Simulator; it came in handy. I really don't remember the next few minutes as we clawed our way up; the downdraft was the worst I had ever encountered. Suddenly we were in calm clear air, and Jeff reduced the power to normal climb. We looked at each other and said nothing. I handed over to Jeff, asked him to inform Tenerife only to get an answer that no one else had complained! I went back and was relieved to see that apart from personal belongings strewn everywhere; there were no injuries. I made a brief announcement, which I hope reassured everyone. One Cabin girl had been sitting at the back looking at the starboard wing tip. She swore it kicked up dust off the ground, twice!

We returned to Gatwick, I filled in a Special Occurrence Report and requested a read out of the flight recorder. This device had become so frightened that it failed to work! My only claim to fame is that now there is a caution note on the Tenerife-South letdown plate – "severe wind shear may occur during approach". No thought given by the Spanish Authorities of being ultra-prepared during northerly winds! I think Jeff and I earned our keep that day.

We night stopped Palma a few times and I used to take the ancient electric train through the mountains to Solle on the North coast for a very pleasant day out. Minorca I think was the most unspoiled. Ibiza (in 1982) was also still uncontaminated by Europe's' young and very peaceful. On the approach to the runway we had noticed the construction of a new hotel. It was obvious that its site degraded the approach path to the runway, noises were made but it continued to grow. At last one day it was pretty well complete but for painting. Then, on my next trip, it had been reduced to a pile of rubble! Rumour has it that it was part of some huge insurance swindle but I never found the answer!

By now the lovely Spanish coastline from Gerona to Malaga was one vast concrete jungle, which I once had the misfortune to experience during an enforced night-stop. We seemed to spend our time (on the holiday routes) taking drunks from one concrete jungle like Manchester etc. to another at Alicante or Gerona: to return the same passengers in the same state back to England two weeks later. I gather its far, far worse now. I remember getting into hot water (!) for telling the passengers, when turning over the beaches of Malaga after take-off, that the ugly brown stain they could see just off the swimming beaches was the towns' untreated sewage outlet! On a more cheerful note I was returning home from Heraklion over southern Italy in good clear cloudless conditions – a rare thing in this part of the world. The sun still had us in its rays but the ground was in deep, purple dusk. Suddenly, every town and village as far as the eye could see erupted in fireworks, presumably some feast-day; it made an amazing sight. I think I waxed quite poetical on the cabin address!

My time in BA was drawing to a close with but six months to go, and I began to write around for a job. My wife said "FitzRoy, you had better find something otherwise you will be unbearable, even more so than you are now!" I felt that eventually I would be happy to go back to instructing at a Club now that Air London had wisely decided to move into the brokering business and pack up its light twin operations; so we looked overseas. I said no to the Middle East; Africa was out of the question. The Far East offered some hope but I was six months too old for Cathay Pacific and Singapore Airlines only required 747 pilots. I must have tried some twenty UK & European airlines – no chance, very demoralising. Then at the last minute Roger Neaves (he of South Cerney fame) gave me a call "How about Brunei"? he said, "You're on", I shouted!

I was going to say that I was very sorry to leave Airtours but that is only a half-truth. Yes, I was very sorry to leave the company of so many nice people and I had been very happy there since the Comet days. But the passengers we carried had changed, frighteningly so. In my last year I had had six arrested, had several thrown off my aircraft for upsetting behaviour to other passengers, and refused to take quite a few more. When I travel now I note that any kind of behaviour seems to be tolerated. The last words I heard from my Flight Manager was something like "Now we will be able to keep some of our passengers!" Anyway, they gave me a choice of flights for my last ten days and I asked Bill Young to join me. We took in all what I call the interesting airfields, Funchal, Gibraltar, some of the Greek Islands. I also got the chance to say goodbye to John Voukalis, Mr. Rojo, our engineer in Alicante and several more. I did my last trip to Funchal and Porto Santo on 19th September 1983 and I became 55 at midnight.

17. Borneo

There was much to do. We had hoped for our usual skiing holiday at Fleines but it was too early in the year for that. Perhaps it was just as well; a broken leg at this stage would have scuppered all my plans. The year before I had come within an ace of breaking something in a hang-glider. A Monsieur Leroubley owned a two-seater hang-glider at the resort and was offering trial lessons. I am told he held the world record for doing 500 consecutive loops in this device! Anyway, we met at the top of the ski lift some 5000ft above the valley floor while my wife waited at the bottom to film the arrival.

The thing about flying a hang-glider is that you do so by shifting your weight, so to put the nose down you haul back on the 'A' frame; totally opposite to normal flying. We started our take-off slide some three yards from the edge of this small plateau that fell vertically down for a thousand feet (there was no abandon take-off drill!). Over the edge, my mentor yelled, "Ze nose DOWN!" So FitzRoy pushes the A frame forward and we stall! After about a couple of minutes we got it sorted and then the sheer enjoyment of flying like a bird struck home. That quarter of an hour of swinging round rocks, catching an updraught here and there was pure heaven and I can understand why people rave about it. My friend talked me through the landing which was a total disaster; my fault, I pushed instead of pulled – old habits, die hard – and very nearly broke a leg! It was a trip to remember.

But I digress again. My wife would have to complete her year of teaching practice (June 84) before joining me but would come out for the Christmas hols. I would return for some leave in February (and a bi-annual medical) and she would return for Easter, so it all worked out quite well. We both looked forward to this new venture in a country neither of us had visited. Brunei is a Malay Muslim Monarchy consisting of two small enclaves of land on the north coast of

Borneo. Oil was discovered here in 1903 and in 1905 Britain took an interest in it and made it a Protectorate until independence was achieved in 1984. During this period the off-shore oil fields were developed, vast deposits of natural gas were tapped and on land large beds of silica were found, giving the Sultan the sobriquet of the Richest Man in the World. There were several small airfields along the coast, mostly developed from airstrips built by the Japanese during the war when Japan occupied Borneo. The main airfield was a modern development quite close to the Capital, Bandar Seri Begawan.

I bade farewell in the first week of October to my three children, who lived with their Mum in Horley. Susan, my eldest daughter, worked at the local vets and had acquired a dog of doubtful parentage called Nearly (she had been nearly put down!) 'Nears', as she came to be known, was really a human being in a black fur coat and was as bright and intelligent as they come. I often took her for walks. On this occasion of farewells she sensed that I was going away for some time, I am quite certain of that, and showed her disapproval by staying in a corner of the kitchen, facing the wall. She did this on similar occasions over the next five years! More about her later.

BA's service to Sydney in those days stopped off at Bandar Seri Begawan, the capital of Brunei, so I had an uninterrupted flight. Disembarking into the warm, damp air at dusk and smelling the familiar aromas of vegetation and jungle convinced me that this was a good move; so much more civilised than the Middle East and beat hands down the vile English winter! I knew that we would love it and so it turned out.

Roger Neaves met me and took me to my new 'home', a bungalow in Kampong Subok, where several pilots lived, about six miles out of town. One of the pleasurable things about Brunei was that there were no ghettos (for want of a better word) of European staff all huddled together as one so often sees overseas, especially in the Middle East. Here in Subok I had a Chinese family as my next door neighbours and I got to know them well – Mama was a marvellous cook! On the other side lay secondary jungle that was home to all sorts of inhabitants who occasionally ventured into the house, including little two-inch brown scorpions, which reminds me of a time a few months later, while standing in the bar of the Mauara Yacht Club, when I felt something on my head. Looking up I saw that I was under a ceiling fan and carried on chatting. A minute later something got onto my shoulder and then hung on a loose fold of my shirt, at which point a man playing snooker shouted "Don't move!" and with one leap swiped "it" off me with his cue. I just had time to turn round to see a writhing black spider (tarantula in most countries) known as a 'bird-hunter' sail out of the open window!

The Company had use of the Malaysian Air Lines Simulator at Kuala Lumpur, so after a few days to get acclimatised and orientated I left for KL to do a base check and instrument rating, then it was into Line Training and route familiarisation flying as a First Officer.

RBA's operating procedures differed considerably from those of BA; RBA stuck meticulously to the Bible according to Boeing and this took some concentration to re-adapt to a new mode of operations. But it was great to be back in the air with the prospect of five more years in a civilised climate working with some really nice people. The money came in handy too. Over the five years I was able to pay off the mortgage on our house and also that of my original home, now occupied by Pam, my ex, and make over the title deeds to her so at least she had a secure roof for herself and our children. I found the local staff, mainly Malay and Chinese, very friendly but one had to adapt to their ways of working; was it Somerset Maugham who said something like 'there is no such word as "hurry" in the East'?

We were a mixed bunch of pilots, as one might expect: New Zealanders, Australians, one Belgian, one from Kenya and of course the Brit contingent, mostly from UK Airlines. We did have several ex-RAF C-130 pilots who had come directly into civil flying, here, with RBA. One was Mike Fox, who became a great friend. He was also a left handed squash player and I never got to win a single game with him! Mike eventually became Head of Flight Operations and after three years when Roger Neaves had retired I became Chief Pilot; but all this was very much in the future. There was one ex-submariner, whom I often thought later should have remained submerged, and a lot of very nice people, together with a few eccentrics, as one might expect out East.

The Belgian, John Keyers, became a good friend. In his much-varied career he had flown for an oil company in North Africa and had visited the crash site of the Liberator "Lady Be Good" in the desert. This aircraft had somehow ended up out of fuel some 200 miles south of the coast, returning from a raid in Italy. Its fate remained a mystery for over ten years until accidentally re-discovered by oil surveyors. Mike Fox had arranged to meet Keyers on Swindon Station when they first joined RBA, and drive him to Luton for their 737 course. When they first met Mike it was hard put not to call him Clouseau (after the Pink Panther films); he had the right hat, raincoat, moustache and look! He even had the right accent, so 'Clouseau' he became! Years later John asked me to meet his niece at Changi one evening and bring her back to Brunei on our late service, I greeted her with the words: "I think you are the niece of Captain Clouseau!"

For my line training and route familiarisation I teamed up with a really nice chap from Christchurch NZ, Tony Westlake. I remember my first trip being to Jakarta, flying more or less over the centre of Borneo to the southwest. Climbing up over the Baram River estuary, which forms the boundary between Brunei and Sarawak, I noticed that the water was a rich brown colour and that this extended at least ten miles out to sea. Tony said he called that 'the lifeblood of Borneo ebbing slowly away' – the irreplaceable topsoil was being washed down by indiscriminate logging on a vast scale. Indeed, we could see thin strips of bright red earth among the mountain forests where new roads where being cut. After heavy rain these narrow tracks would treble in width through erosion.

Over the next five years I would watch familiar mountainsides slowly laid bare, and then set on fire to clean the brushwood, which effectively destroyed the thin nutritious layer (only inches thick) that lies over the marine clays of Borneo. I dread to think what the island must look like now. When I first arrived I heard that a vast area comparable to the size of Taiwan had been decimated by logging in Kalimantan; it was a depressing thought.

Two years later we had a 'drought' in what should have been the NE Monsoon. For three months there was little or no rain and the effect on the rain forest was disastrous. Fires got out of hand, not only in the logging areas but also round Brunei, where farmers took advantage of the dry weather to burn off weeds! For over a month the air was so thick with smoke that aircraft coming into Brunei had to do full instrument letdowns to land in broad 'daylight'!

One of our aircraft was a 'combi' (i.e. all the seats, galleys and fittings were on pallets and the whole lot could be extracted via a large freight door on the port side in front of the wing, thus becoming an instant freighter). My first night flight in this aircraft with Tony was to Changi to pick up a couple of cars for HM the Sultan. I should mention that the Istana (Palace) of the Sultan had a vast underground garage containing, at the time, some 300 cars. These were in the charge of an Englishman known as 'Mike the Mechanic' and I believe he 'exercised' each car at least once a week. The Sultan often drove himself through Bandar to Jerudong Park, his Polo establishment some ten miles to the south of the Palace, at breakneck speed with his motorcycle and escort grimly trying to keep up with him. I once got a good glimpse of him in a Lamborghini with an impish smile on his face!

The last time I had seen Changi was in December 1967 when I was still in the RAF flying Brits. I remember meeting John Cheesbrough again (ex Marham) who was then a Wing Commander and firmly on the ground. I tried to persuade him to join me in civil flying but he remained loyal to the RAF. He did mention, I believe, that the days of RAF Changi were numbered and that rumour had it that it would become Singapore International Airport. It did! Anyway, I could hardly believe my eyes when I saw it for that first time in the gathering dusk. It was vast. The old runway had been strengthened and lengthened and another parallel one added. I believe 80% of it was built on reclaimed land. Changi village had gone, including Ah Lim and his bicycle "restaurant" (all this I found out later) and a new village had been built. The notorious Changi creek was no longer an evil black stream. The old crew transit hotel was still there, having originally been a Jap Officer Mess but was now a Dr Barnado's home. Some of the old street names were still used, Temple Hill Nurses home was still there, sans nurses (!), but otherwise all was very different. There used to be a Chinese restaurant at Bedok (and a radio beacon) on the waterfront which ranked among the most popular on the island. The restaurant is still there but the sea is nearly two miles to the east, such was the extent of the reclamation.

We took off an hour later with a new Rolls and Jaguar in the back and headed for home. Brunei was in the grip of the duty rainstorm and as I broke cloud in torrential rain at about 200ft I saw the runway through the windscreen in a series of gigantic "Catherine Wheels" of light, totally unusable for any landing.

"Can you see OK"? I asked Tony.

"Yes."

"Well I can't see anything, you have control!"

Taxiing-in was nearly impossible; something was smeared across my windscreen which effectively made it opaque. Much later we learned that a new trainee mechanic had used Vim to remove the dead flies but had had only time to do one screen.

In the next few weeks I covered the whole network, Kuala Lumpur, Kuching, Kota Kinabalu, Manila and of course Hong Kong. I found that our Omega/VLF Nav System was not a lot of use in the South China Sea and other areas, due to the position of the transmitting stations. A year later a highly accurate Inertial Nav System was fitted to each 737 – Honeywell Laser Navigation. It was unbelievably accurate and I think we were the first commercial company to buy this equipment. On 6th January I was let loose again on my own.

That New Year saw Brunei become independent with much celebration including a 3 million pound firework display! The historic 100-year-old "Yacht Club" on the riverbank near the capitol, where Somerset Maugham had written some of his novels, was destroyed. This was a great shame, but I suppose it was a reminder of Brunei's colonial past and in that light one could perhaps understand its destruction. This narrative was supposed to be about my flying, but since I was starting a new "mini career" in foreign parts, thankfully not visited by tourists, I thought the reader would not mind too much if I brought in some local colour. After all, five years of one's life at 55 was quite a chunk of time to be away from home.

Thanks to BA Staff Travel my youngest daughter and my son joined me for the Independence Celebrations and a great time was had by all. Although Brunei is a Muslim country it has a large population of Chinese among its citizens. Consequently there were a few stores that sold liquor and the numerous Chinese restaurants which were all licensed. The airline, at that time was also 'wet'. This was to change in four years time as the Religious Affairs Department gradually closed down all drinking establishments. The evening the airline went 'dry'; the late Singapore service went out 'wet' and came back 'dry'! Even then, Customs allowed us to purchase a reasonable amount of booze in Singapore and bring it through.

In February '84 we started a service to Christmas Island (Indian Ocean) which made a nice change of scenery, and it was fun to take my next door neighbours in England out to the Island as already described. So now I could claim personal knowledge of both Christmas Islands! The one I now visited was being eaten away by phosphate mining, how long this was expected to last I never found out. The route from Singapore took one over Krakatoa, thankfully now dormant, but still sending up steam from one or two vents. It was easy to see from the air the evidence of a mountain that quite literally blew itself to pieces.

I remember one evening returning to Changi from Christmas in a really heavy rainstorm. On the 737 heavy rain tends to accumulate on the flat windscreen and looking through it one can get a false idea of one's height near the ground, rather like looking at the distorted lines on the bottom of a swimming pool. On take-off in rain the windscreen would often remain clear until rotation and then the accumulated water on the nose would suddenly move and completely hide the outside world for a second or two! On this approach the rain was very heavy and required a few extra knots of airspeed to keep well above the stall. Over the Bedok marker, which I think was five miles from touchdown on this runway, the aircraft's height was 1500ft AGL – just about right and on the glide path. The Distance Measuring indicators (two of them) both showed us to be about two miles from touchdown.

We pressed on down the glide path and ignored the DME readings. Discussing this later with more knowledgeable people than I, we came to the conclusion that somehow the rain had caused an erroneous readout but I have never found anyone else who had experienced such an event.

It was good to be flying into Hong Kong again: - always fun and a bit of a challenge at times. To help new pilots to the airline I took a series of photos of the approaches to both runways from about five miles out to touchdown. I suppose now they may have a historical value and worth a bit of cash! On one trip I saw my second display of abysmal airmanship (the first being the VC-10 incident at Lusaka) only this time it could have led to catastrophe equalling the collisions of the two 747s on Tenerife North. I was standing on the aircraft steps near the front door watching aircraft landing on Runway 13 about 600 yards away – our parking spot was one of the nearest to the runway touch-down zone. Suddenly an Alitalia 747 came into view from <u>behind</u> the control tower, instead of above it, very low and fast and showing the whole top surface of the wings with the port tip, at the most, ten feet off the ground! The angle of left bank must have been at least forty degrees. The pilot managed to level off and we all fully expected him to go round again. But no, with a thump that must have been heard all over Kowloon, he crunched it onto the runway and stopped just before the end. He must have left his final turn too late and then over cooked it! I dashed inside our aircraft and switched the loud speakers on to hear if Air Traffic had anything to say. (Apparently they thought the 747 was coming in through their windows!) The conversation went something like this:-

Controller (very breathless): *Alitalia XYZ do you have a problem?*
747 pilot: *No, Ees no problem.*

Controller: *We think you do; please report to the Air Traffic Control when parked. Can you taxi?*

747 pilot: *Ees no problem, no problem at all!*

How the 747 pilot got away with it I do no know. He came so close not only in writing his own aircraft off but he could easily have hit two more that were taxiing in from the runway.

While we are on the subject of near disasters, I must admit to getting into a situation that was not entirely my fault but I could have taken action to avoid it. I set off one morning in the Combi to deliver a car to Kuching for the Sultan to use that afternoon on a visit. I took through fuel from Brunei since my final destination was Singapore; this would save time at Kuching. The weather at Kuching was forecast to be clear, but a large thunderstorm parked itself over the field and I had to do a full IFR letdown. This ate into my fuel for Changi, but I was still legal with Johore Baru, about 30 miles to the north of Changi, as my alternative. The weather was good and remained so. However, when I called Singapore over Horsba I was told that I was number seven in a queue to land – very unusual. The reason for this was that one runway was out of action for maintenance and in fact notification had gone out to all stations the night before. Unfortunately, someone in Ops at Brunei had missed this, consequently I had not been informed prior to departure. It was an uncomfortable situation: I would have to use some of my alternate holding fuel. I kicked myself for cutting things a bit fine. Eventually I was number two to land some twelve miles south of the field. What I did not know was that a China Airways Airbus had just declared an emergency on another frequency, because he could not retract his nose wheel after take-off. By the time I was five miles on finals he landed ahead at high speed and burst most of his tyres, successfully blocking the only runway! I overshot, rejoined the traffic pattern at number 9! I had no choice but to swallow my pride, declare a fuel emergency and request an immediate landing at Paya Lebar, now a military airfield some eight miles to the west. Changi sympathised (!) and radar vectored us onto a twelve mile final to PL and we thankfully landed there with not an awful lot of fuel left! If you cut corners in this business you are bound to come unstuck – its Sods Law. There was a humorous side to this; the China Airways crew failed to inform their passengers of their return to Changi, consequently they were greatly surprised that they had reached what they thought was Canton in such good time. However, when the aircraft eventually screeched to a violent halt with smoking wheels they were not amused at being thrown out of it via the emergency escape chutes!

Returning to Brunei that evening with two more cars, I heard a BA 747 bound for Kuala Lumpur call Singapore on VHF with a position report not far from me near Bintulu. I recognised the voice, and asked him to go to "International Natter" on 12345 megs. I asked him if he was Macmillan-Bell.

"It is he", he replied. "Who the hell are you?"

I had not seen Tony Macmillan-Bell since we were on Hastings some thirty years before! Voices do not seem to change with time and his was an unmistakable deep bass. He was on his last flight before retiring and as he slowly descended towards Kuala Lumpur we said goodbye – ships that pass in the night.

Since we are on the subject of communications, our best method of speaking to anyone at home was through Portishead Radio in Cornwall: this was before the days of mobile phones. Using the aircraft's H.F. radio one called up Portishead and they would patch you through to your number on the GPO landline. All this had to be pre-arranged and we were given an account number (paid in UK): the charges were very reasonable. Every month I received an up-date on the best time around Brunei for transmitting; it was usually between 1900 and 2300 local time, and fitted in well with our in-bound flights. I sometimes phoned my daughter and inevitably that human in a black fur coat, her dog Nearly, would be persuaded to bark, to which I replied! This caused no end of amusement to the Portishead operators and no doubt to the hundreds of people who happened to be on the frequency: there is no privacy on the air. I demonstrated this system to an ex-RAF C-130 pilot who had just joined us, by saying, "I must go to HF and call my dog": he thought I was joking! Having got through to Susan she said "Nears, speak to

Dad" and back came a few barks to which I replied in like manner. The look on my colleagues' face was priceless, and he said not another word for the rest of the flight. I think he saw Mike Fox the next day and told him; Mike said, "yes, I know, we all get like that after a couple of years!" He should know, he had befriended a chicken as a pet, but this unfortunate creature could only run backwards!

Staying with animals, we had three stray dogs that slept in our carport at night and got fed: Wagger, Scarface and Lady. Animals, especially dogs get a rough time in the East and though these three remained with us for nearly five years they would never let me get close to them. Which brings me back to Fox. Mike's Amah, a Phillipina, complained one day that she had been bitten by an animal whilst on the loo in her quarters(!). On close inspection (by Pauline, Mike's wife) they were indeed deep bite marks on her posterior. After a thorough investigation which included lifting septic tank covers and other unpleasant activities, the culprit was eventually found in a sewer pipe and chased back into the jungle – a two foot long Monitor Lizard!

In 1985 I became Flight Safety Officer just in time to represent the airline at an ICAO Seminar in Vancouver; life is tough when you have power! The thing lasted three days and I was able to tack on 14 days leave, taking a week in Vancouver and a week in Hong Kong. I had arranged to meet Trish in Vancouver, who had been visiting her parents in England. The night she was due to land I had a call from BA Traffic to say that all staff had been off-loaded for commercial reasons, but the next flight looked O.K.

'Ah well,' I thought, and returned to the bar. About forty minutes later I had a very strange feeling and I said to my companion, "She's here, I know it," and shot off to the foyer. Sure enough, she was just coming through the entrance.

"I knew you would be here," I said, to which she replied, "And I knew you would be waiting!"

I asked how on earth she avoided being off-loaded!

"Ah yes…" she said, "I just fluttered my eyelids at the captain and got the jump seat!"

We had a great few days and took in Sproat Lake the home of the last two remaining Martin Mars flying boats, now converted to forest fire water bombers. One boat had been Admiral "Bull" Halsey's transport during the war in the Pacific and was named 'The Hawaii Mars'; we spent a fascinating hour looking over it.

And so to Hong Kong, where I met up with Nigel Best (ex Air London) now with Cathay Pacific and George McBain (ex-Airtours) with his hair just as long as ever. We had a good day out with him on the Cathay Pacific yacht; George had joined Cathay soon after I left Airtours. For a few hours we thought we were millionaires – sipping gin and tonics while a crew of three ran the boat and topped up the gin! Then it was back to Brunei and work again…

In May '85 the company had signed a contract with Britannia Airways for the loan of several First Officers on one year tours. One of the first to come out was Angus Mundie, whom I had last seen on Vanguards. When he returned to Britannia he got his command and eventually became boss man of their Glasgow base. It was good to see him and meet his wife Marie-Louise. He was a keen cross country runner, so was Marie-Louise, and they joined the local branch of the Hash House Harriers, who enjoyed running through the jungle! Needless to say, I abstained – the last time I had done any serious running was in 1954, fleeing from a very bent Vampire at Valley! – but Trish did achieve 25 runs before we left.

I didn't mind walking, though, and one day a party of us climbed a local hill of some 2,000 feet (Buket Teraja). Just prior to setting off up the track we heard a low but loud buzzing sound. A swarm of bees drifted our way and we all beat a hasty retreat to our cars. Stings from bees are high on the list of causes of death in the jungle, followed by falling trees and snake bites; the other nasties come way behind. Anyway, we later sweated our way to the top and I must say it was worth it for the view.

On the subject of bees, I later had a swarm fix themselves to the nose and cockpit windows of a 737 parked on the ramp at Brunei. We shut off the air conditioning and APU, closed everything, got overheated and called for help. I could not see out of the cockpit windows for bees. The fire truck came to our aid, its crew grinning broadly at our predicament, and turned on a fire hose. It was then our turn to be amused as the fire truck disappeared down the ramp pursued by a very angry swarm!

On one afternoon Kuala Lumpur service, I had a request from Traffic for the jump-seat for a BA engineer on holiday, one Jaroslav Muzika. On the way over he told me he had been a fighter pilot in the RAF during the war and on return to Czechoslovakia had escaped from the Reds in an Antonov biplane. This rang a bell and I asked if he escaped with Jan, who in 1954 was an Air Traffic Controller at Lyneham. He was all smiles, "of course" he said. "I suppose you didn't trust the French either, and advocated getting to England first! "Of course" he replied. After the war he became an instructor and went out to RAF Heany in Southern Rhodesia, where my old friend John Cheesbrough had done his training. It turned out that he had been John's instructor on Harvards! I had a Chinese co-pilot that day, Sebastian Newn, who listened to all this in utter amazement! On another Kuala Lumpur flight a few weeks later waiting for the returning passengers to finish boarding, Daisy, one of our best Chinese chiefies, came onto the flight deck in a state of hysterical laughter.

"You not believe this Captain, but an Englishman is on board with a cat on his head!"

I took a peep round the flight deck door, and true enough there was the cat sound asleep on this mans head. I said to Daisy, "No booze ... for the cat, I mean". The cat remained in situ occasionally casting a baleful eye at the other passengers. At Brunei the last I saw of it, was still on the man's head as he cleared customs!

Still talking of cats, one of our Captains called Alan had a Brunei cat which he worshiped. I must tell you that most Brunei cats have a deformed tail usually with a right-angled kink in it. Alan's cat was no exception. Alan went on leave and Mike and I undertook to look in on the cat now and then and feed it. One day Mike found the cat dead. We talked this over; how were we going to explain this to Alan who would only accuse us of neglect! Mike had the brilliant idea of freezing the corpse with legs extended and then place it behind the front door an hour before Alan's return, so that when he opened the door he would think he had killed it. I think this solution was arrived at after several cold beers; I hope so otherwise the reader will think that we were all "troppo"! Needless to say we had to tell Alan as soon as he returned!

We now started a twice a week service to Darwin, always good to do and escape from the "East" for a night. On my first flight I was amazed at the transformation of the town that had taken place since I last visited, flying a Hastings in '54 – from one of tin shacks to a really nice city. A destructive hurricane had wrecked the town (1958?) and the opportunity was taken to start afresh. In fact I like Darwin, especially in the "dry" season, and my wife and I once had a super holiday in Kakadu National Park. Darwin still showed evidence of the railway that once joined it to the mining town of Birdup about 200 miles to the south; and I never did find out why it had never been extended to the rail-head at Alice Springs! Our alternate for Darwin was "overhead holding fuel" but on the way down Dilli, in East Timor, had a good runway but a somewhat volatile political regime; I am glad we managed to avoid using it!

That holiday in the Kakadu was one of the best we had ever had. From Darwin it was a six hour drive to the Park Headquarters and to the only Rest House. Here we joined small conducted tours in 4 x 4 mini-busses to the various scenic spots, usually taking from dawn to dusk. Twin Falls was one of these and to get there required a two hour drive along the foot of the Arnhem Land escarpment. Once at the river it was into our "bathers" and with our belongings in small inflatable dinghies we swam, paddled our way upstream through a gorge which led to a wide amphitheatre surrounded by high cliffs, down one tumbled the two hundred foot twin falls into a large pool.

A small spit of sand made a good beach and there was plenty of shade from scrub trees. It was one of the most beautiful settings I have ever seen and of course only accessible in the dry season. One of our newly employed Captains later caused the Immigration Service at Darwin to become exceedingly volatile! On his first night-stop he was asked by the Passport Officer the standard question, "do you have a criminal record?" To which he replied "No, I did not know it was still a requirement"! This not very original reply landed him in the cooler overnight and Mike Fox was hard pressed to persuade the authorities to let him out to bring the aircraft home the next day.

Returning on one flight about half an hour out of Darwin, I heard an aircraft call up with his position report which I relayed to Darwin. His height struck me as odd – 2000ft, and it was going to take him four hours to do just over 300 miles! It turned out that the pilot was flying a Puss Moth from the UK to Oz in celebration of some epic flight of the thirties. I asked him if anyone had warned him about the sharks in the Timor Sea which he thought was an unkind question! Years later at Duxford at one of our Air Shows, I heard the pilots voice again, and turning I said "Timor Sea and sharks" to which he replied "RBA"! It was Henri Lambouchere from Diss, a much-respected expert on DH Moths and their restoration.

Apart from taking the odd spot of local leave and spending week-ends in Singapore, we looked to the sea for relaxation. Brunei had lovely pristine, sandy beaches and the outlying uninhabited islands in Brunei Bay were often visited. However, there were a few snags, sand flies for one. Sand flies abounded in their millions and we had to continually spray ourselves with insect repellent when by the water. The sea harboured on occasions, box-jellyfish which could kill small children; even a tiny sting from this creature was extremely painful. The beaches were great places for barbecues and parties and some of us, Roger and I included, invested in local *prahus* (boats) with out-board motors and so frequently visited the outlying islands. Christmas was always celebrated here, and I even managed to water-ski again for the first time since leaving California where, although I say it myself, I had become a bit of a dab-hand on one ski. This time I could only manage on two!

There were other places of interest; the remains of the Brookton Colliery on the coast near Maura, closed in 1929 that once provided fuel for the coaling station at the turn of the century – was one. The No.1 shaft was still open and one could peer down the 60° slope about one hundred feet to the water level. It had been a dangerous and very wet mine to operate, similar to the one on the northeast coast of Labuan Island, thirty miles farther to the east. On the island of Rusukau Besar in Brunei Bay, lie the graves of some of Ferdinand Magellan's soldiers who died on the first known visit of Europeans to North Borneo in 1521, all marked out in stones taken from the ship's ballast.

Evening entertainment was limited to some excellent restaurants in Bandar; Thai, Chinese, Korean, Indian and of course Malay; but no music! There was the Sheraton Hotel which had a pool and a good restaurant and once a year we were allowed to hold a Company dinner-dance on New Years' Eve; otherwise such goings-on were confined to one's home. We (all of us) therefore entertained a lot, and being from so many diverse backgrounds, our evening gatherings were always interesting and fun. The Sultan also generously allowed pilots and families the use of the swimming pool and restaurant at Jerudong Park which was a nice relaxing place to visit. To get there one passed the entrance to Jerudong Jail, the local Nick. On the door there was a notice which read "Entry by prior permission only!" If one wanted a couple of evenings of Western relaxation then Singapore was only an hour and a bit by air. Raffles Hotel at this time was still unspoilt (i.e. no air-conditioning) and almost in its original layout apart from the main entrance which had been changed during the Japanese occupation. It was a place of tranquillity, and we often stayed there in preference to the chilly atmosphere of the more modern hotels. Old Singapore was rapidly disappearing and I am glad that we made the effort to see it in time.

Labuan Island lay two hours away by 50ft launch and offered a more relaxed and quieter atmosphere than Singapore, and we spent many days here. Kota Kinabalu (Jesseltown) was but an eight minute flight by 737 and from there one could hire a car and drive south-wards towards Mt. Kinabalu, the highest peak in this part of the world, at 14,000! We did once try to reach Sandakan to see the goril-las (Orangutans) but the road had been damaged by flooding and so we stopped at Ranau. It was here that the only six survivors of the infamous death march of 2500 Australian and Commonwealth POW of the Japs from Sandakan to Ranau in 1945 were found by a local Dusun farmer and cared for.

Two of the six returned in 1985 to meet the farmer again (now 80 years old), an event well covered in the local papers at the time. In the centre of the town is a stone monument that really represents the slaughter of all those prisoners by the Japanese; it is to an Australian who was tied to a post and beaten to death on the same spot. His steel helmet tops the stone cairn above a bronze plaque. Thinking again of the wartime past, I was amazed to see when I first arrived in Bandar, an eight foot bronze statue of Sir Winston Churchill standing in front of a semi-circular building that housed a Churchill Museum. Apparently the Sultans' father had been a great admirer of Sir Winston following the liberation of Brunei in 1945, and this was his show of appreciation.

I seem to be wandering away again from my central theme! Borneo is known as "The Land Below the Wind" because it lies within five degrees of the equator and is therefore exempted from typhoons! In fact a remarkable lady called Agnes Newton Keith wrote a book about Borneo with that title which is a fascinating account of life out there before the war. She wrote a sequel called "Three Came Home", about her survival with a four year old son and husband, in the Jap Internment Camp in Kuching, notorious for its death rate of 50%. Nevertheless, strong winds do blow in Borneo but are mainly confined to thunderstorm activity, which I suppose represented our worst flying weather problems and, of course, heavy rain. We did have a tornado one night which left a trail of destruction five miles long and a few hundred yards wide, and removed the top of Mike Fox's house leaving Mike and Pauline in bed unharmed, and with a good view of the stars! When flying it was mandatory to have serviceable radar in order to avoid the storm cells: I remember the poundings we used to receive when flying Hastings in thunderstorm areas without it, thirty or more years ago.

Flying to Manila was always interesting; air traffic in those days was not of the best and on more than one occasion I had been "lost" on their radar and came too close to the hills that lie to the east of the airport. Another time I broke cloud under radar over a Military air display in time to see one aircraft flick out of a loop! But the Philippinos did make superb ice cream and I used to bring gallons of it back to Brunei. We once took ten days leave and spent part of the time exploring the island of Corrigdor and sailing round Fort Drum better known as the "concrete battleship". These were two of the most evocative battlefields that I have ever visited.

My youngest daughter Rosie, decided that she would take a year away from home and go round the world! I said I would get her the required staff tickets on the promise that she would not backpack, a past time that was already becoming highly dangerous for young girls especially in Australia. Like me, she is a bit of a train freak and flew to Bangkok and later went to Singapore by train, quite an epic trip. Together we "trained" on the only railway left in Borneo, the Kota Kinabalu to Tenon narrow gauge via Beaufort and the Padas River gorge in Sabbah. Built in 1909 for the inland tea plantations it was one of the most memorable journeys I have ever made; I hope it is still in being. Then I flew her to Darwin and she bussed to Alice, climbed Ayers Rock and took the famous Gan train for a two-day ride to Melbourne. One of the strange things about Australian railways was that some states used tracks of different gauge to their next door neighbours; I believe in some cases they actually changed the carriage bogies going from one state to another. I remember noticing in Perth that the rail track consisted of three rails to accommodate out of state trains! After nine months in New Zealand Rosie eventually came to Sydney where she worked for a few months in the famous Doyles Fish Restaurant and then returned home via the USA and my family in Connecticut: it was the sort of trip that I would have loved to have done!

By the end of 1985 the Airline Board had been given the go ahead for the expansion of our operations. While traffic rights etc were being negotiated an order was placed for three 757s from Boeing (paid in cash!) and crews were withdrawn from the 737 fleet and new recruits taken on to cope with future long haul operations. It was the end of an era for the airline. Training was done at Seattle and at the

Singapore Airlines simulator facility at Changi. I had less than three years to 60 when this was put into effect; not long enough to justify another very expensive conversion. I didn't really mind; the older you get the less attractive long-haul flying becomes. Roger Neaves retired and went home, I bought his magnificent bamboo cocktail bar out of his house (unfortunately bereft of booze) and took his job over: as Chief Pilot. And so, late in life, the trappings of power from behind a desk were mine again, all mine – a far cry from that last job at RAF Marham.

Roger did his last flight to Darwin and I came with him as F/O: it was a great final trip. Before I took over from Roger I had made a deal with Mike Fox, my boss, that I should get to fly at least twice a week and in fact I managed quite a bit more. Part of my job was to deputise for Mike at the weekly Management Meetings and I came to know many of the Malay and Chinese board members. It was a fascinating experience to attend these events being only one of two white faces the other being our Chief of Maintenance. As CP I was responsible for supervising rostering, training and the day to day running of the Airline. I must say I viewed my appointment with mixed feelings – maybe I would not be up to the job, after all, my experience in this new environment was limited to an Air Taxi Company! Mike Fox was away quite a lot recruiting new pilots and keeping an eye on our first local pilots undergoing training at Kidlington, Oxford. I like to think we made a good team and I could not have had a better friend with whom to work. We shared a secretary, Mrs Gina Lim usually known as Mrs Potter why I cannot remember but she was a brilliant secretary.

One of the first things I had to organise as chief pilot was the acceptance of some Ansett pilots for 737 line training prior to that company buying the aircraft. Thus I met up with Ron Austen from Sydney and we became great friends. We later spent a very pleasant week with them in Sydney meeting up with Rosie when she returned from New Zealand, and in 1993 my wife and I made a "world tour" taking in Sydney and New Zealand and renewed our friendship with them and many other ex RBA friends—Ron took me on the jump-seat on a service to Norfolk Island, a fascinating spot, once a penal colony, and home of the famous Norfolk pines.

In 1986 we had, or should I say His Majesty the Sultan and Yang Dipertuan Negara Brunei Darusalaam, had a visit from the Red Arrows who put on a display at the Jerudong Park Polo ground that was truly brilliant and would have made an Air Display Safety Committee of today cover their eyes! It was good to see the Royal Air Force so expertly represented. Later that year the airline started a flying club with one Cessna 172 and I was able to do some instructing again, and of course we could hire it out for joy rides down the coast to places like Seria and Miri. It made a welcome change, Trish loved flying in it, and was getting to be quite competent in straight and level and gentle turns.

The 757's started to arrive in the middle of the year with two Boeing pilots to assist in line training and base flying. One was Gene Bolin who had been, amongst other things, a B58 Hustler pilot in S.A.C. at about the time that I had been at Mather AFB. We had a lot in common and have become close friends. I obtained authority to do some base flying with him, after all, as Chief Pilot I should at least have a rudimentary knowledge of the workings of the 757! It was a good excuse to get my hands on this great aeroplane and I spent several happy trips flying it with Gene. Gene stayed in Brunei about ten months during which time he married his long time Swedish girlfriend, Bodil, and they were often in our company in the evenings.

We did our best to interest ourselves in local celebrations and occasions, always colourful. The festival of Hari Raya celebrates the end of Ramadan. Over a period of three days the Sultan's subjects can go to the Istana (Palace), take breakfast and shake the Sultans hand. I always attended this ceremony and joined the thousands who thronged to the palace. One got a very good glimpse of the inside of this vast structure and I think our local staff and management appreciated the gesture.

We occasionally had RAF VC-10s in with soldiers for the Jungle Warfare course that was run by the Brunei Army and the resident Ghurka regiment. They would rotate these chaps about every two months and they seemed to leave a lot thinner than when they arrived! I always tried to meet the aircraft in case there was someone I knew and one occasion the Captain was a Squadron Leader Bob Humphreys, whom I had last seen on Beverleys as a sprog co-pilot. He gave me a searching look and eventually said, "you are Ken Fitz-Roy", "Yes." He continued "I remember you at Nicosia! You had just returned form Kyrenia after a night out, got in the aeroplane, took-off and handed over to me for the next four hours to Malta while you snored your head off"! "Bob" I said, "have you been harbouring this grudge all these years? "Yes I bloody have" he replied! We had a good evening together at my house and parted friends! Trish said to me later that it must have been quite a night out in Kyrenia! The next evening we had several friends round for drinks including the Foxes. We had had a thunderstorm in the late afternoon but now the sky had cleared and a light mist was forming along the valley and for once was cool though very humid. After dinner, sitting on the veranda with smoke pots going to keep the insects at bay conversation turned to the past and since we all came from very different backgrounds we all had different tales to tell. On this occasion John Keyers (Clouseau) related his visit to that Liberator crash in the North African desert: the "lady be good", and his hairy flying for the oil companies out there. Trish was always interested by these tales and afterwards said to me "you know, you should record these evenings they would make a fascinating book"! I suppose I have always had those words in the back of my mind and that may have prompted me to write these few words fifteen years later.

Slowly but surely plans were made to wind down the 737 fleet and when I left we just had the one – the Combi primarily for freight and, of course, new cars! In 1987 we sold a 737 to Lanchile in Santiago and against much muttering from the remaining 737 crews I elected to ferry it out there; after all there is no point in having power and not abusing it! I took with me a ground engineer and F O Sebastian Newn, our Chinese senior local pilot. Bas would shortly be doing his command course and a trip like this was just the ticket for him.

We left Brunei on 27th August for Nandi (Fiji) refuelling at Port Moresby. We stayed in the Nandi airport hotel, the Mocambo, which our flight engineer on Hastings 330 had tried to burn down in '53. After discreet enquiries I found that no one remembered the incident! On to Tahiti the next day where I had carefully planned one afternoon, night-stop and full day recuperating from the stresses of crossing time zones. On the way I was able to ease north of track a bit to overfly Bora Bora again which merely confirmed that it must have lost its charm judging by the numerous hotels along the shore. No, I did not want to go back. The following night was a long hop to Easter Island which we would reach with barely "island holding fuel" if we were lucky: I see it took us five hours and ten minutes. We tanked up to the limit at Papeete Airport including topping up the outer tanks from over-wing hoses to squeeze a few more gallons in. It paid off. We got to the island around dawn and after breakfast the station manager gave us a three-hour tour of the island and its giant statues. Easter Island in 1987 was still untouched by the worst of tourism and lacked roads and a hotel; indeed I think the SM's Land Rover was the only vehicle that I saw. No doubt things have now changed. Then onto Santiago, another four-hour leg, to be made really welcome by our Lanchile hosts. We spent two full days there during which we made a trip into the Andean foothills, bought lots of lapis lazuli trinkets, sampled several bottles of excellent red wine and developed a healthy respect for the local tipple – Pisco Sours! We flew home via Buenos Aries and Los Angeles where we had a night off and I was able to see a couple of old friends from my March AFB days, then home on the first of the month, very weary.

At the end of September I managed a few days leave in Hong Kong with the Bests, Nigel now being firmly established in Cathay Pacific, and a couple of days in Macao. It was while we were there that I realised Trish had lost a lot of weight. She said she had been a little under the weather over the last few weeks and put it down to the usual common tummy bug. However, as a precaution, I got her an appointment with our Doc who set her up on the same day with a specialist. The news was not good; she had a lump in the colon and he recommended immediate return to the UK for exploratory surgery. We got ourselves home the next night on BA and two days later she was operated upon and a malignant growth successfully removed. However, a year's course of chemotherapy was prescribed, this to involve mild doses one day a month.

Needless to say I felt as if someone had kicked me into a bottomless pit; Trish took it all in her stride with a courage that I do not have. Our oncologist said she could return to Brunei each month providing there were no side effects and this is what she did, returning to the UK for treatment. By June all traces of cancer were gone but we still had four more treatments to go.

During this period we continued to spend the odd quiet week here and there; at Frasers' Hill in Malaysia and on the slopes of Mt Kinabalu. We made plans for my "retirement" at 60 in September. I got wind of an opening going in Birmingham with a feeder airline operating Jetstreams, the operations officer of which had been a Navigator on 511 Squadron on Britannias. This sounded a good option. I also heard from one of our new pilots, an ex-Boscombe Down test pilot, Russ Peart, of a job (unpaid) with the Fighter Collection at Duxford, flying their B-25 Mitchell. Trish said "whatever else you do, take this, for this will give you more pleasure than anything else you have done!" How right she was; but that was in the future. Another option was Connectair, a charter operation out of Gatwick using three Short 360s and in the end I accepted a job with them.

In the months that followed Trish completed her first novel which was published in 1989; her mother was a well known novelist so Trish had obviously inherited her flair. One day in August I did the KL evening service to meet Trish off the BA service from London. I met her in the terminal; she was in a wheelchair and had collapsed leaving the 747. With great help and kindness from the Malaysian health people I got her on board and flew home, my mind in turmoil. She had rallied a bit and I got her home to Subok where her daughter was staying with us. By midnight things had got worse and I called an ambulance.

This narrative is no place for a tale of woe or for me to write about it, which I find difficult to do. In the weeks that followed her kidneys started to fail and it was thought best to rest them through dialysis and get her home as soon as possible. Doctor Chin, her doctor, managed to get her strong enough to stand the journey, albeit on a stretcher. Wives of our pilots were wonderful in keeping her company in the hospital while I tried to snatch some sleep. Anyway, we left Brunei in early October by 757 for Singapore to a huge send-off of staff and friends. BA Staff Travel came up trumps and organised a curtained-off bunk at the rear of the 747 and I had the help of a nurse who was travelling home on leave. At Heathrow we were met by an ambulance organised by Tony Mack of Air London and Trish was in the renal ward at the Royal Sussex Hospital in Brighton within two hours of landing.

She improved a lot in October and in early November but then took a sudden dive. In mid December she declared that she had had enough; her oncologist concurred: scans showed that "it had escaped". On 18th January she had her last dialysis and then three days of doing things that had been denied her, a Chinese meal, swimming in a neighbour's pool and three nights at home. I drove her to hospital on 20th and she died free of pain with the dignity she so richly deserved on the 22nd. Later we scattered her ashes, as she had wished, on Ashdown forest, a free spirit again. There have been times when I wished I had had the courage to join her.

18. Home to 'the Shed' and the Fighter Collection

After the funeral, I thought that the only way to beat the aftermath was to go back to work. I had tried to cater for this in October and November when we still had hope that Trish would recover, by reading at home (and in the hospital!) the Short 360 manual. It took my mind off things a bit and I kept my sanity. I even managed to pass the ARB exam at the beginning of November and got myself base checked. Trish was delighted and I really thought that maybe, just maybe, things would improve. It was not to be and I took leave from Connectair. The Chief Pilot, Rex Shilton, kindly kept the job open for me. Perhaps I should mention that now that I was over 60 my commercial flying was limited to aircraft with a maximum weight of 20,000kgs and the Short 360 and 330 both fell within this limit. Another proviso was that the combined ages of the two pilots should not exceed 120 years! This all meant that I had to exchange my fully automated and modern 737 for an aircraft that had a 1950 radio and instrument fit, no autopilot, unpressurised, i.e. flying below 10,000ft and a potential killer in the right hand seat in his first multi-engined commercial aeroplane! I would not have missed it for anything and in my first year achieved nearly 800 hours flying, mostly training, which I enjoyed immensely, but it was hard work with a lot of night flying. Slowly but surely life improved.

During the last few weeks of my wife's life I had employed a nurse, Sally Laing, to come in for a couple of hours a day and help her. Sally proved to be a tower of strength to both of us. She only lived a few hundred yards away and we became good friends; indeed she began to stick me together again. And so a week after the funeral I returned to Connectair where Rex Shilton gave me a few sectors with a Training Captain and sent me on my way again. I shall always be in his debt for letting me fly again so soon.

Following Russ Pearts' mentioning of the Fighter Collection at Duxford and their need for a B-25 pilot, I made contact with them. I had a talk with one pilot, Jack Brown, who lived near by and learned that the aircraft was on the American register; fortunately I still had a valid FAA Commercial Licence, type rated for the Boeing 377 now a bit of a dinosaur! This led to an interview with "Hoof" Proudfoot, Chief Pilot, and Stephen Grey, the Boss. To my intense joy they decided to take this old duffer on and I teamed up with John Romain on the B-25. John later gained fame as the engineer who restored the Blenheim, only to have an idiot wreck it (with John inside) at Denham. So he built another one! There must be forty years difference in our ages and yet we got on famously, at least I think we did. I learned a lot about display flying from him and on how to handle old aeroplanes, and I shall always be glad we teamed up together. When the display season started in May I flew the Mitchell with another pilot, John Larcombe, a couple of times and then, with John Romain, after we had taken our FAA type ratings on the beast with John Crocker, the FAA examiner. I remember John looked at my FAA licence (issued in 1954) and muttered that it looked more like a historical document! I reproduce here an article I wrote for the *Fighter Log*, The Fighter Collection journal, I hope it will be of interest and I am allowed this indulgence. It was called, "A day to remember;" I wrote it in 1991, the first of a series which now form part of this book. I have taken authors license in mixing my first trip with John Larcombe with my type rating.

A Day to Remember

Let me tell you about a lady that I met one day nearly two years ago. I first saw her in the hangar, standing alone near the western end, the roof lights glinting on the Perspex. Then the hangar doors rolled open and with the bright sunlight streaming in I moved closer and gazed up at her. Her lines, though functional, flowed smoothly from her blunt nose, over the neatly fared-in cockpit and down her long straight back broken only by the mid-upper turret. The two Wright-Cyclones under-hung on the gull wing gave her an air of aggressive-ness that warned predators that here was someone not to be trifled with. I walked around her, the two point fives in the turret reminding me of the sting in her tail. Not the feline elegance of the Mosquito here, but a more mature, purposeful look which gave me the impression that she could tackle any task and do it well, a fact well borne out by history. I doubt if there is another aeroplane that has had so many varied roles, medium bomber, torpedo bomber, gun-ship, tank buster, photo-recon to name but a few. When fitted with a 75mm gun in the nose she was the only aeroplane ever to carry a cannoneer as a crewmember to feed the weapon!

The front hatch was already open, so I ducked down and stood up inside. The old familiar smells of hydraulic, petrol, oil and paint assailed my nostrils. Not the pungent aroma of the Lancaster or the Shackleton but a more gentle scent very much American. It was quite intoxicating.

Climbing up into the Navigator's compartment, I was amazed at the pristine appearance of her interior, giving the impression that she was not long out of the factory; a false one, our Mitchell is forty seven year old. Stepping up into the cockpit I eased myself into the seat and relaxed. Oh joy, Oh joy, a long smooth nose to look over once more and the companionship of two large Wright - Cyclones to lend one courage and purpose! I got my Pilots Notes out and started on the checklist, but my mind wandered…

I remembered Jimmy Doolittle's affection for the Mitchell and what he had made it do. Prior to the carrier borne Tokyo Raid in 1942 and with the help of the Bendix Corporation he fine-tuned the engines. Dootlittle demonstrated that a B-25, fully laden, could get off the ground in 250ft. He achieved this by using full flap and maximum power (plus a bit) before releasing the brakes – on land! All sixteen B-25s, took off from the carrier Hornet on 18th April 1942 bound for Tokyo without incident, including one aeroplane flown by Lt. Lawson, who forgot to lower his flaps! The raid did little damage but did much to restore American morale. There is now no doubt that the raid also led to the rather precipitate decision by the Jap High Command to launch a retaliatory offensive that would become the Battle of Midway which marked the start of the decline of the Rising Sun...

I met John Crocker for briefing that same morning and took to him straight away. Here was a man who loved his flying and his aeroplanes. After a chat we got down to business – a Crocker Briefing. Lots of question, a memory struggling to recall piston engine handling and other things. Then it was out to the Mitchell, now parked on the peri-track and a thorough walk-round, the inquisition never far away! Then with pitot cover and nose-wheel pin in pocket, up to the cockpit, the lower hatch shutting with a satisfactory "clunk".

A wave to Peter on the deck and power came onto the bus-bar; the ship now alive and we were ready to start. I tried to remember how loud four Centaurus had sounded but I was not prepared for the bellowing roar that was soon to occur! Carbs wetted, starter engaged, bringing that strangled whine so peculiar to American radials. "Mesh" and the left engine turned and coughed out some blue smoke as a cylinder fired, soon to be joined by others in a joyous cacophony of noise. Ground power out and with the generators on line, we were ready to move.

Taxing out I did my best to remember to go easy on the brakes – no anti-skid in 1944, but my feet seemed beyond control as we lurched from side to side down the peri-track, seeking the centre line. Lining up and parking on the end of runway 27 I am sure I heard John breathe a sigh of relief! The run-up on the Mitchell is simple and logical and quickly completed; an eye being kept on the oil and cylinder head temperature for over-heating.

At last, with a hand on the throttles and 44" of boost we were off. The Mitchell can be persuaded to leave the ground in a very short distance but a take-off speed of 100 mph is recommended bearing in mind the Safety Speed is 150 mph. Once airborne, wheel brakes 'on', gear up, levelling off to get that magic 150 mph as soon as possible, a very different procedure to going for a noise abatement climb that is standard airline procedure these days. That first take-off is something

I will remember for all times; it was as if forty years had been swept away and I was back in the era of Hercules and Merlin's again.

The Mitchell is stable in all axes though with an aft centre of gravity and full wing fuel it becomes slightly unstable longitudinally, a fact to be remembered in transit flights. The rudder and elevator controls are responsive at all speeds but become heavy as speed increases, the ailerons are light in feel below 160 mph but become heavy and stiff above 200 mph. The trims are very sensitive and must be used with care.

John introduced me to stalls (very gentle and conventional), high speed flight, tight turns, display manoeuvres – the B-25 was designed with a +3.5g and – 2.0g flight envelope at weights up to 26600 lbs! We then went into engine failures and feathering drills, critical speed exercises and at last, with sweat pouring off me, we returned to Duxford for circuits and landings. Like all similar types of this vintage, the Mitchell has a tendency to become very nose-heavy on the last stages of the final approach as the speed decreases, but the elevators remain powerful and responsive. Initial approach up to the end of the base leg is in the order of that magic speed again, 150 mph decreasing to 110 mph on finals, with full flap. Providing the correct speeds are flown then the aeroplane is very easy to land and once the mainwheels are on the ground the nose can be "held off" to increase aerodynamic drag, then lowered gently onto the runway before the elevators become ineffective. Short-field landings are a bit more demanding because at slower speeds and high power settings the aeroplane tends to yaw from side to side. I found this phase of the conversion quite interesting as airline pilots simply do not do such exercises and it must have been thirty years since I had done any for real on large aeroplanes.

We taxied in, with a little more finesse this time, stabilised the engine temperatures and shut down. I opened the side window and listened to that long forgotten sound of a hot engine cooling. I was reminded of another time long ago when the last sixteen RAF Lancasters were ferried from St. Mawgan to Wroughton to be broken up.

Not one was saved: an act of sheer vandalism for which the RAF was responsible.

The Mitchell is as famous in its own field as the Lancaster and we are indeed lucky to have one in the Collection. We are also very fortunate and privileged to both maintain and fly this superb aeroplane and play our part in this unique flying museum – The Fighter Collection. So now I added another type on my licence even older than the Boeing 377!

In the meantime I got stuck into flying the Shed and doing line Training again. One has only to look at a Short 360 to understand the origin of its nickname. All the fuel was in the fuselage ceiling thus simplifying load sheets. We carried newspapers most nights to and from Paris and mail to Stansted and on to Liverpool and return. At Gatwick the Royal Mail Van was usually in charge if a well built young "Amazon" lady who reminded me a bit of the Russian Political Commissar at South Cerney in 1965. But by golly, she got things moving and aircraft were loaded and unloaded pronto!

The Shed did have one or two quirks. Having a pneumatic wing de-ice system it follows it did not take kindly to heavy ice. The large strut from the wheel sponsons to the wing were not catered for and could accumulate well over an inch of ice (as well as on the sponson) and could cause excessive drag. I recall going into Manchester once with nearly full power to maintain the ILS glider path before lowering flap! It reminded me of the performance of the Argosy some twenty years previously. In crosswinds it could be quite a handful requiring a delicate (!) combination of crabbing and into-wind wing "down" to achieve a successful landing – on one wheel! Its rate of climb when fully loaded was not the greatest either. Box Hill near Dorking was on track after take-off for a northerly destination. I was very familiar with the winds along the North Downs since in my Redhill days we were often aero-towed there in an Olympia sailplanes to waft up and down between Dorking and Redhill in a strong southerly wind: If one had the courage one could sometimes return to the airfield if one could get up to about 1800ft above it, over Redhill. It meant crossing the gasometer with about five hundred feet to spare. I only tried it once! Otherwise we landed out, in a field. I digress. One night in a Shed turning north we hit the updraft near Dorking, and then the downdraft from the curl - over thirty seconds later. It quite alarmed my student in the right-hand seat so I waxed eloquent on the reasons why. I must have sounded pompous!

My friend Peter Westbury from Air London days was in a syndicate operating a Boeing Stearman bi-plane. Indeed I had flown this several times when on leave from Brunei. There was no way that I could afford to join but thanks to the generosity of the owner, Ian Craig-Wood, a good friend I was able to subscribe a small sum each month and occasionally fly the aircraft paying for fuel and landing fees etc. My thanks go out to him, too. I now availed myself of this heaven sent opportunity to fly a real "fly by wire" aeroplane, and have continued to do so, though now we operate a Tiger Moth. I was able to take Sally up a few times and once we went to Compton Abbas for lunch to see an old chum from Rhodesia days, Phil Pickford. It was a cold day and Sally in the front seat complained bitterly about a draft coming up from the floor; this let to an extensive and fruitless investigation to find the cause. Some months later John Turner, another Stearman pilot, suggested to Ian that the non-standard windscreens that had been fitted to the aircraft some years previously should be replaced by the original ones and that he was able to get hold of a pair and would fit them. The current windscreens were made of a large single piece of Perspex bent round the front of the cockpit and were twice the height of the original ones. The result of the change apart from the enhanced looks were amazing. Gone was the draft in the front seat, the indicated airspeed was up by 5 knots at the same power settings and rudder effectiveness improved no end, especially with the tail on the ground during the landing run when the Stearman was prone to ground-looping. Anyway, Sally was impressed by her new found comfort and later sampled the delights of sitting on the rather uncomfortable jump-seat in a Short 360 to Guernsey with me driving.

John Romain and I did several displays in '89, Alconbury was one, Lakenheath another and of course the Duxford shows. I really could not believe my luck, this was the high spot of my flying career. I was sorry to put the beast "to bed" at the end of the season but May would soon be round again. I think the transit flights to the various shows were perhaps the most memorable for us in the Mitchell. We usually flew as lead ship navigating (map-reading) and to go thundering along with perhaps a Spitfire, Hurricane and P-47 on one side, Hoof in the Mustang on the other plus a P-63 and P40, over the countryside was an exhilarating experience. Our social life at shows was great fun; I suppose we all thought that we were back in the RAF again at half our ages! In the air things were different. Hoof and Boss kept a tight rein on discipline.

Meanwhile I continued to earn my crust with Connectair which in 1990 was taken over by Air Europe and became Air Europe Express. We expanded a bit, moved offices onto Gatwick from a house we had occupied in Horley, and were paid a bit more! But the happy working atmosphere remained. On one trip to Antwerp (20-9-90) our stewardess (we usually only carried one) sprung a surprise. Tapping on the sliding cockpit door to the chicken shed (flight deck) she stood back as I opened it. I was greeted by thirty passengers singing "happy birthday to you" and Sally, our girl, holding a cake with, thankfully, just one candle – a large one. I was very touched; some of the passengers were, too, I think, especially those who could not speak English!

Jersey and Guernsey saw a lot of me, I think the company flew twice a day to the Islands. I managed to see Jock Hare who now flew for Aurigney and had done some of my 737 line training in Airtours and had later joined RBA. Which reminds me that someone once said that RBA stood for "Retired British Airways"! Tony Morgan's home in Guernsey (who had been with me in Khartoum with a broken Beverley) was also a frequent port of call.

We had several two day events in the B-25 that year and in June, in the company of half a dozen fighters flew to La Ferte Alais, just south of Paris for a three-day event at the home airfield of Jean-Paul Salis. These were always much looked forward to events, and I was able to exercise my rather rusty French. The weather was kind, the flying great and Jean-Paul gave his usual welcome hospitality. On Monday 4th June we started to stream back to Southend and Duxford. The first to go were John Larcombe in the P-63 and Jack Brown in the P-47. It was my turn to fly home, with John and some ground crew. As I taxied out having watched the first pair leave I heard a voice on the radio say, "he's on fire", then "has crashed, it's non-survivable, I am going on to Duxford to see Marianne". It was Jack Brown, who had seen the P-63 trailing smoke and crashing. We were stunned, and I returned to our parking area and shut down. Someone took off and surveyed the crash site, about ten miles to the west and returned. Stephen took charge and we were later dispatched home. I do not intend to dwell much on this sad event suffice to say we were, and are, a very close knit bunch and felt the loss of John Larks very keenly. It was a reminder that old aircraft sometimes bite and one only has to look at the accident statistics during the war to confirm this. Still, we had all lost a good friend.

I flew the TFC Beechcraft Baron a bit which we used for transporting urgently required spares and personnel to air shows especially when the B-25, which could carry about six, was not required. I found it much faster than the Aztecs and Twin Comanches I had flown with Air London, but again it was a lot more expensive to buy and operate: our Baron was an ex-Hamble one. In mid June I returned to Cosford in the Mitchell for a show; it was my first visit since I had joined the RAF there in 1952. Later that month saw us at Swanton Morley, a return for me after a gap of 27 years. I managed to get my youngest (Rosie) daughter on my transit flight: We met up with an old friend, Alfred Warminger. I should have mentioned him before since he was Rosie's godfather(!) and I used to go gliding with him at Swanton Morley when I was serving my sentence at Marham. He had had a EON 419 in those days and I got my hands on it now and then. He owned a Tiger Moth too, which he used for towing and we spent many happy hours towing each other. Alfred had two claims to fame: he had held the office of High Sheriff of Norwich and had nearly been shot down in a Hurricane over RAF Horsham St Faith at night, during the war, by an intruding ME 110. Swanton Morley was followed by Brands Hatch and West Malling, where I took my late wife's parents because Hugo had been an air gunner on Lancaster's during the war (at 40!) and I was able to introduce him to the Battle of Britain flight Lancaster whose crew made him welcome. It had been a bumper display year, now it was back to the winter and the Shed!

Flying continued in Air Europe Express, we were very busy right through the winter. In January one morning I was returning from Antwerp into a seventy knot headwind at 6000ft when I called the Company crossing Dover. They said that Gatwick showed eighty knots across the runway, was I landing?! We diverted to Stansted where the wind was more or less down the main runway at a steady seventy. I think a lot of people got caught out that morning judging by the chatter on the radio, after all, Gatwick's forecast had been for forty knots and more into wind! We landed, no flap and stopped in about the length of a tennis court with hardly any brake at all. I managed to taxi onto a high-speed turn off still nearly into wind but no way were we able to turn. Air Traffic allowed us to park and sent handlers to tie the aircraft down. The next problem was to get the doors open and this was only achieved with the aid of several men; we remained on the aircraft. On my right about four hundred yards away were three large tanks, standing some 15' high. One had collapsed but the other two looked like getting ready to roll in our direction and we sat with our eyes glued on this potential disaster! Gradually the wind abated a bit and by 1900 we were able to take-off and hop over to Gatwick. The M11 looked like a battlefield with lorries on their sides everywhere. The M25 traffic was stationary and formed a complete red and white illuminated necklace round London in the gathering dusk. It had been quite a day!

On 8th March '91 I was returning from Rotterdam early that morning and nearing Gatwick I called Company for my stand number. There was a pause then a familiar voice said "Park in the Freight area and we will send a coach. Lock the aeroplane up, chock it and go home, the company has gone bust and we have all been fired"! To me this was totally unexpected but not to others in more lofty positions – most had, we learned later already fled! I saw Rex later and he admitted he had smelt trouble but only a sniff. I mentioned that we in Air Europe Express, had been doing well. "Agreed" came the reply, "that was what the barman on the Titanic thought until they hit the iceberg"! So now I was out of a job – fired! No back pay no nothing! I became a chauffeur to an old lady in our village who paid me four pounds an hour and I must say I quite enjoyed it. It was a bit like that lovely film with Jessica Tandy, "Driving Miss Daisy".

Duxford season opened in May with a check ride on the B-25 with Johnny Crocker and then to La Ferte again, for four days. We returned via Le Touquet to pick-up Nicky Grey, our Boss's son who had gone in there with a over heating engine in a Spitfire. The weather got rather poor but we managed a low level departure under cloud to mid-channel going round ships (by the bows, the seagulls always congregate at the stern) rather than over them; I felt as if I was back in the Kipper Fleet. At mid point the weather cleared as predicted and we pressed on home

In June the Boss and his son Nicky, had a show to do in Roudnice, an airfield just north of Prague, and asked me to fly the Baron as mother ship I was grateful, still being out of work! We did it all VFR routing via Charlerois both ways. The Czechs made us very welcome to this, their first display since the withdrawal of the Russians and the collapse of the USSR. Many old veterans of the Battle of Britain and the war turned up in faded blue uniforms carefully and lovingly preserved. Some had been imprisoned by the Reds on their return in 1945 and this was the first time that they had been able to wear their uniforms so proudly again. It was a very emotional experience for some including ourselves and I am so lucky to have been there. Nick was showing one old pilot his Hurricane. As he got into it he said, "I only flew the Hurricane once but I didn't land it – I got shot down"! It was at this show that I saw my first Mig 29 flying. It was a breathtaking display. This was a conventionally powered fighter—no computers or fly-by-wire gizmos and yet it put up a display that would have put a Tornado to shame. We were all sorry to say goodbye and return home. I believe a very senior RAF officer was later heard to comment "That we should have bought the Mig 29 for the Air Force. It is simple, half the cost of the Tornado and just as good"! I would echo those words.

Good news awaited me. The previous management of Connectair, who had moved to Air Europe, were going to salvage our little company. We were to be called Euro World which became City-Flyer under franchise to British Airways (Again!). We started operations in mid June with one 360. Gradually it got going and in mid July I was able to say goodbye to "Miss Daisy" and take up my rightful employment: - the pay was better, too! Our route structure was much as before and it was good to see the same old faces again; in the case of the Captains the same very old faces. Which reminds me that at Antwerp once, a passenger came up to my side window and knocked. I opened it and he said "I just wanted you to know how reassuring it is for me to see someone up front with nice short grey hair instead of some long haired youth!" Who says appearances do not count!

A couple of more shows and the season closed for Duxford. By now Sally and I had decided to marry in the New Year but things did not quite work out on schedule. On 3rd December I was scheduled to operate a double Gatwick – Guernsey and for once it was not a training flight. The first two sectors were made in the trail of a cold front and very rough, with Guernsey offering it's usual 30-knot crosswind! The last sectors were at night in crystal clear weather and relatively smooth air – for a Shed! We had a full load of happy punters on board looking forward to Christmas. I did not relish my festive season: the CAA had written to me to say that a minor irregularity had been picked up on the ECG during my last medical and though they were happy (!) to let me fly I should have my next one in February at Aviation House. It was a glorious night with every star and planet in the sky clearly identifiable; the ground a mass of coloured lights. I was reminded of the shock that I had when I first started night flying on my return from Brunei. Whereas five years before one could identify Buckingham, Coventry, Milton Keynes etc, by the shape of their lights, now it was one mass of lighting from London to

Manchester, such was the ever-increasing sprawl of urbanisation. Even here over Hampshire and Sussex, Brighton now seemed joined to London. I landed at Gatwick, my usual "smoothie" – not difficult with a trailing-link soft undercarriage, and taxied in. Our punters wished us well, I thanked the crew, all two of them, and headed for home. Little did I know that that was to be my last commercial flight.

I had some mild chest pains in the next few days and Sally insisted I saw my doctor. The upshot of it all was that on January 2nd I was in the London Bridge Hospital being told by Mr. John Keats an eminent surgeon, that my plumbing was 70% stuffed and that I required three by-passes, at least! Would an appointment in three weeks suit? At this point Sally, a mere nurse informed him that it would not suit, and that she was not prepared to risk taking me home in this shape. Mr. K gave a thin smile, got on the telephone, and said "how about tomorrow morning"? And so it was.

I much resented not lasting out until 65 (only by 14 months) and viewed the sudden cessation of flying, a way of life to me, with many misgivings. The more I thought about it, the less I liked it; I suppose I was too wrapped up in my own misery to think how lucky I was to have been diagnosed early and grateful for having been able to continue private health care, courtesy of British Airways, I hope the reader will forgive my selfishness. I had had an unbelievably varied flying career and for that I am very grateful, but retirement was the one thing in the world that I have always dreaded and now it had come with little chance of even flying for pleasure.

However, there is one thing I look forward to. The remnants of my RAF pilots course, about a dozen of us, plan to meet for the first time since we parted company on our return to England on the 20th February 2003. We meet at Cosford, where our service began, on 20th February, fifty years to the day of our wings presentation: I hope we can recognise each other!

I returned to Duxford in the spring and helped Hoof with the air shows administration and represented TFC as a "safety man" in the Tower during displays, and generally tried to make myself useful. Everyone was very kind, the Boss especially and I was sneaked on board the B-25 on the odd occasion. John Romain re-introduced me to the T-6 after a gap of forty years and I was; and still am, taken for an "airing" in Ian's Tiger Moth so I cannot complain. I was reacquainted with 'Bee' Beaumont whom I had not seen since my Warton trips with Air London. I was bemoaning my lot one day and he took me to one side, "you know, Ken," he said, "we all have to stop sometime"! I felt better after that!

19. Post Flight

Sitting at my desk looking out onto Ashdown Forest, my thoughts turn back to the past. Yes there had been some dark moments as there are in anyone's life, but I am glad to say that it is the more humorous ones that I remember best; some of these have gone down in these pages, some I have to leave unsaid and there they must remain!

People have often asked me what I had enjoyed most in my flying. The answer is difficult to quantify. That introduction to aerobatics in a Harvard in Rhodesia on a moonlight night was one of my earliest thrills. Flying the Air 100 sailplane to 24,000 was my high (sorry!) spot in gliding. There are of course several milestones which a pilot never forgets: First solo, presentation of Royal Air Force pilot's brevet, the first time you fly as Captain of a crew and if you become an instructor, the first time you send a student pilot on his first solo; providing he survives! In my early overseas flying it was fun to see the world sliding by from just a few thousand feet; the modern day traveller is denied this, sitting at 40,000ft. Seeing from a Hastings that wonderful Castle of the Kraks in Syria for the first time, appearing against a backdrop of mountains silhouetted against the rising sun is something I remember especially well. Flying low over the sea in a Shackleton always fascinated me: I love the sea and from the air the seascape changes every few miles in colour and surface even on a day of flat calm, in a full gale it is something else. To come across one of the Queens going full tilt into the long Atlantic swells was a wonderful sight too.

Driving the Beverley (it had to be driven not flown!) also has a fond place in my memory, especially on the long cross-desert legs we used to do, he Navigator up front map reading from a chart that still had tracks marked "Lawrence 1916"! But if I had to choose a winner it would be my three years with SAC. Strong memories up front in a

KC-135 with a B-52 hooked up behind, gradually reducing power on our inboard engines (better response to a "Break Away") to maintain .72m as the fuel transferred, listening to the '52's engine power gently increasing and decreasing as it maintained its position twenty five feet underneath us, the overall noise level slowly getting louder as its weight increased. Listening to Charlie quietly calling the fuel states to the completion of the off-load and to Jim the Boomer's calm voice talking to the B-52 pilot, calm even in turbulence or cloud, when things could get hairy very quickly. Watching Fred's hands on the throttles ever ready for a "Breakaway" call. I was indeed fortunate to have had such a first class crew.

Inevitably there have been a few incidents that have caused me concern, ranging from a momentary feeling of real fear when the engine of Chipmunk 373 decided to quit over foggy Cambridgeshire, (on a Sunday, too; moral here!), to a gradual unease increasing to a cold feeling of despair when utterly lost in that Anson; suddenly replaced by an unbelievable feeling of relief when Jersey showed up! Running low on fuel in an aeroplane can quickly undermine any feeling of well being for two reasons; the first is obvious the second is that it is bound to be your own stupid fault! That Brunei-Kuching-Singapore flight is a classic example of what not to do. But this is all very minor stuff compared to the experiences of some of my wartime elders and betters with whom I was privileged to enjoy my early flying.

The Britannia was also a great aeroplane, very different from any other large four engined aircraft I have flown, a joy to fly as long as you had an engineer on board who understood the electrics. But most of all it is the comradeship and friendship that I found in the Royal Air Force that I value most: many staunch friends with whom to keep in touch, many no longer here.

Civil flying was very different and looking back had I been able to continue flying in the RAF. I would probably have stayed on. There were compensations; flying the Comet for one, and spending most of my civil years in BEA Airtours which had a working atmosphere not too dissimilar to that of a Squadron. Much more I have already said but I must add that my 737 days, both in the UK and in Borneo were among the best. The '73 is a great little aeroplane and I spent more time on it than on any other type, eight years to be precise.

More gazing out of my study window; a woodpecker on the bird feeder. It has been difficult to keep to my intended central theme of aviation without allowing some of my private life to intrude, after all, behind every man there is usually the support of a woman, well, this was the case in my day! The parting from my family still causes me much sadness for what I have missed. The courage of Trish right through her battle with cancer was something that I doubt I can match when I reach the departure lounge. Then to find Sally and be returned to near normality with understanding was more than just luck. How she puts up with this cantankerous old duffer I do not know!

There is a little more to tell. Sally and I got married in July '92. Angus and M-L Mundie came to the wedding as well as John and Paddy Cheesbrough (best man), and Sally's parents and family. Her father, Squadron Leader Laing, of course had done some of my conversion flying onto Canberra's at Bassingbourn in 1959! My children came too, I am glad to say. For my birthday that year Sally organised a surprise present. She drove me down to Sheffield Park Station, the home of the Bluebell line steam railway and handed me a footplate pass! This was the realisation of my boyhood dream (indeed that of every boy of my generation!), Sally came too; in a First Class carriage! For my 70th year she somehow persuaded Peter Kynsey to take me in PV 202 a two seat Mark IX E Spitfire, I could not believe my luck. We took off from Goodwood for Half-Penny Green: Peter had a display to do nearby; so I got out. On his return we refuelled and flew back to Goodwood with Peter giving me a bit of dual. Then I had 20 minutes trying my hand at aerobatics, which confirmed for me that everything that pilots said about the Spitfire was true. One did not fly the Spit in the true sense, one was part of it and it seemed to respond to your every thought and intention. It was just pure magic and an experience that I shall remember forever. I am now wondering if Sally is planning an 80th birthday present in the Space Shuttle! On reflection and in the light of recent events I may have to refuse the offer! I did however, get an interim 75th birthday present. I went over to Lasham that day to lunch with Wally Kahn: Wally was one of the first Surrey Gliding Club members to make me feel welcome when I first joined that club at Redhill so long ago. Anyway, between the two of them they had organised a trip in an all-glass fibre 18m Cirrus sailplane with the owner Phil Phillips. It was a glorious day with Thermals up to nearly four thousand; I had an hour of pure heaven and managed an odd loop to boot. The day was crowned when I found a red kite circling in a thermal at 3000 feet. I joined him for several minutes. Flying in the company of such birds, and to be accepted, is always a privilege to be cherished.

I continued to help at Duxford and at the air shows where I stood in for Hoof in the Tower while he was flying. On 14th July '96, he was displaying our P-38, "Happy Jack's Go Buggy", and had just completed a barrel roll approaching the airfield and immediately started a second one: totally unlike Hoof who always insisted that one was the limit. He failed to recover and crashed on the airfield and was killed. Whether the second roll was self-induced or the result of a control fault (the P-38 has power boost on the ailerons) was never determined. Suffice to say it was a very black day at Duxford.

From then on I took over pilot rostering and Pilot's records (from home) to help our temporary Chief Pilot, Jack Brown, who had a full time job running an airline. This continued for some three or more years during which time we acquired our present CP, Peter Kynsey who has more than filled Hoof's shoes. A new secretary arrived in 2000 in the shape of John Larcombes' daughter Jane, who took over the admin reins and my rostering activities and brought TFC into the 20th Century on computer! I am glad to say she is still with us for a better administrator would be hard to find. It was good, too, to have a 'Larks' back in the fold. We also saw Hoof's two sons on the team as well, Ian and Lee.

In the mid nineties the CAA took a closer look at Air Display safety. We all had air display Authorisations for our various aircraft renewable every year with a CAA delegated examiner; the area now under scrutiny was the actual flying performed at a show. It needed monitoring, preferably by ex-display pilots or similar qualified ones. We thought that by closely watching display flying we might be able to detect in good time a particularly dangerous tendency in a performance, in time to prevent an accident, especially in formation aerobatics such as tail-chases. To this end flying control Committees were formed with the Chairman given the powers to stop a display and have the aircraft landed. Flying over crowd lines and below authorised heights etc, could also be watched. In all, I think that the FCCs achieve considerable success but of course it is impossible to quantify. Accidents do still happen – that's life! I am still a member of the Duxford FCC and I occasionally fill in elsewhere. I feel that I am paying back into flying a little something for all the pleasure I have had from it.

There are so many people to whom I owe a debt of gratitude that I do not even know where to begin. From the unknown Group Captain who let me continue Service flying having made a 'horlicks' of my Vampire course in 1953, to Hoof who visited me after heart surgery, chased the nurses, and nearly caused the steel staples in my breastbone to fly apart through laughing, and to Sally without whom none of this would have been written: I can but offer my grateful thanks.

20. Epilogue

We had that 13 Course pilot's reunion at RAF Cosford on 20th February this year. Of the 16 new pilots that returned from No.5 FTS, Southern Rhodesia, ten turned up, mostly with their wives I am glad to say, plus John Cheesbrough with whom I had travelled from Winchester. Two had died, four had gone "missing", one, our reunion organiser Peter Lewis, was at home recovering from surgery but with us courtesy of BT: one had declined.

The RAF at Cosford did us proud with a tour of the station and Museum and then lunch in the Mess. Later we repaired to a local hotel for our Dinner and night-stop. Even after 50 years we easily managed to pick up the threads again; time had not dimmed our memories nor marred the camaraderie that had existed between us. Our subsequent careers had differed wildly: three had remained in the Service flying Lightnings, Jaguars, Hunters, Meteors and a few more. One had had to leave his Jaguar courtesy of Martin-Baker and thus became the oldest RAF pilot to eject—just a few days short of his 53rd birthday. Quite a few, myself included, went civil, and one went into Civil Air Traffic.

We hope to meet again but I think that might be a shade optimistic on our part! I know that we will all now keep in touch.

I guess that just about wraps up my tale. I could ramble on about the past – a few regrets here and there; maybe I should have spent more time on the ground after all! Now that it is over I know what I miss most: life on a Squadron, there is none better. To end my flying with the Fighter Collection was a bonus, the icing on the cake, and for that opportunity to come my way a little late in life; I thank my lucky stars!

Photographs

Gliding at Gutersloh, 1947.

Redhill Aerodrome, looking east from T-21.

T-21.

'Splash' at play.

15.04.51 – First solo flight in AFOZ, Jean Bird attending.

South African nationals, 1952. From left to right 'Hoffie' (Base Commander),
Cilla Lasch, Roy Forman, Helli Lasch.

Helli and Air 100

Cockpit of Air 100.

Diamond Height Day!

Scratch one Tiger.

Author in Harvard 68.

20.2.53 – Wings Parade; Group Captain Cassels attending.

The remains of 13 Course prior to Wings Parade.

Tarrant Ruston 1953 – author (left), 'Bengy', Hines.

It was cold at 18,000 feet.

Hastings Mark II.

Loading jeeps for dropping.

Pamela and our Talbot.

Moonraker's tow car and trailer, Hamilcar workshop.

Author in Moonraker's Gul IV, 1955 Nationals, Lasham.

Gull IV instrument panel.

The team. L to R Author, Fred Ord, Stan Wills (pilot), Ted Morris, 'Chiefy' Owen, 1955 Nationals.

Hastings 338 to Fiji – Roy (nav) map reading.

Loading 'Striker' frame and patient at Changi.

Hastings navigator and engineer back to back.

338 at Fiji and passengers: No.3 engine still feathered!

MR Course, St Mawgan, Sept 55. Author 5th from right, middle row.
[courtesy of RAF St Mawgan]

T-Class submarine snorkelling near Malta.

Pilot's view of Shackleton's port wing.

Avro Anson. [courtesy of B McKee]

'Robbie' in WG 529.

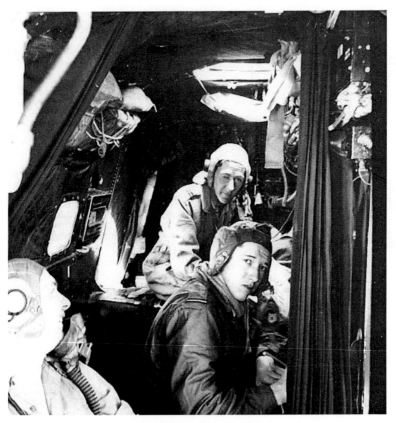

Maurice and Phil navigating.

Author flying 'C' in nine ship formation.

Bora Bora. Top: Annette Ellacot, PC 'Coco', Wg Cdr Tillings, M Pensard
(gendarme. Bottom L-R: Maurice Smythe, Reg Castle, Wg Cdr Surtees, Grp Cpt
John Aysford, Jim Kearney, Robbie Robinson. Taken by the author.

Christmas Island. View of the reef from camp area.

Malden Island test, 19.6.57. Everyone got a copy as a 'thank you' from AWRE.

Gilbert islanders show an interest in WG529.

Bora-Bora.

Madame Bouchine's four star hotel, Bora-Bora.

SS *Captain Hobson* arrives at Bermuda.

53 squadron 1958. Wng Cdr Bas Taylor (centre) seated. Author 4th from left, seated. [courtesy of RAF Abingdon]

Beverley in para-drop role.

Embarking paras.

Blackbushe – Chas (nav) in the hatch.

Picking up the last Beverley – Brough May 1958.
Eric 'Timber' Woods extreme right.

Beverley in heavy-drop role, rear doors removed.

Strubby, May 59. Meteor 8 and friend.

Canberra conversion, Bassingbourne, July 59.

Friends on Meteor 7, Strubby.

Martin-Baker test rig.

Eric Reeves (cockpit) and John Williamson – 1959 Nationals.

Pam, Ian and Susan in snowy California! 1959.

RCAF NAMAO tankers of the 320th line up on alert.

My crew: standing l to r – Moi, Bruce Rowlands (CP), Dave Siegal (N)
squatting – Jesse Klahn (E), Georges Caccahanas (boomer) Radio op.

KC-97 and B-47 hook-up [courtesy of Boeing].

Gliding at Bellows Field, Oahu.

B-52 climbing away after refuelling.

Wet take-off of KC-135A.

Crew J-10 Mather, author on left, Fred Holtgrave (CP), Charlie Martin (nav),
Jim Watland (boomer).

Flight planning!

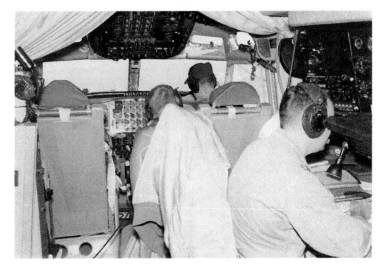

Flight Deck of KC-135.

B-52 hook-up as seen by the boomer.

Homeward bound on RMS *Queen Mary*.

Wide awake commander!

WD-373 now in civil guise and flown by John Romain [courtesy of ARC].

N'Dola – Zambian oil lift.

Fifty-six 42-gallon drums of fuel in Brittania.

Britannia flight deck.

Loading fuel drums at Nairobi.

Transit mess, Changi – now a Barnardo home.

Approaching RAF Gan.

'Hadar' and crew, John Cragg second from left.

Hastings 520 RIP, Gan 1967.

Beagle 206 showing window screens.

Beagle 206.

Comet at Tenerife North.

Aztec at Le Touquet – L-R Trish, Jan and Bill James DFC.

Author doing outside checks! San'a, Yemen.

Airtours 707 in Syrian Arab colours, San'a, Yemen.

Heavy landing, Fleines.

Merchantman.

Merchantman flight deck.

Train in Damascus from circa 1910.

Castle of the Kraks, near Hamma, Syria.

Watermills at Hamma, Syria – as old as time.

River Kwai Bridge, Thailand.

Wartime Japanese loco on the Kwai Bridge.

It pays to make a careful outside check!

Trish on the Vancouver-Victoria Ferry, 1986 holiday.

Royal Brunei Airlines 737.

Sultan's Palace, Brunei.

1984 – with Sebastian Newn, now a senior training manger.

Final turn to runway 13 at Kai Tak, Hong Kong.

Bill and Janet James bid farewell to Christmas Island.

Wayside halt Kinabalu railway, Sabah.

Turning finals for Kinabalu, Angus Mundie.

With Trish on the Flight Deck of the Hawaii Mars.

Hawaii Mars in flight, Victoria.

Hawaii Mars moored.

Roger Neaves' last trip.

The first 757 arrives.

Russ Sparks and crew.

War memorial at Ranau.

The mighty shed!

Distracting the refueller.

Tracey dispenses tea with the 'dog kennel' in the background.

Sally in the Stearman.

Another surprise discovered on an outside check!

Family outing to Le Touquet, 1983 – Susan, Pam, Rosie, Ian and Me.

La Ferte Alais, 1990.

The Author, 1989.

Fighter Collection line-up at Mildenhall, 1990.

Fighter Collection 1989, Stephen Grey second from left.

Following the fighters.

En route somewhere.

B-25 en route somewhere.

Mark Hanna in a BF109, Dieppe 1990.

Nick Grey in a Spitfire.

The Boss in his Bearcat.

B-25 flight deck, West Malling 1989.

Rare picture of chief pilot 'Hoof' Proudfoot working!

Last Moth Minor G-AFPN

Too many cooks! John Larcombe extreme right.

The Boss laying down the law. On his left, Author, John Romain, Jeanne Frazer and Hoof (courtesy of Nick Grey).

Author sampling a Meteor again, Hurn 1999.

Back in a Harvard after 40 years courtesy of John Romain.

Author celebrating 50 years since first solo – 15.4.01.

Leading the flock.

Doing my stuff with John Romain.